PITT LATIN AMERICAN SERIES

PITT LATIN AMERICAN SERIES
Cole Blasier, Editor

SELECTED TITLES

Argentina in the Twentieth Century
David Rock, Editor

Authoritarianism and Corporatism in Latin America
James M. Malloy, Editor

Constructive Change in Latin America
Cole Blasier, Editor

Cuba in the World
Cole Blasier and Carmelo Mesa-Lago, Editors

Discreet Partners: Argentini and the USSR Since 1917
Aldo César Vacs

The Giant's Rival: The USSR and Latin America
Cole Blasier

The Hovering Giant: U.S. Responses to Revolutionary Changes in Latin America
Cole Blasier

Juan Perón and the Reshaping of Argentina
Frederick C. Turner and José Enrique Miguens, Editors

The Overthrow of Allende and the Politics of Chile, 1964–1976
Paul E. Sigmund

The Politics of Mexican Oil
George W. Grayson

The Politics of Social Security in Brazil
James M. Malloy

Public Policy in Latin America: A Comparative Survey
John W. Sloan

Revolutionary Change in Cuba
Carmelo Mesa-Lago, Editor

Social Security in Latin America: Pressure groups, Stratification, and Inequality
Carmelo Mesa-Lago

Urban Politics in Brazil: The Rise of Populism, 1925–1945
Michael L. Conniff

THE STATE AND CAPITAL ACCUMULATION IN LATIN AMERICA

Volume 1: Brazil, Chile, Mexico

Edited by

Christian Anglade and
Carlos Fortin

UNIVERSITY OF PITTSBURGH PRESS

© Christian Anglade and Carlos Fortin 1985

All rights reserved. No part of this publication
may be reproduced or transmitted, in any form
or by any means, without permission

First published 1985 by
THE MACMILLAN PRESS LTD

Published in the U.S.A.
1985 by the University
of Pittsburgh Press,
Pittsburgh, Pa, 15260

Printed in Great Britain

Library of Congress Cataloguing in Publication Data
Main entry under title:

The State and capital accumulation in Latin America.

(Pitt Latin American series)
Includes bibliographies.
Contents: v. 1. Brazil, Chile, Mexico.
1. Saving and investment—Latin America—Addresses,
essays, lectures.   2. Latin America—Economic Policy—
Addresses, essays, lectures.   I. Anglade, Christian.
II. Fortin, Carlos.   III. Series.
HC130. S3S83   1985   338.98   84–12015
ISBN 0–8229–1144–2 (v. 1)

Contents

List of Tables	vi
Preface	ix
List of Abbreviations	xi
Notes on Contributors	xiii

1 The State and Capital Accumulation in Latin America: a Conceptual and Historical Introduction
 Christian Anglade and Carlos Fortin   1

2 The State and Capital Accumulation in Contemporary Brazil
 Christian Anglade   52

3 The Political Economy of Repressive Monetarism: the State and Capital Accumulation in Post-1973 Chile
 Carlos Fortin   139

4 The Financial Constraint on Relative Autonomy: the State and Capital Accumulation in Mexico, 1940–82
 E. V. K. FitzGerald   210

Index   241

List of Tables

2.1	Brazil: growth rates, 1968–73	54
2.2	Brazil: growth rates, 1958–61	55
2.3	Brazil: budget deficit, public savings and inflation, 1958–62	59
2.4	Brazil: income distribution in Brazil, 1960, 1970	68
2.5	Brazil: rate of growth of industrial production, 1972–79	71
2.6	Brazil: savings and inflation, 1971–79	78
2.7	Brazil: growth of loans to the private sector, 1970–79	79
2.8	Brazil: rate of growth of the money supply and of inflation	81
2.9	Brazil: balance of payments deficit: summary accounts, 1971–79	83
2.10	Brazil: growth and profile of the external debt, 1970–79	84
2.11	Brazil: distribution of assets and profits among firms, 1976	90
2.12	Brazil: domestic savings and capital formation, 1971–79	92
2.13	Brazil: wage distribution by sectors, 1977	98
2.14	Brazil: balance of payments deficit: summary accounts, 1979–82	107
2.15	Brazil: global expenditure of the federal government, 1979–82	112
2.16	Brazil: operational deficit of state companies, 1979–82	112
2.17	Brazil: domestic savings and capital formation	117
2.18	Brazil: income distribution, 1960, 1970, 1980	123
2.19	Brazil: the wage structure, 1980	124
2.20	Brazil: rate of growth of inflation and INPC, June–September, 1983	126
3.1	Chile: public investment in fixed capital, 1961–69	145
3.2	Chile: distribution of the equity of industrial stock companies by type of shareholders, 1967–69	146
3.3	Chile: state control over industrial enterprises, 1970–72	148
3.4	Chile: financial deficit of state enterprises, 1971–73	149
3.5	Chile: real salaries and wages, 1970–82	163

List of Tables vii

3.6	Chile: unemployment, open and total, 1970–81	163
3.7	Chile: public expenditure excluding debt as a percentage of GDP, 1969–70 and 1974–82	165
3.8	Chile: evolution of public expenditure, 1970–79	166
3.9	Chile: real internal interest rate and interest rate for external credit, 1975–81	168
3.10	Chile: index of real dollar rate of exchange for imports, 1973–81	169
3.11	Chile: copper prices, 1970–82	170
3.12	Chile: balance of payments, 1974–81	171
3.13	Chile: number of public enterprises, 1970–77	173
3.14	Chile: revenue of state enterprises as percentage of GDP, 1978–82	174
3.15	Chile: financial operations of public enterprises, 1978–82	176
3.16	Chile: financial operations of the consolidated public sector, 1978–82	177
3.17	Chile: indicators of welfare, 1974–81	182
3.18	Chile: distribution of payments to capital by main sectors, 1960–81	186
3.19	Chile: sources of savings, 1970–81	190
3.20	Chile: authorised and actual foreign investment by sectors, 1974–83	191
3.21	Chile: public and private shares of gross domestic investment, 1970–81	191
3.A1	Chile: gross investment in fixed capital as a percentage of GDP and index of per capita domestic investment in fixed capital, 1960–82	204
3.A2	Chile: sectoral shares of GDP, selected years, 1907–82	205
3.A3	Chile: payments to labour as percentages of domestic income, selected years, 1940–81	206
3.A4	Chile: annual rate of change of GDP and per capita GDP and index of per capita GDP and per capita industrial value added, 1960–82	207
3.A5	Chile: variation of the consumer price index, 1950–82	208
3.A6	Chile: foreign debt and reserves, 1960–81	209
4.A1	Mexico: sectoral growth and expenditure composition	236
4.A2	Mexico: gross fixed capital formation by institutional sector	237
4.A3	Mexico: sources of savings	238

List of Tables

4.A4	Mexico: public sector accumulation account	238
4.A5	Mexico: external debt	239
4.A6	Mexico: functional distribution of income, 1940–80	240

Preface

The origins of this book go back to the 1978 Conference of the Political Studies Association of the UK when Christian Anglade convened a session on the state and capital accumulation in Latin America with papers on Chile by Carlos Fortin and on Brazil by Anglade himself. The papers exhibited an uncommon degree of similarity in approach, and this, together with the response of the small but incisive group attending the session, led us to think that the topic was worth pursuing with a view to a volume of case studies covering the more industrially advanced countries of the continent.

We were further encouraged later that year when Fortin submitted a revised version of his paper to a seminar on the state and industrialisation in Latin America held at CEDLA in Amsterdam. Also presented to the seminar was a paper on the state and capital accumulation in Mexico by Valpy FitzGerald, and again the coincidence of issues and approaches was striking. FitzGerald agreed to produce a case study based on his contribution to the seminar, and other papers were commissioned on Argentina, Colombia and Uruguay.

A number of intervening factors delayed progress in the project until 1981. By the end of that year, however, the Brazilian and Chilean case studies were growing into medium length monographs, and the volume as a whole was far exceeding the original format. The idea of a two-volume book covering all South American countries – except Paraguay, a special case – plus Mexico was then discussed and agreed. Further papers were commissioned on Bolivia, Ecuador, Peru and Venezuela, and the editors undertook to write a substantial introduction presenting both historical materials and the conceptual framework.

We believe this attempt is now particularly timely. The collapse in the eighties of the export-oriented models that had been adopted by many Latin American countries in the preceding decade – and which had in some cases been hailed as 'economic miracles' – has once again put the question of the role of the state in accumulation in the periphery at the top of the agenda. In some instances, such models had retained an industrialising bias, while in others the objective had been to specialise in the export of primary products. In all cases, however, two features appeared: a growing dependence on inflows of foreign financial capital to make up the balance of payments deficits due to increased imports of capital and intermediate or consumer goods; and a stepped up role for the state, whether in an essentially repressive capacity or combining also a role in direct production and accumulation. An evaluation, therefore, of the chances of capitalist development in Latin America in the light of the export-oriented experience calls for an inquiry into the presence of the state in capital accumulation, into the complex interaction between the social and political struggle and the economic mechanisms of accumulation and into the pattern of relations between the internal accumulation processes and the world capitalist system. This is what this book attempts to do.

The first volume includes a historical and conceptual introduction and case studies of Brazil, Chile and Mexico. The second volume contains case studies of Argentina, Bolivia, Colombia, Ecuador, Peru, Uruguay and Venezuela plus a concluding chapter in which the editors attempt to draw together the arguments of all country chapters to suggest some tentative conclusions of relevance to the whole of the continent and, it is hoped, to other Third World industrialising regions.

The intellectual debts of the various authors are recorded in each of the chapters. The debt of the editors to Mrs Rosalind Woodhouse and Ms June Yates for the patient and careful typing of the manuscript is gratefully acknowledged here.

Christian Anglade
Carlos Fortin

List of Abbreviations

ABC	Santo André, São Bernardo, São Caetano
AFL–CIO	American Federation of Labor–Congress of Industrial Organisations
ALALC	Asociación Latinoamericana de Libre Comercio
ARENA	Aliança Renovadora Nacional
BEFIEX	Comissão para a Concessão de Benefícios Fiscais e Programas Especiais de Exportação
BNDE	Banco Nacional de Desenvolvimento Econômico
CACEX	Carteira de Comércio Exterior
CDE	Conselho de Desenvolvimento Econômico
CEBRAP	Centro Brasileiro de Análise e Planejamento
CEDLA	Centro de Estudios y Documentación Latinoamericanos
CEPAL	Comisión Económica para América Latina
CIA	Central Intelligence Agency
CIDE	Centro de Investigación y Docencia Económicas
CIEPLAN	Corporación de Investigaciones Económicas para Latinoamérica
CORFO	Corporación de Fomento de la Producción
CP	Communist Party
CVRD	Companhia Vale do Rio Doce
DIEESE	Departamento Intersindical de Estudos e Estatísticas de Salários
DINA	Dirección de Inteligencia Nacional
ECLA	Economic Commission for Latin America
EEC	European Economic Community
FGTS	Fundo de Garantia do Tempo de Serviço
FGV	Fundação Getulio Vargas
FIBGE	Fundação Instituto Brasileiro de Geografia e Estatística
GATT	General Agreement on Trade and Tariffs
GDP	Gross Domestic Product

GNP	Gross National Product
IAPI	Instituto Argentino de Promoción del Intercambio
IBGE	Instituto Brasileiro de Geografia e Estatística
IBRD	International Bank for Reconstruction and Development
IDB	Inter-American Development Bank
IFDA	International Foundation for Development Alternatives
IMF	International Monetary Fund
INPC	Indice Nacional de Preços ao Consumidor
IPEA	Instituto de Planejamento Econômico e Social
INPES	Instituto de Pesquisas
ISI	Import substituting industrialisation
LAER	*Latin America Economic Report*
LIBOR	London Interbank Offered Rate
MAP	Movimiento de Acción Popular
MDB	Movimento Democrático Brasileiro
NAFINSA	Nacional Financiera Sociedad Anómina
ODEPLAN	Oficina Nacional de Planificación
OPEC	Organisation of Petroleum Exporting Countries
ORTN	Obrigações Reajustaveis do Tesouro Nacional
PEMEX	Petróleos Mexicanos
PMDB	Partido Movimento Democrático Brasileiro
PNAD	Pesquisa Nacional por Amostra de Domicílios
PND	Plano Nacional de Desenvolvimento
PRI	Partido Revolucionario Institucional
PSBR	Public Sector Borrowing Requirements
PT	Partido dos Trabalhadores
SEPAFIN	Secretaría de Patrimonio y Fomento Industrial
SEST	Secretaria para o Contrôle das Estatais
SPP	Secretaría de Programación y Presupuesto
SUMOC	Superintendência da Moeda e do Crédito
USAID	United States Agency for International Development
VAT	Value Added Tax

Notes on the Contributors

Editors

Christian Anglade is Lecturer in Government and Director of the M.A. Programme in Latin American Government and Politics, University of Essex. He studied politics and economics and holds a degree in politics, a *licence ès lettres* and of a DES in Political Science from the University of Toulouse, France. He has taught at several universities, both in Europe and in Latin America. He has written on Latin American politics and political economy.

Carlos Fortin is Fellow and Deputy Director of the Institute of Development Studies at the University of Sussex. He holds degrees from the University of Chile and Yale University, and has taught at the Latin American School of Political Science and Public Administration (Santiago), the University of Chile and the University of Essex. He has published articles and papers on the political economy of the role of the state in development, particularly in the field of natural resources.

Contributor

E. V. K. FitzGerald is Professor of Economics at the Institute of Social Studies in The Hague. He read PPE at Oxford and did his doctorate in economics at Cambridge, where he was Assistant Director of Development Studies. He was adviser to the Mexican government between 1976 and 1979 and has published papers on the fiscal problems of Mexico, US–Mexico linkages and the experience of the Depression. He is currently seconded as economic adviser to the government of Nicaragua.

1 The State and Capital Accumulation in Latin America: a Conceptual and Historical Introduction

CHRISTIAN ANGLADE and CARLOS FORTIN

The concept of capital accumulation is as old as political economy itself. Curiously, though, it was not until the mid-1970s that it began to feature significantly in analyses of Latin American development.[1] To be sure, the major contributions of Latin American economists in the 1950s and 1960s included treatments of issues of capital formation, and many of the relevant discussions were couched in political economy terms.[2] But the emphasis tended to be on the consideration of abstract variables such as the aggregate level of savings and investment opportunities.

The introduction of the language of accumulation – which is partially to be explained in terms of the growing impact of neo-Marxist approaches – meant a shift towards a more concrete exploration of the class structure and of the social conflict concerning the creation and appropriation of social surplus. This, in a way, both reflected and superseded the common distinction whereby capital accumulation refers to the building of capital reserves for purposes of investment and subsequent expansion of production, while capital formation refers to the investment of those reserves in fixed capital. In the sense discussed here, the notion of capital accumulation includes both, although emphasis is placed on questions about the origin of the surplus and about control over it: how is accumulation financed? Which economic actors – the multinationals, the state, private domestic capital and its various fractions – control decisions that affect the direction of accumulation by sectors of activity and the choice of technologies? What are the effects of the pattern of capital accumulation on the possibility of continuing expanded reproduction of the system?

The shift, therefore, is not simply one of terminology. It involves going beyond the purely 'economic' analysis of saving and investment to consider the concrete social actors who shape, and are also affected by, the process of accumulation. And, in the case of Latin America, this implies primarily a reassessment of the role of the state. Although discussions on the role of the state in Latin American development are nothing new,[3] it is only rather recently that systematic attempts have been made to link its role as an economic actor with its character as an institutionalised arena for political struggle, and to take advantage of theoretical contributions that seek to relate the two to processes of accumulation and expanded reproduction.

This is precisely what the case studies that follow attempt to do. Before moving on to them, though, it seems useful to review – if only briefly – the main available theoretical contributions concerning both the question of accumulation in the periphery of the world capitalist system and the analysis of the role of the state in accumulation. We shall then offer a historical account of the role of the state in Latin American development and will conclude with an assessment of the main features of the contemporary process of accumulation in the three countries covered in this volume.

THE DEBATE ON CAPITAL ACCUMULATION IN THE CAPITALIST PERIPHERY

The question whether the countries in the periphery of the world capitalist system could undergo a process of capitalist development was not a matter of debate before the 1950s, either in liberal or in Marxist economics.

The basic assumption of liberal economics is that free international trade results in a general equilibrium, with every country specialising in the production of those goods in which it has a relative cost advantage. In this context, trade is considered a rational choice, since it allows each country to maximise the use of the factors with which it is best endowed. As a result, each country gains through the international division of labour. Because the initial – providential – endowment of factors of production is not the same for all countries, some are inevitably less developed than others, but all share in the benefits of the system.

On the other hand, the assumption of classical Marxist theory (notably in the writings of Marx and Lenin) was that the contradictions within the capitalist mode of production were responsible for the expansion of capitalism from the centre towards the periphery, as a result of which the latter would eventually catch up with the industrial countries. The equalisation of the levels of capitalist development was only a question of time.

It was in the 1950s that both assumptions began to be challenged, particularly in Latin America.

The Early Debate in Development Economics

Based on an analysis of the more developed among the underdeveloped countries, the Economic Commission for Latin America (CEPAL) first questioned the general equilibrium virtues of the international division of labour, by emphasising both the tendency for the terms of trade to deteriorate for primary producing countries, and their dependency on 'traditional' (i.e. non-manufactured) exports.[4] To these external obstacles to economic development were added other – internal – ones, closely related to the first, since their existence had been reinforced by the imposition of the international divison of labour on the primary producing countries. This had helped to maintain in them archaic social and political structures, and a highly unequal distribution of the factors of production (land). Although not radical – in the sense that it believed that capitalist development was still possible for the Latin American countries provided some essential reforms were introduced both in the trade relations with industrial countries and in the internal structures of the Latin American societies – the CEPAL critique was a blow to the consensus surrounding the axiomatic optimum of the capitalist system at world level.

Partly sparked off by this challenge, development economics began to produce models and recommendations which focused on those policies most likely to allow underdeveloped countries to make better use of their own resources in order to achieve development. These theories make the same monistic assumption as classical Marxist theory, i.e. that the development of capitalism in the periphery is only a question of time. Unlike Marx and Lenin, however, Lewis and Rostow do not believe that this is due to contradictions in the capitalist system, or accept the notion of an expansionist tendency resulting from the need to resolve them. They suggest instead that capitalist development is a possibility open to all countries which have a sufficiently favourable factor endowment and which are prepared to implement the 'right' policies. When the two are combined, capitalist development must follow in 'stages' according to Rostow.[5]

Lewis made an important contribution to the analysis of the process of capital accumulation in underdeveloped countries when he addressed himself to the key problem of the distribution of the surplus (in the sense of the difference between the price of goods and their costs of production). The starting point of his analysis is that most underdeveloped countries have limited capital resources but an unlimited supply of labour concentrated in the subsistence agricultural sector. This situation, which results from the presence of large numbers of low productivity, low wage workers in agriculture being attracted by the prospect of higher productivity and better paid jobs in industry, helps keep industrial wages low, since 'the wage which the expanding capitalist sector has to pay is determined by what people can earn outside that sector'.[6] The existence of a labour surplus tends to generate a situation in which, he suggests, the capitalist surplus grows while the average wage remains constant. Through reinvestment, this surplus will help the capitalist sector to expand further, absorbing more labour from the subsistence sector, thus producing a larger surplus and so on, until the supply of labour from the subsistence sector is exhausted. Before this point is reached, higher wages in the industrial sector would tend to slow down profits, which would reduce the rate of investment and the absorption of surplus labour. When all surplus labour has been absorbed, the wage level will begin to rise nominally, but further increases in productivity will continue to widen the gap between wages and profits, thus maintaining the rate of accumulation.

The central assumption in Lewis' model is that profits are the only source of savings, or – rather – that only those savings resulting from profits are invested. This classical assumption of a perfect identity between the investment rate and the rate of savings from profits means that inequality alone in the distribution of the surplus is not sufficient for the economy to expand. In typical classical mistrust of the landowners, it must be an inequality in the distribution of income in favour of profits, not rents.

Several criticisms have been made of Lewis' model: (i) it contains a serious internal contradiction since, given the level of wages and the rate of savings anticipated, it would inevitably suffer from insufficient aggregate demand, which would reduce profits; (ii) his native capitalists are idealised versions of 19th century protestant-type entrepreneurs acting in a context of perfect competition instead of being submitted to the greater monopoly power of foreign capitalists whose accumulation behaviour is not primarily a function of the features of the host country economy; (iii) the assumption of a higher saving and investment capacity of the capitalist classes as compared to the non-capitalists is based on the earlier historical experience of industrial societies and does not take into account the fact that – in contemporary underdeveloped countries – the capitalists have easy access to external outlets for capital accumulation, which the non-capitalist classes have not. The latter's savings can conceivably be channelled into domestic capital accumulation to a larger extent than those of the capitalist classes, and should therefore be encouraged rather than systematically ruled out.

But these are academic criticisms. What matters is that Lewis' recommendations concerning the optimum distribution of the surplus for the purpose of economic growth have been put into practice in many underdeveloped countries which are trying to achieve rapid growth through industrialisation. The relevance of his theory to Latin America is particularly obvious, since – with the exception of Argentina and Uruguay – all the countries of the area have a labour surplus in their subsistence agricultural sector. This labour surplus has played – and continues to play – a crucial role in their models of growth and capital accumulation, to the point that it is suggested here that they could not be understood without reference to it. Lewis's theory is frequently invoked as a justification for the low wage policies enforced in those countries. Whether a distribution of national income increasingly favourable to profits necessarily generates higher rates of capital accumulation is one of the questions which this book proposes to investigate.

In general terms, the position of most development economists concerning the 'best' model of growth and capital accumulation for underdeveloped countries has shifted along two axes: (1) export of primary commodities versus industrialisation, and (2) balanced versus unbalanced growth.

As already suggested, concentration on the production of primary commodities exports was for a long time the key recommendation of liberal economics, for which the initial factor endowment should determine the specialisation of each country. But, in the 1950s and 1960s, CEPAL's analysis combined with an emerging new international division of labour to shift the emphasis on industrialisation, first through an acceleration of import substitution, and then through export promotion. The idea, immediately attractive to the decision-makers of most underdeveloped countries, was to reduce their dependence both on industrial imports and on traditional exports. This was to improve the situation of the balance of payments and to set in motion a more autonomous and more reliable model of capital accumulation than the traditional one based on primary exports.

This debate on the most suitable specialisation in the nature of production was – and still is – frequently related to another debate concerning the advantages and disadvantages of 'balanced' and 'unbalanced' growth.

The ideas developed by Hirschman in favour of an unbalanced model of growth have been influential with both national decision-makers and international organisations since the 1960s, for the same reasons as those which explain the popularity of the industrialisation model, of which it is a more elaborate expression. Based on the same argument of the scarcity of capital resources in underdeveloped countries as used by Lewis, his model advocates a concentration of all resources in one sector of the economy, namely the modern industrial sector, thus deliberately increasing the unbalanced pattern of growth. If the modern industrial sector is chosen, it is because it has what Hirschman calls the 'largest linkage effects', capable of spreading development both forward and backward to the other sectors of the economy. In the context of capitalist development, the choice of this sector is also necessary to attract private capital investment. After a first stage, when growth will be more unbalanced and the distribution of income more concentrated, Hirschman suggests that the 'linkage effects' will begin to operate and, somehow, pull the economy together in a process of development.[7]

As in the case of Lewis, Hirschman's ideas were well received in Latin America, which provides us with several tests of the validity of his model. Without pre-empting the findings of the different policy evaluations contained in this book, it seems that – in general – the mechanisms which are supposed to put the 'linkage effects' into motion do not work. On the contrary, the tendency is for the modern sector to grow faster while the other sectors lag behind. This is hardly surprising since the high profits yielded by the modern sector continue to attract private capital which does not find any motivation in other – less profitable – forms of investment. The state has thus to move in, to fill those 'empty spaces' in production and to increase the level of public subsidies to those sectors of production which – like agriculture – do not attract private capital. When it does not, there tends to be an accentuation of the disequilibria within the economy and eventually a slowing down of growth in the modern industrial sector as well. In most of Latin America, the result is that the growth potential of manufacturing industry is reduced by the persistence of the low productivity levels of agricultural production for the home market and by the widespread poverty of the rural population.

This is the recurrent problem with the solutions of classical inspiration which have been implemented in underdeveloped countries with a view to promoting development. They are adopted because they promise economic growth and propose to solve the problem of insufficient domestic investment by intensifying capital accumulation through a greater shift of income distribution in favour of profits. They are thus economically attractive and politically acceptable to the dominant classes of most underdeveloped countries. Internal demand obviously suffers from such patterns of distribution of the surplus, but this is not considered to be a problem; on the contrary, low wages are one of the main advantages that these countries enjoy in their export promotion policies, and a growing external demand should more than compensate for insufficient demand at home, with the added advantage of helping out with the balance of payments.

Beside being based on the assumption of pure and perfect competition and free trade, this strategy is also based on an evaluation of production costs which tends to overestimate labour costs and to neglect the costs of technology transfers for underdeveloped countries. Today moreover, it would seem that the financial crises of those Latin American countries which have tried to follow this recommendation have also demonstrated that export promotion is not an unquestionable panacea for sustained growth, even if one is prepared to overlook the heavy social costs that it entails. Yet, it is presented to them both as the path to development and as the solution to the present crises.

While recognising that the only way in which the Latin American industrialising countries have been able to reduce their trade deficit recently has been through cutting their imports down to levels that are not sustainable, and while admitting that their potential export growth is more limited than that of the Asian industrialising countries, the bankers' recommendation for Latin America continues to be export promotion and, at home, monetary restrictions and wage restraint.[8] It is made clear that IMF support and some renewal of international credit entirely depend on these priorities being fully implemented. The examples to be followed are those of the Asian industrialising countries, where export/GNP ratio averages 35 per cent against 15 per cent for Latin America. Since the adoption of austerity measures throughout Latin America has done little to improve export records over the past few years, to propose to step up austerity even further almost amounts to saying that authoritarian solutions will have to be stepped up as well. This is a more likely outcome than the one implied by the suggestion that wage restraint should be reinforced and contradictorily predicting at the same time that 'governments that give first priority to exports will be best placed to provide steadily rising living standards to their people'.[9]

Recent data on GDP growth rates and prospects for Latin American and Asian industrialising countries highlight the difficulties involved in relying on export promotion in a context of recession, protectionism and intense competition for export markets. The GDP record of all Latin American countries in 1982 compares unfavourably with that of the Asian countries and, with the apparent exceptions of Argentina and Colombia, the projections for 1983 are all negative for Latin America and positive for Asia. In practice – as this book will examine for Latin America – the problem of adequate demand for an expanding industrial production is not always easily solved by relying on export promotion, and insufficient aggregate demand remains one of the main causes of the crisis which affects most of the industrialising countries of the area.

Not all development economists have been advocating unbalanced growth, low wages and an exclusive reliance on exports. In the 1950s, when the debate really started, authors like Nurkse recommended balanced growth between industry and agriculture, while others – like Strassman – argued, against Lewis, that the more nearly equal the distribution of income, the more likely was economic growth. Later on, Furtado, from a structuralist rather than a neo-classical perspective, also argued that – in the specific case of Latin America – it was the lack of sufficient consumer demand which caused stagnation and prevented development; in other words, the alleged negative savings effects of a more equal distribution of national income would be a stimulus rather than an obstacle to growth.[10] More generally, the argument about the compatibility of growth and redistribution of income was forcefully revived in the early 1970s by Chenery and others.[11] But, possibly because these views were contrary to the prevailing orthodoxy and certainly because they were unacceptable to the dominant classes of the underdeveloped countries, their impact on policy making was limited.

The Marxist Debate

Among Marxist economists and social scientists, the debate on capital accumulation in the capitalist periphery has been between those who – against the classical Marxist assumption of an equalisation of the capitalist mode of production at world level – argued that capitalism was blocking development in the Third World, and those who – returning to the classics – criticised the thesis of the 'development of underdevelopment' of the Third World as being both empirically unfounded and theoretically inconsistent.

The assumption made by Marx and Lenin on the development of capitalism in the periphery was challenged in the 1950s by Baran, who argued that the expansion of capitalism to backward countries had not allowed them to develop. Because it had encouraged primary exports and discouraged industrialisation, it had helped traditional dominant classes to remain in power, as a result of which the available surplus had not been used for productive investment. Elsewhere, together with Sweezy, he developed the idea that – at its monopoly stage – capitalist expansion to the periphery was motivated by the search for higher profit rates which were repatriated to the centre where they were necessary to resolve the basic underconsumptionist contradiction. The constant extraction of the enlarged surplus made available in the Third World through the expansion of monopoly capital allowed the centre to continue to accumulate and develop at the cost of the non-accumulation and underdevelopment of the periphery.[12]

It was basically the same idea that was further developed by the brand of 'dependency theory' associated with the names of Amin, Frank and Wallerstein.[13] For them, the processes of economic reproduction in the dependent countries are but the local expression of a process of capital accumulation in the centre which feeds on surplus extracted from the periphery. The closer the links between the centre and the periphery, the less likely it is that the periphery will achieve capital accumulation. Links with the centre actually 'underdevelop' the periphery. In this they agree – albeit through a different theoretical route – with Emmanuel, who made perhaps the most original contribution to economic dependency thinking by using the labour theory of value to explain the relative fall in the international prices of exports of underdeveloped countries. Emmanuel, however, did not regard this fall as inherent in centre–periphery relations and therefore was considerably more sanguine about the possibility of capitalist development in the periphery than the 'development of underdevelopment' writers.[14]

The 'development of underdevelopment' argument prompted a reaction in the 1970s which found its origin both in the observation of trends different from those predicted by the argument and in a demand for a more rigorous theoretical framework for the analysis. The influential work of Warren highlighted the success of a number of underdeveloped countries in undergoing rapid industrialisation[15] and – more generally – the fact that the growth rates of the less developed countries as a whole during the 20th century 'compare favourably with the growth rates of the now developed countries in the early years of their development'.[16]

The basic premise of this 'return to the classics' is the notion that for Marx, economic development is measured only by the development of the productive forces of society.[17] Since there is ample evidence that the productive forces are developing in many countries of the Third World, increasing the socialisation and the productivity of labour and thus enlarging the capacity of those economies to produce goods and services, development is taking place. That this development of the productive forces engenders contradictions and increases social inequalities is not surprising; this is part of every process of capitalist development. Similarly, that crises occur is inevitable, since they are the recurrent outcome of the contradictions of the capitalist mode of production.

The orthodox Marxist critique of the 'development of underdevelopment' approach succeeded in exposing the latter's fundamental weakness, which is to see dependency as a necessary and sufficient determinant of underdevelopment. The critique itself, however, accepted the oversimplified definition of the issues introduced by the 'development of underdevelopment' approach. Their notion of economic development is a highly aggregate and undifferentiated one, in effect regarding it as synonymous with growth of industrial output. They argue that, since capitalism is one, its development in the periphery necessarily follows the same patterns as it did in the centre and that crises and contradictions in that process are evidence that economic development is underway. Thus, the critique does not concern itself with identifying the specific features of capital accumulation in the periphery – including the interaction between 'internal' and 'external' factors – and the extent to which they might differ from those of accumulation in the centres of the capitalist system. This, however, is the crucial set of issues. While the characterisation of capital accumulation in the periphery can only be undertaken in terms of concrete, historical cases and with full regard for the social and political context in which accumulation takes place, the relevant issues can be identified in a more general manner.

1. A first set of issues has to do with the sources of surplus for accumulation in the periphery and with the origins of the savings mobilised: is accumulation based primarily on absolute surplus value and the superexploitation of labour, as was the case in the first stages of accumulation in the central countries, or on increases in productivity resulting from the introduction of more advanced technologies (relative surplus value), as is the case in contemporary industrialised economies, or both? Is accumulation based on domestic savings? What is the role of foreign inflows, and what form do they take: direct investment or financial flows, or both and in what proportion? Have these flows changed over time and what has been the recent dynamics of those changes? The latter question appears essential to characterise the case of many industrialising countries of the Third World in general and Latin America in particular in the context of the eighties.
2. Closely related to the preceding set of issues is the question of control over the accumulation process: to what extent does it lie within or outside the national society? What are the roles of multinational corporations, the state and local private capital in accumulation? Here, the critique of the impact of multinational corporations on Third World development remains relevant.[18] Their degree of control is important because – in the nature of the situation – there might be fundamental decisions about accumulation made by individuals and groups who are not themselves part of the society where accumulation is taking place, and who will therefore respond but indirectly to the internal social and political process. It is also important because of the nature of multinational corporations as economic actors whose logic of accumulation is global rather than national; thus, their control means that the operation of the law of value within the national economy is overridden by the operation of the law of value internationally, and this will have concrete consequences for other sets of relevant issues, such as the choice of sectors for expansion and the choice of technologies.

3. A third set of issues has to do with the sectors in which accumulation takes place. The basic distinction here is between the consumer goods sector (Department II in Marxist terminology) and the sector producing capital goods and intermediate inputs (Department I in the Marxist vocabulary). In which one does accumulation concentrate, and what is the pattern of control in each of them? In this connection the hypothesis has been put forward that, inasmuch as peripheral accumulation is dominated by multinational corporations, whole areas of production will tend to be reserved for other locations within the global corporate strategy, and this will affect particularly the location of capital goods industries; the accumulation circuit in the periphery will thus tend to be incomplete.[19] Within the consumer goods sector, the multinationals will also tend to reproduce the spread of products that they exhibit in the home market, thus influencing the pattern of consumption in the peripheral society and giving rise to the need for policies of income concentration.

4. This raises the question of the market for which the output of the production added through accumulation is primarily destined: is it the internal market or is it the export market? This will be a function of the pattern of control over accumulation, of the potential size of the internal market, of the level of accumulation reached and of the overall economic policies implemented by the state. An accumulation process oriented towards the internal market and coexisting with regressive income distribution policies might encounter problems of insufficient aggregate demand that might require a shift to exports. The shift might progressively free the accumulation process of its dependence on internal demand – and therefore might become compatible with policies of superexploitation of labour – but only at the expense of increasing external vulnerability. This is particularly important as the expansion of world trade and of international liquidity in the second half of the 1960s and the beginnings of the 1970s gives way to the global recession, the contraction of world trade, the protectionist tendencies and the financial crisis of the 1980s. It simply might not be possible for Third World countries to attempt to reproduce the pattern of export-oriented accumulation that was proclaimed as the path to development in the preceding decade.

5. A final set of questions concerns the issue of technology and technological choice. The type of accumulation that obtains in peripheral countries – in terms of control, concentration on given

sectors and market orientation – will determine the degree of technological dependence of the process. A capital goods sector controlled by multinationals and oriented to exports will require, to remain competitive, the introduction of frequent technological changes, because of the rapid obsolescence of technology in the advanced economies. The dependence of the process of accumulation on access to advanced technology and the cost of technological transfers for the peripheral economy will increase. In effect, multinational corporations will always have a preference for advanced, labour-saving technology, since it entails externalities and economies of scale at world level for them. This choice of technology might, in turn, increase the problems of employment and insufficient aggregate demand for the host economy.

In summary, the exploration of these various sets of issues – whose interconnection should have, furthermore, become apparent from the preceding discussion – could provide a richer and at the same time more accurate picture of the degree to which a given process of capital acumulation in the periphery is relatively solid and self-sustaining or, by contrast, is highly vulnerable to external shocks. As already indicated, such an exploration can only be done in concrete terms, and paying special attention to the level of capital accumulation which prevails in the peripheral society in question. In this sense, it is not in dispute that accumulation in the periphery proceeds through the unfolding of contradictions and their resolution through crises. However, what must be emphasised here is the extent to which crises and contradictions in peripheral capital accumulation differ from those that accompany accumulation in the centre. While, in the latter, crises are mechanisms of control and resolution of the contradictions of accumulation and the subsequent restructuring of capital re-establishes accumulation at a higher level, in peripheral capitalism contradictions and crises are magnified by dependency. The response of international capital to an intensification of internal contradictions in the periphery is often an interruption of accumulation and a restructuring elsewhere. Both the magnitude of the crisis and the time required for restructuring and recovery are amplified; eventually the process might well lead to a breakdown of accumulation altogether.

Thus, what is required is an overall political economy assessment of the model of capital accumulation on which industrial growth is based in specific peripheral countries and of the costs and benefits of growth for the different actors in the process. This is a question that has to be examined within the social and political context in which the process of accumulation takes place. The choices and the decisions which shape that process are political as well as economic, and to opt for a particular pattern of social distribution of the national income is an essentially political decision. In this respect an influential contribution has been made by the approach of 'dependent-associate' development put forward by Cardoso,[20] which recognises the specificity of peripheral capitalist accumulation and its dependent character. It has not, however, fully incorporated the implications of the changes in the world economy and in the nature of dependency which might significantly modify its basically optimistic prognosis about the future of capital accumulation in countries such as Brazil.[21] From a concentration on investment capital and profit returns in the 1960s, the emphasis shifted in the 1970s to financial flows and interest payments. This has important consequences for both the central and the peripheral countries. On the one hand, it makes returns to international capital independent of specific productive enterprises in the periphery: interest and capital repayments are due whether the debtor economy is doing well or badly. The risk inherent in direct foreign investment is in that way transferred from the centre to the periphery – although, of course, the risk of default in the medium or long term become, if anything, greater given the overindebtedness incurred by some peripheral countries. On the other hand, the shift involves the peripheral state in a direct way in the process of dependency. While most of the credit is contracted by the private sector – including some local subsidiaries of multinational corporations – the state becomes increasingly the financial mediator between the local economy and international capital; government guarantees to private loans tend to become the rule rather than the exception. In this way, the state sees its room for manoeuvre reduced at the international level. A new form of dependency is thus introduced, one that is not adequately accounted for by 'dependency theory', as it is basically a theory of the internationalisation of productive capital. This new form of dependency means a new form of vulnerability of the processes of capital accumulation in the periphery, and casts further doubts about their ability to continue in a progressive and cumulative way. These recent developments are another reason why a reassessment of the role that the state plays in capital accumulation in the capitalist periphery is required.

THE STATE AND CAPITAL ACCUMULATION IN PERIPHERAL CAPITALISM: SOME CONCEPTUAL NOTES

There is little dissent among students of development on the proposition that the state plays a central role in the process of capital accumulation in peripheral societies. The consensus disappears, however, when it comes to the question of the definition of that role, its bases and its determinants; there we find at best inconclusive, albeit often enlightening, debate, at worst ideological polemics. Very often guidance in the conceptual intricacies of the role of the state in capitalist reproduction is sought in Marxist theory, offering, as it does, a powerful point of entry into the question of the relationship between civil and political society, between the economy and the state.

The Marxist theory of the state, though, is itself undergoing a crisis; undeveloped in the writings of Marx and Engels, and with the important contributions of Lenin and Gramsci trapped at crucial points in the immediate urgencies of their political praxis, it reached the second half of the present century in some disarray. As a result, the contemporary theoretical discussion on the state within Marxism exhibits all the features of vigorous internecine debate associated with not as yet fully constituted theoretical fields.[22]

For all these serious problems, Marxist theory still offers the most promising conceptual framework to undertake the difficult task of locating the state within the process of expanded reproduction of capitalism in the periphery, especially if it is understood to cover – as it should – not only self-styled 'orthodox' viewpoints but also contributions which, while broadly recognising a Marxist lineage, are none the less prepared to depart from the received doctrinal body. In particular, the Latin American contributions on the 'bureaucratic–authoritarian' state – notwithstanding some of the weaknesses of the concept – represent an indispensable point of reference for some of the central conceptual questions.[23]

The following notes will not presume to attempt to provide the missing theory of the capitalist state in Marxism. Their purpose – at once more modest and, we hope, more relevant – is to raise some of the fundamental issues that a class theory of the role of the state in peripheral capitalist reproduction should tackle, and to review briefly the ongoing debates surrounding them; in the process, it will attempt to suggest some conceptual tools to deal with the concrete analysis of the state in Latin America as they are exemplified in the case studies contained in the two volumes that make up this book.

Two Meanings of the State

Our starting point is the recognition that the concept of the state in the Marxist tradition contains two meanings which, although closely related, are nevertheless distinguishable. On the one hand, the state expresses the domination of a given combination of classes and fractions of classes on the rest of the society. Notions such as 'the social bases of the state' or 'the class nature of the state' make reference to the state in this sense. On the other hand, the state is a set of institutions and personnels through which class domination – which is not exhausted in the state – is expressed.[24] The personnels include high executive and legislative office holders as well as civilian and military bureaucracies, collectively designated sometimes as 'state managers',[25] and the managers of state enterprises, whose status is peculiar as in some instances they are held to constitute a new fraction of the dominant class, the 'state bourgeoisie'.[26] The state in its institutional sense is often referred to as the 'regime', thereby emphasising the formal structures of political authority – parliament, executive, judiciary – but including also the mechanisms of mediation between those structures and the citizens, notably the party system.

Recalling this distinction may help us break through the inconclusive debate between those observers who, emphasising the apparent continuity in the dependent capitalist character of the Latin American state – with the exception of Cuba – claim that fundamentally it remains today the same as it was in the post-war period; and those others who, looking especially at the military dictatorships of the Southern Cone, speak of break, discontinuity, 're-foundation'.[27] A comparable polarisation takes place when the question is whether there are 'essential' differences between those dictatorships and the more democractic regimes in the continent.

The distinction alerts us to the possibility that both statements about the degree of continuity of the Latin American state might be correct; is it perhaps a question of the state as an expression of class domination being the same, but its institutional embodiment having changed between the forties and the eighties? This seems to be the view of Cardoso who writes that the essential feature of the dependent capitalist state in Latin America is that it pursues policies aimed at accelerating capital accumulation through controlling the labour force:

> But, in this respect, there are obvious similarities between the Mexico of the PRI and the Brazil of the Institutional Acts imposed by the

military. In both cases the policies aim to achieve rapid capitalist development, while the governments feel in the long run that continuing worsening of income inequality and dependency do not affect the historic destiny of their respective nations. Indeed, using these criteria, even such democratic countries as Venezuela and Costa Rica have the same type of capitalist state. In these two countries there is likewise a socio-economic exclusion of the majority. There are similar models of economic accumulation (control of wages, patterns of income distribution) and even similar favourable policies toward multinational corporations. Thus the state, when seen as a basic pact of domination, is a comparable capitalist state in all of these countries.[28]

But then the notion of the state as an expression of class domination seems to have lost discriminating power. It exhausts itself in the recognition of the capitalist and dependent character of the Latin American state. This is, of course, a non-trivial statement, but its implications should be pursued further and in a way that distinguishes different paths to capital accumulation within a capitalist – i.e. exclusionary – general type. In other words, while Cardoso is precisely correct in that the *type* of state in Latin America – or at least in those countries with more advanced industrial economies – is the same, capitalist and dependent, we need a theory of the *form* of the state that can differentiate among various patterns of dependent capitalist accumulation.

Type of State, Form of State, Form of Regime

Such a theory is available in the contribution of Nicos Poulantzas and his distinction between the type of state, the form of state and the form of regime.[29] The type of state is determined by the mode of production which is dominant in the social formation in question. The capitalist state is a type of state, as distinct from, for instance, the feudal state; the dependent capitalist state – corresponding to peripheral capitalist social formations, such as the Latin American countries – is a variant of the overall type of capitalist state.

The capitalist state can, however, take on various forms, basically corresponding to the stages of development of the capitalist mode of production. Poulantzas' classification of stages in the capitalist mode of production and the corresponding forms of capitalist state (private capitalism/liberal state; monopoly capitalism/interventionist state; state monopoly capitalism/'strong' state) is debatable and in any case probably not fully applicable to peripheral capitalism. The criteria to differentiate between forms within the type of capitalist state are, however, illuminating:

1. the power bloc, including (i) its composition: the classes or fractions of classes which are included in the power bloc, not necessarily in the sense that they actually control the state apparatus (classes in charge) but in the more fundamental sense that it is their interest that is being furthered by the state; (ii) its index of hegemony, that is the interests of the class or fraction what prevails within the power bloc and which serve as the point of articulation of the interests of the other members, albeit in a conflictive manner; (iii) the nature of the contradictions and concrete relations of force within the power bloc: what are the principal aspects of the contradiction between classes and fractions within the power bloc and *vis-à-vis* the classes or fractions outside it?;
2. the specific form of intervention of the state in the economy and the corresponding incidence of the economic in the sphere of the state.[30]

The definition of the form of the state in terms of the power bloc in Poulantzas appears close to the conceptualization of the state as a 'pact of domination' in Cardoso. However, Cardoso's concern with a class domination that does not pass through the state, introduces a certain ambivalence in his views on whether the 'pact of domination' can vary fundamentally within a dependent capitalist state.[31] In this respect, Poulantzas' notion of form of state is closer to Lenin's – and the classics' – concept of 'state power', defined in terms of the class or fraction of class that holds power, as distinct from 'state apparatuses', including the state personnel and the 'functions' of the state, which Lenin defines as technico-economic, political, ideological, etc.[32] We shall come back to the issue of state functions below, to suggest that the fundamental role of the state in capital accumulation is an element of the form of the state, intimately linked to the composition of the power bloc and its index of hegemony, and to the level of development of capitalist productive forces. By contrast the so-called coercive, ideological and welfare 'functions' of the state are in fact the bases of domination of the existing structure of authority and therefore belong properly in the characterisation of the political regime.

Poulantzas' conceptualisation of the regime basically coincides with the one suggested above, i.e. the formal links between the various structures of the state and the mediations and representations provided by political parties. Forms of regime include all the variants of democratic arrangements (constitutional monarchy, republic, presidentialism, parliamentary system, two-party, multi-party, etc.) as well as politically exclusionary regimes: authoritarian, corporatist, fascist, etc. Cardoso is right in this sense when he suggests that the 'bureaucratic-authoritarian state' is in reality a form of regime, not of state. We would also agree with his emphasis on the notion that there is no simple, univocal correlation between the form of the state and the form of the regime.[33] On the other hand, the degree of compatibility between different forms of dependent capitalist state and different forms of regime is a valid and highly relevant topic for concrete analysis.

The Functions of the Capitalist State

How can we further categorise the notions of form of state and form of regime to come closer to the interaction of the political and the economic in the process of capital accumulation? Raising the question of the role of the state in capitalist accumulation faces us with the vexed issue of the functions of the capitalist state. There are several attempts at conceptualising those functions, both for the capitalist state in general and for the state in peripheral capitalism. Some are hampered by the fact that what appears to be sought is less a conceptualisation of functions than of the bases of domination or the means through which the state secures compliance and the maintenance of the system as a whole and of subsystems within it. Thus, Mandel suggests that the functions of the state are repressive, integrative and technical;[34] Poulantzas, in the same vein, categorises the functions as coercive, ideological and economic.[35]

In other cases, the two criteria (functions and bases/means) are mixed in a single framework. Altvater, for instance, identifies as state functions: (i) the provision of general material conditions of production ('infrastructure'); (ii) establishing and guaranteeing general legal relations, through which the relationships of legal subjects in capitalist society are performed; (iii) the regulation of the conflict between wage-labour and capital, and if necessary the political repression of the working class; (iv) safeguarding the existence and expansion of total national capital on the capitalist world market.[36] Clearly the third function is in a different category from the other three: the legal order can serve different purposes, including, for instance, the regulation of the conflict between capital and labour.

The well-known and influential framework proposed by O'Connor is also relevant here. He suggests that the functions of the state in contemporary advanced capitalism are accumulation and legitimation, and that a fundamental tension exists between them, since both take up resources. State expenditures promoting accumulation (social capital) are projects and services that increase the productivity of labour power (social investment, such as infrastructure) or lower the cost of reproduction of labour (social consumption, such as social insurance); state expenditures required to maintain social harmony (social expenses) fulfil the legitimation function: the clearest example is the welfare system, but expenses on law and order as well as on external warfare are also classed here. Specific expenditures will often fulfil both functions, but the basic tension is always present and, together with the fact that socialisation of the costs of accumulation and legitimation is not accompanied by socialisation of profits, it leads to a fiscal crisis of the state: state expenditures tend to increase more rapidly than the means of financing them.[37] O'Connor's solution largely avoids the confusion between functions and means, but, on the other hand, it neglects the coercive aspects of state domination, which are somewhat incongruously placed within the legitimation function; as it happens, the coercive aspect of state power is of paramount importance in peripheral capitalist societies, as this book will attempt to show.

Finally, Evers has proposed another conceptualisation which has the double advantage of deliberately avoiding the confusion between functions and means and of being geared to the case of the state in peripheral societies. He suggests the functions of the state in the capitalist periphery are: (i) guarantee of insertion in the world market; (ii) imposition of general market rules; (iii) guarantee of availability of labour; (iv) guarantee of general material conditions of production. He then identifies four means of state action: (i) money; (ii) the law; (iii) ideology; and (iv) violence.[38] Here the problem is more with the categorisation of means than with that of functions – although we shall try to improve on the definition of functions below; the means listed seem to belong in different levels of abstraction and possess non-comparable characteristics. Thus, while the state has the monopoly of law-making and of legitimate violence, it does not have the monopoly of the production of ideologies nor, in effect, of money; the law, on the other hand, can itself be a means to regulate money or produce ideology or prescribe legitimate violence.

It would seem, therefore, that none of the approaches reviewed provides by itself a fully satisfying framework to deal with the question of the functions of the state; they do, of course, provide valuable insights, as the references to them in the contributions to this book below should show. However, what is required is an attempt to bring together the insights in a more comprehensive framework specifically addressed to the understanding of the role of the state in capital accumulation in dependent capitalist societies and the links with forms of political regime. While the contributions to these two volumes do not adopt a single, unified conceptual apparatus, they revolve around the kinds of issues raised by the framework that we now turn to presenting.

The Roles of the State and the Bases of Domination

The starting point for such a framework is the notion that the dynamics of accumulation in capitalist societies are given by the extent to, and the way in, which surplus value is extracted from labour by capital, and the manner of its subsequent apportionment among the various fractions of capital. The state will play various roles in the process, albeit with different degrees of intensity and in different ways. The roles themselves will be contradictory since, through them, the state becomes deeply involved in the class struggle at the economic level, including the conflict between fractions of classes. These roles are:

1. Guarantor of the conditions for the maximisation of the surplus value to be extracted by capital as a whole. This confronts the state directly with the working class, but, as suggested, the confrontation is ambivalent. The fundamental facet of this role is the control and disciplining of labour through regulations, restrictions on wages, etc. at points involving, as Altvater suggests, political repression of the workers. There is, however, another facet in the form of a minimal protection of some workers against excessive exploitation that could threaten the expanded reproduction of the labour force; the provision of welfare and labour legislation establishing workers' rights are elements of this facet. This is not to imply that workers' rights are a result of the logic of capital accumulation requiring the protection of labour; in concrete terms, most rights of the workers in capitalist societies have been won by the workers themselves through hard struggle.

What we are saying is that some degree of protection of labour against the behaviour of individual capitalists is functional to the maintenance of exploitation. In some cases the state has in fact taken the lead in providing such protection, although in peripheral capitalist societies, this protection tends to be granted selectively to those workers employed in the more modern sectors of production whilst the rural labour force frequently continues to be left outside. In so doing, the state introduces divisions within the popular classes which reduce their potential for political action and thus guarantee yet another condition for the maximisation of the surplus value for capital as a whole.

2. Interventor in the process of the sharing of surplus value among various capitals. This confronts the state with particular fractions of capital, but is again ambivalent in that, with respect to some, the relation is one of support, with respect to others, of antagonism. In this role, the state alters the distribution of surplus value among capitals as determined by the operation of the law of value and in this way orients the process of accumulation in given directions. Through the various instruments of economic policy, such as monetary, taxation and fiscal policies, distribution of income and credit, price regulation and subsidisation, the state can promote, for instance, industrial capital with preference to agrarian or financial. Also included in this role is the provision of infrastructure, which is viewed not as a form of support of 'capital in general' but as a form of promotion of fractions of capital. A particularly important element in this role in dependent capitalism is the management of the external sector, through foreign trade regulations, exchange and currency regimes, the management of external indebtedness, as well as the links with international capital through, for instance, foreign investment regimes.

3. Accumulator in its own right, which involves the development of direct productive activities in areas in which private capital is also interested. This role is also ambivalent in at least two respects: (i) the taking on of an accumulator function by the state is functional to the expanded reproduction of capital as a whole, but at the same time confronts the state as a competitor with private capital, whether local or foreign, whose own opportunities for accumulation are constrained by the presence of the state; (ii) in many cases, the involvement of the state in direct production in apparently competitive areas is in effect a form of subsidisation of private accumulation through the devalorisation of state capital. Whether the role of the

state is effectively one of accumulator or of subsidiser of the private sector is a question for concrete analysis.

The hypothesis running throughout the contributions to this book is that an exploration of the three roles of the state as indicated above is required to ascertain the form of state that obtains at a given point and its dynamics. As implied above, the definition of the roles is systematically linked to the other element in the characterisation of the form of state, namely the composition of the power bloc and its index of hegemony: the interests of which fractions of the dominant class are being furthered by the state and which one among them is paramount and serves to articulate and organise the whole (the hegemonic interest)?

In terms of the characterisation of the regime, we suggest that the relevant features for purposes of conceptualising the interaction with the process of capital accumulation are what can be called the bases of domination of the regime. Political theory, whether of the Marxist or the structural–functionalist varieties, seems to agree that the basis for the operation of political regimes is always a combination of coercion and of voluntary compliance. Functionalism will stress the voluntary or habitual element, while Marxism will emphasise the fundamentally coercive character of any form of state. Still, the notion that the capitalist state develops a complex apparatus of ideological control to allow for the reproduction of the system of domination is very much present in the writings of Marxist political theorists, notably those of Gramsci. Our proposed conceptual framework makes use of this fundamental distinction and adds a third category, namely the extent to which domination is made possible or at least less conflictive by means of the state provision of welfare. Welfare is understood here in a broad sense, including not only the provision of social services, such as social security, health, social welfare, education and training, housing, but also state regulation of private activity which directly alters the immediate conditions of life of individuals or groups: taxation policies, social legislation, consumer protection, building by-laws, obligation of minimal education for children, etc.[39] 'Welfare' may in some cases help reduce potentially disruptive forms of popular mobilisation and is therefore an added mechanism of control to be placed alongside force and ideological manipulation. As in the case of the accumulation functions, all three bases of domination are present in all states, but their relative importance and the complex interaction between them vary. Specific apparatuses and activities will also probably relate to more than one basis of domination: the armed forces specialise in coercion but at points might operate as structures for the creation and dissemination of ideologies;[40] welfare arrangements have ideological implications as well as, in some cases, coming closer to coercion in their control over individuals' material well-being.[41] Paralleling the point concerning the specification of the form of state, the form of the regime includes reference to the composition and interrelation of the classes and groups in charge of the state – the 'state managers' – who, in many instances, will not be recruited from the dominant classes, and who might develop non-class forms of behaviour, interests and loyalties: the bureaucracy, the military, etc.

We suggest that the particular combination of roles of the state *vis-à-vis* accumulation at a given point in time is a function of both the context of capital accumulation in the society and the level of political and social conflict associated with it – including the conflicts related to the constitution and development of the power bloc; and that the combination of roles adopted will in turn act upon, and be affected by, the bases of domination of the political regime and the composition and behaviour of the groups in charge of the state. This, it should be stressed, does not in any sense imply a determinism of the political by the economic. The process of capital accumulation is seen as the structural framework within which options for action and policies are offered to concrete social actors; there is no implication that the actual options chosen are pre-determined by capital accumulation. In other words, the underlying logic of capital accumulation, including its objective determinants and constraints, are expressed in concrete terms through the conflicts and struggles of social actors whose courses of political action are a function not only of the structural features of capital accumulation but also of their perspectives and goals – which, of course, include their definition, correct or false as the case may be, of the process of capital accumulation and of their own interests. To paraphrase Marx's words, although men's struggles and actions do not take place 'under circumstances chosen by themselves, but under circumstances directly encountered, given and transmitted from the past', they still 'make their own history'.[42]

The Relative Autonomy of the State

This leads us to the last conceptual point regarding the state raised in the case studies that follow: the question of the relative autonomy of the state.[43] It has already been indicated that the fundamental role of the state in capitalist society is to express and further the domination of the capitalist class over society as a whole; more specifically, the various forms of the capitalist state express and further the domination of the fractions of the capitalist class that make up the power bloc under the hegemony of one of them. This immediately raises a problem: the particular interests of the various fractions of the dominant class are not only different but are often in conflict. The state therefore needs to have some autonomy from any of the fractions of the dominant class to be able to express the interests of the dominant class as a whole. In addition, the ideological claim of the state to represent the interest of society as a whole can only be credible – and therefore operate effectively as ideology – if the state incorporates some of the interests of the dominated class; again, this requires a degree of freedom or autonomy. In this sense, therefore, the relative autonomy of the state can be conceived as the degree of independence of the state managers *vis-à-vis* the social bases of the state; the extent to which they can pursue the common interest of the classes and fractions of classes that make up the pact of domination even against the interests of any of them separately, and the extent to which they can pursue their own interests *qua* distinctive social group. This is, of course, a problematic formulation, in that it does not specify how far the autonomy can go without changing the nature of the state; the danger of a 'hyperfunctionalist' reading thus suggests itself, whereby everything the state managers do must be functional to the dominant interests. There is also the difficult question of the extent to which the 'state managers' constitute a coherent group with common interests and a degree of continuity, and not just a functional social category comprising various changing interests. These issues, though, are best dealt with in concrete terms, and the case studies in these two volumes address themselves to them in various levels.

There is another dimension to the notion of relative autonomy, and it has to do with the question – touched upon above – of the relations between the economic and the political. There is no simple determination of the form of regime by the form of state or of either by the features of the process of capital accumulation; on the other hand, as suggested, the accumulation process sets the structural framework within which the form of the state and the nature of its intervention in accumulation are determined; the two, in turn, set the framework for the various options concerning the form of the regime. The limits within which various types of accumulation can coexist with different forms of state and regime are, again, a question for concrete analysis of the sort exemplified in the case studies that make up this book.

Finally, the notion of relative autonomy can be understood in an external sense: what is the room for manoeuvre of a given nation-state in the world system? Despite the ideological emphasis of some international relations theories on 'interdependence' as the organising principle of inter-state relations,[44] the reality of the differences among states in their autonomy with respect to other states and other actors, such as international financial organisations or the international banking system, is all too evident. On the other hand, the point to be emphasised here is the need to avoid conceptualising inter-state relations as if states were homogeneous and self-contained actors. The class nature of the state must be integrated dialectically with the insertion of the nation-state in the world system; it is not only a question of whether the state has become more autonomous in the world but also of which classes and groups within the state have become more – or less – autonomous. The studies in this book suggest that the contemporary Latin American state might be acquiring an increasing degree of autonomy *vis-à-vis* the dominant classes in civil society but that – at the same time – it is facing growing external constraints as a result of foreign indebtedness and the operation of the world financial system, which reduce its capacity for autonomous decision making.

With these conceptual precisions – as well as these open questions – in mind, we can now turn to our brief account of the historical background to the role of the state in capital accumulation in Latin America.

THE STATE AND CAPITAL ACCUMULATION IN LATIN AMERICA: A BRIEF HISTORICAL RETROSPECT

A survey of the historical role of the state in the process of capital accumulation in Latin America runs into two problems.

The first problem concerns a tendency among most social scientists who have written on Latin America to overemphasise the role of the state in Latin American societies before the 20th century. The 19th century Latin American state is frequently portrayed as an almost 'Leviathanesque' – even though dependent – entity ruling over civil society through the centralising policies of constantly expanding bureaucracies. In the case of a majority of Anglo-American writers, this vision fits well with the idea of a fundamental difference between their own pluralistic political cultures and the Latin tradition of a strong central power. This is alleged to have reinforced a trend transplanted in Latin America between the 16th and the 18th century by a Spanish crown which managed to impose on its own colonial territories a centralisation and absolutism which had always been challenged in the metropolis. For the many Latin American social scientists who share this vision of a strong state tradition in Latin America, the motivation is often to establish clear areas of difference with the USA, which inevitably leads them to overstate a commonality of culture with their own sources of colonisation and intellectual inspiration.

The second problem refers to a belief – popularised by a school of dependency theory but widely accepted beyond it – that whatever surplus that was generated in Latin America was transferred abroad, thus not allowing for any domestic process of capital accumulation.[45]

Both views are exaggerated. Historically, the state has been less powerful and also less autonomous *vis-à-vis* civil society than is often implied. Until the 20th century, its structures were modest everywhere, and the control held over it by landowning oligarchies well entrenched. This was not only due to the economic power of the landowners but also to the social fabric of those traditional societies. Even in the case of Chile, where the foreign ownership of the mines and the growth of the mining surplus had meant that agriculture participated less and less in GDP in the second half of the 19th century, the early centralisation imposed by Portales and the unusually large (by Latin American standards) development of the state machinery did not prevent the landowners from maintaining tight control over the state and, when threatened in their hegemony at the end of the 19th century, from starting a civil war which overthrew President Balmaceda.

If state power can be measured by the degree of intervention by the state in society and by the degree of relative autonomy of the state *vis-à-vis* civil society, then the state was weak in 19th century Latin America. Its institutions were more or less an outgrowth of the dominant landowning interests, both in Congress and in the Presidency, with little or no autonomy *vis-à-vis* those interests, and performing both an administrative and a legitimising role for the dominant minority.

But to understand this role, we must first examine the evidence concerning the presence or absence of a domestic process of capital accumulation in Latin America during the 19th century.

The Process of Capital Accumulation in 19th Century Latin America

For the brand of dependency theory associated with the notion of the 'development of underdevelopment' the absence of a domestic process of capital accumulation in 19th century Latin America was the direct consequence of the surplus transfers from Latin America to Europe, which left the former totally deprived of the surplus that its own economies were producing. This was in turn the outcome of the historical articulation of the Latin American economies with the industrial economies of Western Europe, imposed during the 19th century through the system of international division of labour which assigned to Latin America the role of producing raw materials and foodstuffs for export. In this way, the international division of labour established inevitably and conclusively the conditions for the dependence of the Latin American countries. Dependence is seen as a consequence of imperialism. As such, it is a one-way process determining both the type and the limits of growth of Latin American economies in accordance with the requirements of the advanced capitalist societies.

The evidence, however, presents a considerably more complex picture. The nature of the model of growth adopted in Latin America until 1930 (and largely pursued afterwards as well) could be summarised as follows: since the production of primary commodities was designed for exports, growth and thus profits depended exclusively on the volume of external demand, as a result of which there was no need to increase the size of the domestic market. This, plus the fact that all the Latin American economies (with the exception of Argentina and Uruguay) disposed of 'unlimited supplies of labour' meant that there was no need either to distribute income as wages, which in turn generated a high rate of profits; this tendency was reinforced by a system of land tenure based on the latifundia-minifundia complex. In other words, a low productivity sector was functional to an overall high level of profits. On the other hand, growth depended on the variations of external demand, in what became a cyclical process of prosperity and recession for all the Latin American economies until 1930. From this point of view, a diversification of investments and thus of production would have had stabilising effects both on capital accumulation and on the balance of payments. However, while some foreign capital was attracted to invest in Latin America, as a rule domestic capital was not. Two arguments are frequently advanced to elucidate this apparent contradiction.

One is the high rate of conspicuous consumption of the dominant classes of the area. The other is the reference to a lack of entrepreneurial mentality. Both arguments imply the existence of patterns of irrational behaviour among the Latin American dominant classes, which must be challenged. If conspicuous consumption can be easily substantiated through the grandiose lifestyles of the Latin American dominant sectors during the period of the export boom, to conclude that all profits were wasted in this way seems to be a case of misplaced ethnocentrism, in that it assumes that only a 'Protestant ethic' type of consumption pattern is compatible with capital accumulation; instead, we know that there were large capital transfers abroad from most primary export economies in Latin America during the period 1850–1930. The other argument, the lack of entrepreneurial mentality, can only be assessed in the context of the overall rationality of the behaviour of the Latin American dominant classes in which – as we shall show below – the maintenance of the stability of the social order was paramount.

As a matter of fact, some industrial development took place in several countries before 1930.[46] It was first the large profits made from exports and then the development of an urban tertiary sector that constituted the basis of the monetisation of the economy as well as its limitations, since both the export of profits and their capitalisation in the tertiary sector reduced the domestic rates of monetisation. Outside Argentina, Uruguay, and to some extent Southern Brazil, wages were too low to contribute to monetisation. But, partial as it was, the monetisation of some Latin American economies offered the basis for industrialisation to start. That basis was used when, due to the cyclical nature of all export economies, a recession in exports was followed by a devaluation, through which imported goods became more expensive and thus local production of the same goods more competitive; the higher profits made on import substituting goods were thus the basis of some industrial development. Another cause of such development was the First World War, when the export of manufactured goods from Europe was considerably reduced. However, in spite of these favourable conditions, industrialisation remained fairly restricted until 1930. Why?

If we examine the nature of industrial production in the 19th century, we can see that industrialisation almost always started with textile, food, and beverage industries, that is with industries producing for a potentially large market. These products correspond to a demand that can easily be enlarged, since the income level at which demand appears for them is relatively low. Nevertheless, not only were their spill-over effects very modest, but these industries also developed large unused capacities of production until 1930.[47] Therefore, it appears that it was not the lack of capital resources but the way in which income was distributed that explains the limited industrialisation of Latin America until 1930. In other words, the lack of industrial expansion was a consequence of the cheap labour policies implemented through most of Latin America. However, if the patterns of income distribution explain to a large extent the genesis of the process of underdevelopment in Latin America, they were also perfectly 'rational' for the Latin American societies of the time.

We wish to suggest that, within the context of the 19th century Latin American societies, the decision of the Latin American capital owners not to invest in industry can be interpreted as a 'rational' choice on the grounds of the stability of the social and political systems in which they had acquired a dominant position, and which – through low wages – allowed them to benefit from high rates of profit.

The stability of traditional societies is based on the maintenance of a complex network of social relations in which positions of status and power are accepted and basically unquestioned. Those in turn represent the basis on which a system of domination can be established. In Latin America, the different forms of labour subjection inherited from colonial times were apparently abolished in many countries after Independence.[48] Slavery and serfdom no longer obtained formally, but in practice, the existence of a labour surplus in agriculture and the social distance that isolated labour from the rest of society made it possible to continue to enforce feudal and neo-feudal relations of production, whose *de facto* maintenance, although contradicting the law, was legally protected. In those societies, this represented much more than a source of high profits: it was the basis of their system of domination and an essential element of the stability of the social order. Changes in it could only have had destabilising consequences for the whole system. For the well-informed dominant classes of those traditional societies, industrialisation appeared as an ethically desirable form of progress but also as a considerably disruptive process for the stability of the social order.

As P. P. Rey writes: 'There is ... one reason which can induce the bourgeoisie to voluntarily slow down the enlargement of its relations of production: it is the fear that such an enlargement might precipitate a social revolution.'[49]

The Primary-Export State

In those traditional societies based on export economies, conditions did not exist for the state to acquire a relative autonomy *vis-à-vis* civil society. In some countries, the sphere of state intervention in society became larger than in others, mainly due to its redistributive function, as in the case of Chile,[50] but this was not sufficient to change the patterns of its control by civil society.[51] Even the occasional occurrence of external wars, which had been instrumental in the process of relative autonomy of the European states, did not play a significant role in this respect in Latin America, since those wars did not affect the basic stability of the traditional order. In that context, the state performed essentially the functions of guarantor of the basic conditions for private capital accumulation and of interventor on behalf of the interests of the dominant classes as a whole.

The performance of these functions was facilitated by the absence of a conflict between the Executive and the Legislative. Given the very narrow limits of political participation, both the President and Congress could easily be identified with the same dominant interests, and thus conflicts between them were unlikely outside secondary matters of constitutional procedure. Exceptions to this norm were extremely rare, and always involved a reformist President being opposed by a Conservative Congress. There were only three such cases: in the early 1890s in Chile, under Balmaceda, where the conflict resulted in a civil war in which Balmaceda was defeated; and in the 1920s, in Argentina under Irigoyen and in Chile under Alessandri, where the advance of the middle class sectors that they represented met a Conservative opposition in Congress which led to military takeovers.

The administration by the state of the interests of the dominant class was efficient, but it was also flexible enough to guarantee the stability of the system.

Its efficiency consisted in the passing of legislation designed to serve directly the interests of the dominant class and to guarantee the conditions of private capital accumulation: (i) to ensure the further concentration of private landownership through the confiscation of religious properties and Indian communal holdings and the sale of public lands, always acquired at a fraction of their appraised value;[52] (ii) to maintain the system of debt peonage and of other forms of labour subjection to the landowners;[53] (iii) to consolidate internal debts; (iv) to borrow from abroad in order to guarantee the investments in infrastructure that were necessary for exports or congenial to the lifestyle of the dominant classes but which the latter were not prepared to finance themselves; (v) to introduce tax systems in which there were no taxes on land; (vi) to allow for an increasingly large share of agricultural income to be derived not from agricultural production but merely from landownership, through land rent.[54]

Efficiency was also reinforced by the degree of relative flexibility that was built into the social systems. That flexibility was expressed in the considerable use of cooptation which coexisted with the vertical links of loyalty and patronage that are characteristic of traditional societies. These are an essential element of the stability of the social system in that (i) they work against the articulation of horizontal or class interests in society. The most likely form of social mobility is individual, i.e. through the position that an individual of lower status is capable of reaching within a series of vertical structures, as a result of the advantages that he might receive from his loyalty to the clan, the *patrón*, or one of his intermediaries; (ii) by so doing, they create the illusion that society is more open than it really is, and thus they increase the stability of a system of domination which, somehow, they legitimate.

Those traditional societies changed very little before 1930. The changes that occurred affected those countries in which – in the latter part of the 19th and in the early part of the 20th century – there was a development of urbanisation and thus of the 'middle classes', intensified by immigration from Europe.

But industrialisation remained very limited in Argentina, Brazil, Chile, Mexico, even more so in Uruguay and Colombia, and almost absent everywhere else. Both the urban middle classes and even the small industrial working class were rather easily accommodated in those traditional societies where – outside Argentina – the presence of a labour surplus in agriculture always accounted for low industrial wages. The continuation of the primary export model of growth and capital accumulation was not questioned, and the export state kept guaranteeing the conditions of private capital accumulation through a mixture of coercion and cooptation made easy by the social control maintained over rural labour.

The Populist State[55]

The primary export model received its first real challenge with the world economic crisis of 1930. Throughout Latin America, the immediate consequence of the 1929 slump was a crisis in the balance of payments due to the fall in external demand for primary commodities. The first priority was therefore to try to reduce the effects of that crisis. For most countries of the area, this proved an impossible task: they had exclusively relied upon primary exports until 1930, and they had no alternative policy at their disposal. For some other countries, an alternative existed. Those were the countries in which a 'spontaneous' process of industrialisation by import substitution (ISI) had started before the crisis.

After 1930, they started using their previously unused productive capacity to accelerate their process of ISI, both to satisfy an internal demand for manufactured goods which could no longer be imported and to set in motion a new model of growth and capital accumulation. This model was 'new' in at least one respect: internal demand – which had formerly been irrelevant to growth – was now an essential component of it. We could thus expect the patterns of income distribution to be radically changed, particularly since the acceleration of ISI was taking place under conditions of labour intensiveness in production. We could also expect the move away from the primary export model to have far reaching consequences for the system of domination: the replacement of the model of growth could be likely to produce the 'bourgeois revolution' which had been delayed for so long, or perhaps even to represent the evidence that such a 'revolution' had finally succeeded in overthrowing the political domination of the landowners, with whom the interests of the industrialists could only clash.[56]

This is where the presence of a labour surplus in the agricultural sector played – once again – a crucial role in transforming a conflict which might otherwise have arisen between primary export and industrial groups into an alliance between them. From being potentially antagonistic, their interests were made compatible and even complementary by the availability of an 'unlimited supply of labour'.[57] Through keeping wages low in industry, the agricultural sector contributed to a process of capital accumulation within the industrial sector. In the agricultural exporting countries, this in turn did not put on export profits the stress which would have been produced by higher wages in industry forcing a reliance on capital transfers from agriculture to provide the capital required for industrial investment.

The only case in which the latter situation obtained was in Argentina under Perón. The absence of a labour surplus in Argentine agriculture maintained wages relatively high in industry. This led the Peronist government to enforce capital transfers from agriculture to industry in order to compensate for an insufficient rate of capital accumulation in the latter. This policy, implemented by the State Export Board (IAPI), consisted of buying cheap from the agricultural producers, selling at higher prices abroad, and investing most of the difference in industry. It could only provoke the discontent of the landowners, constantly squeezed on their profits.

Elsewhere, a further justification for keeping primary export profits high was found in the essential role which those profits played in ISI by paying for the cost of purchasing industrial inputs abroad. With the protection of traditional export interests perfectly in tune with ISI, the political systems which emerged were thus the expression of alliances made between the owners of capital in both sectors of production. Outside Mexico (which had made its agrarian-based revolution in 1910) and – to a lesser extent – Chile, they were not the result of 'class alliances' around an industrialisation project, but of intra-class alliances between sectors of capital, with the expansion of middle and low urban income groups being instrumental to the stability of that alliance.

We can evaluate the validity of this argument *firstly* by looking into the ISI policies adopted by the so-called populist regimes which emerged after 1930, and, *secondly*, by trying to assess the extent to which the populist policies favourable to labour reduced or – on the contrary – reinforced the pattern of inequality in the social distribution of the surplus between capital and labour.

1. *Promotion of ISI or Protection of the Traditional Exports Sectors*
   In the agricultural exporting countries, the measures adopted in the context of ISI policy making seemed as much designed to protect the interests of the export agricultural sector as to promote industrialisation.

   Until the mid-1950s, protectionism was the main stimulus to industrialisation, but – surprisingly – there was a high level of protection for export products as well. Contrary to what might logically be expected, the products on which the heaviest import duties and charges were payable in Latin America usually included all or almost all those which were traditionally exported by each of the countries of the region, and which were therefore produced on a sufficiently competitive basis to make any form of protection presumably needless.[58]

   In industry, consumer goods alone received tariff protection, while industrial inputs were allowed free entry, regardless of the fact that at least some of them could have been produced locally. There were two good reasons for this: (i) the local production of inputs was not attractive to the industrialists because – in the short run – it offered lower rates of return than the production of finished products; (ii) the larger the number of stages of production protected by tariff duties, the higher the price of manufactured goods on the market and thus the smaller the profits and/or the demand. One can then appreciate that a different use of tariff protection – which could have been made to discriminate less unilaterally against the import of manufactured outputs and more against certain types of inputs – could, at an early stage, have had considerable effects on the further development of industrialisation. Similarly, one is also tempted to agree with Hirschman that 'the high customs duties on their outputs, combined with low (or negative) duties on their inputs, could almost be seen as a plot on the part of the existing powerholders to corrupt or buy off the new industrialists'.[59]

This pattern of trade control was repeated for the exchange control mechanisms, which affected the traditional export sectors much less than is usually assumed; if the overvaluation of national currencies sometimes affected the export sectors, it was more often the result of errors in the implementation of very complex multiple exchange rate policies than the consequence of a deliberate policy. On the contrary, the concern for protecting the export interests was such that it often led to the adoption of measures combining overvaluation with inflation.

Furthermore, the populist state in the type of countries discussed did not mobilise domestic resources for investment purposes in a manner congruent with an ISI policy:

(i) There was no subsidised credit for industry, and most of the credit available was charged at commercial rates by a banking system used by primary exporters as another outlet to enlarge their own profits.

(ii) Whilst domestic savings continued to be exported or deposited in bank accounts instead of being invested in industry, taxation was not used as a means to force savings and to channel investment towards industry. The regressive tax systems changed very little, and land remained either untaxed or grossly undertaxed. This neglect of one of the most essential instruments of a policy of industrialisation in a process of 'forced' ISI was clearly indicative both of a limited policy orientation towards industrialisation and of the concern of policy-makers not to infringe upon the profits of the traditional export sectors.

(iii) In the 1950s and early 1960s, the insufficiency of domestic investment became such that – in addition to calling in foreign capital – inflation was used as a method of forced savings, in spite of being more difficult to control and less efficient than taxation in channelling savings towards industry. In the 1970s – as we will see later in this book – and contrary to orthodox expectations, inflation did not produce the higher savings rate which it is 'normally' supposed to produce and, by increasing the price of basic foodstuffs, it negatively affected the volume of aggregate internal demand for manufactured goods, thus making it more difficult to maintain the levels of production and industrial investment.

2. *Populism as a Technique of System Adaptation in Labour Surplus Economies*

At first sight, the populist regimes of Latin America seemed to be the expression of a class alliance against the former system of domination. Their rhetoric certainly was, and many of their policies also brought some improvement to large sectors of the urban working class, through labour legislation, welfare programmes, minimum wage policies, etc. However, for the dominant classes, the impact of those reformist measures was more than compensated for by their positive effects on the distribution of the surplus and on social stability.

What happened to the distribution of the surplus was precisely what Lewis suggests must happen under conditions of labour surplus, with the capitalist surplus growing while average wages remain constant, and any increase in productivity further widening the gap between the share of labour and that of capital.

This tendency was reinforced by the regressive nature of tax systems and by the high rate of inflation which affected in particular the industrialising countries of the area in the 1950s and 1960s. Both had the effect of eroding the nominal wage increases granted by the populist governments, and, by reducing real wages, they accelerated the rate of surplus extraction from labour and they precipitated the crisis of populist regimes gradually caught in the web of their own contradictions.

As could be expected, the result of a constantly growing capitalist surplus was to reinforce class differentials. In addition, the labour conditions under which this was taking place was also enlarging sectoral differentials among wage earners. This is another direct consequence of the presence of a labour surplus in an economy undergoing industrialisation. The trend towards an increase in wage differentials between agriculture and industry was further strengthened by a deliberate policy pursued by all populist governments and which consisted of a selective granting of welfare and other benefits to some categories of workers to the exclusion of all others. Rural labour was always forgotten in the distribution of those benefits: (i) minimum wages for agriculture either did not exist or – when they did – were not implemented; (ii) social security and pension scheme benefits were restricted to industrial labour; (iii) the right to form a trade union was not even recognised for rural workers in most countries, and they continued to be submitted to the same forms of paternalistic coercion that had always been applied to them.

The maintenance of remarkably constant patterns of exploitation of rural labour by the populist regimes of the labour surplus economies of Latin America was probably the most important single variable in the process of adaptation of their former system of domination and in the stability of the populist alliances: it was ultimately the source of a growing capitalist surplus, and it acted as a factor of division within the working class. For most of the urban wage earners, the terms of reference by which an improvement of their conditions was measured were the conditions of labour in agriculture. The cost at which the cooptation of urban labour could be achieved was thus considerably reduced by the existence of increasingly large differentials which tended to separate them away from their original reference group.

The Crisis of the Populist State

As we have seen the stability of the populist alliances was based on two elements: (i) within the alliances, a growing surplus from which both landowners and industrialists could benefit; the exception being, as suggested above, the case of Argentina; (ii) social support for them was provided by the urban working class and sectors of the urban middle class, who received material advantages in their standard of living which represented the objective basis for popular mobilisation.

Both elements contained potential contradictions whose development eventually led to crises.

1. The underlying contradiction of the first concerned the capacity of the model of growth adopted to maintain a satisfactory share of the surplus for the two partners in the alliance. This capacity began to be doubted in the 1950s by the industrialists who started complaining about the insufficiency of investment facilities in industry and of demand for industrial goods. The first insufficiency was caused by inadequate government policies to promote industrialisation, namely by the absence of a system of subsidised credit. The second was a consequence of a low level of wages in the agricultural sector, due to the patterns of land tenure. The development theory of CEPAL supported their argument by linking industrialisation to agrarian reform; but – outside Chile, which made it a priority after 1964 – agrarian reform was always resisted throughout Latin America in spite of the mounting dissatisfaction of the industrialists, whose part of the surplus was constantly narrowing.

   The investment solution was found in the opening up of those economies to foreign capital. But – after welcoming it at first – many entrepreneurs soon came to realise that they were not equipped to face the competition of foreign firms, and many local firms were quickly absorbed. More than ever, they saw the solution to their problems in an expansion of the market. Their insistence on agrarian reform and the unwillingness of the landowners to accept any changes in the systems of land tenure introduced a serious element of conflict within the populist alliances.

2. The material basis of the social support enjoyed by the populist regimes depended on both industrial employment and industrial wages expanding regularly. However, the techniques of production began to change rapidly in the 1950s and 1960s with the entry of foreign capital and, from labour intensive, industrial production became more and more capital intensive, i.e. labour saving. Unskilled but also semi-skilled jobs tended not to be provided any longer by an expanding industrial production, and unemployment grew. Working class support for the populist state inevitably suffered from this development, particularly since it was combined with a fall in real wages due to rising inflation. Even nominal wage increases began to be more difficult to obtain since higher wages were often seen as the main single cause of inflation.

These adverse trends affected all industrialising countries of Latin

America in the 1960s. Everywhere, they were simultaneously responsible for a declining rate of capital accumulation and for popular unrest. The latter gave rise to 'new' forms of working class mobilisation which were no longer functional to the stability of the social and political system, especially since any form of popular discontent began to be seen against the background of the Cuban revolution.

These contradictions within capital and between capital and labour soon acquired a political dimension both in Congress and between the Presidency and Congress. Of the three countries discussed in this first volume, Mexico avoided this type of open clash as the control that the PRI exercised over these conflicting interests appeared unshaken. In Chile, the conflict found its expression in Congress and through strike action, and at the end of the decade in the electoral mobilisation leading to the election of Salvador Allende as President; in Brazil the reaction, albeit less radical, was perceived as a threat to the stability of the social order. In the latter two cases military coups intervened to pre-empt the threat.

The occurrence of the Cuban revolution and the failure of the Alliance for Progress contributed to this process: the first by making the always potentially dangerous lower classes appear as an even greater threat all over Latin America; the second because – by insisting on the urgency to introduce both tax and agrarian reforms – the Alliance had antagonised the dominant classes which were not prepared to accept the challenge to their privileges which these reforms entailed. They preferred less iconoclastic models of development, and were attracted by the model of unbalanced growth discussed above, which had a considerable influence in the 1960s with inter-American and international agencies and banks. Apparently, the goal had not changed, and it was still argued that the expansion of the internal market was necessary to stimulate industrialisation. But the means by which this was to be achieved were different. The emphasis was now put on free trade as well as on measures capable of attracting foreign investment in the industrial sector. International integration was also sometimes – as in the case of ALALC – conveniently substituted for national integration. The contradiction inherent in trying to integrate together very unintegrated economies raised a few criticisms, which pointed out that an integration of the problems would certainly not lead to very positive results; however, because it was economically fashionable and politically safe, formal steps towards Latin American economic integration were taken.

But the most important developments were taking place at another level, made possible by the new political conditions created by the outward rejection of the populist formula – first expressed in the Brazilian military coup of 1964 – and the replacement of 'reformism' by authoritarianism throughout the area.

LATIN AMERICA IN THE 1970S AND 1980S: THE STATE AND THE MODEL OF INTEGRATION IN THE WORLD ECONOMY

The preceding section has offered a highly general and stylised account of the role of the state in capital accumulation in Latin America up to the period of import-substituting industrialisation. Only at such level of generality can the account be defended as being common to the countries discussed in the two volumes that make up this book. A detailed discussion of specific cases would show a picture of considerably more complexity and variation in terms of timing, particular features and outcomes. The chapters of this first volume undertake just such an analysis for three of the most industrially advanced countries of the continent, and those variations then become apparent.

Even more strikingly, when it comes to the characterisation of the process in the post-ISI period – which is in effect the main concern of the case studies – it appears that no comparably general and stylised common description is warranted. There are, to be sure, important features that are present in all the countries discussed in these two volumes. Thus, the response to the exhaustion of the import-substituting model and to the parallel social and political pressures upon the 'populist state' seems to involve in all cases some attempt at increased integration in the world capitalist economy in the form of an export orientation and an 'opening' of the national economy to the rest of the world. In all cases there is a strong presence of international capital, and the state combines a stepped up role in economic management with an essentially repressive character and/or an increased role in direct production and accumulation. In all cases there appears to be a subsidiary role for the local bourgeoisie, under either industrial or financial leadership, and an exclusion – in varying degrees – of the popular sectors from the fruits of growth and from political participation. And in all cases, the crucial point of expression of the contradictions of the model seems to be the management of external financial relations.

But there the commonality ends. Two polar types seem to emerge from the case studies,[60] approximating the concrete conditions of two countries, with all the others placed somewhere along a spectrum whose coordinates, however, are not linear; the choice of analytical emphasis of the chapters, therefore, varies. Brazil, on the one hand, is often characterised as a case in which integration in the world economy and an export oriented model are accompanied – particularly after 1968 – by an attempt at stepping up local accumulation. The system aims at increasing levels of technological complexity. The dynamic agent in accumulation is the multinational enterprise but the state plays a central role in defining the conditions for the operation of the multinationals and also takes on a role in accumulation itself through state enterprises that might associate with foreign capital in particular projects. Local capital accepts a dependent position *vis-à-vis* multinational-state expansion, but it is a position involving some dynamism. Thus, the peculiarity of the dependent capitalist state in this variant is that its social bases are composed of the internationalised fraction of capital, the local bourgeoisie and the managers of state enterprises, the 'state bourgeoisie'. With respect to the popular sectors, the new model is economically more exclusionary than the populist state. It no longer aims at the defence of the internal market, and its concentrating effects on income distribution are serious.

Chile, on the other hand, is characterised as a case in which the disintegration of the import-substituting model and the 'compromise state' leads to a model oriented towards primary production for exports, with a downgrading of industrial development and of the industrial bourgeoisie and the dismantling of the productive apparatus of the state. The social basis of this type of model is perceived as composed of the financial and commercial fractions of the local bourgeoisie in alliance with international – primarily banking – capital. The basic role of the state is defined in terms of repression of the popular sectors; the impact of the model is extremely exclusionary, entailing not only the reduction in the standards of living of the workers but a decrease in the number of industrial workers as such and the accompanying growth of the 'marginal' sectors.

Chapters 2 and 3 by Anglade and Fortin, while recognising the broad features of the two models described, introduce significant qualifications to the outlines proposed above. Anglade begins by tracing the origins of the post-1964 economic model in Brazil back to the import substitution–populist period, and particularly to the Kubitschek administration (1956–61). He argues that there is a fundamental continuity between the model and Kubitschek's attempt at rescuing an ailing process of capital accumulation by attracting foreign capital and increasing state activity to fill the 'empty spaces' in production. The very success of the attempt (there also was an 'economic miracle' in the second half of the 1950s in Brazil) created the conditions for its demise: the capital-intensive technology brought in by the MNCs led to a crisis of insufficient demand, and increased state expenditure was not able to revitalise demand but only created inflation. This, in turn, exacerbated social and political tensions and disrupted the 'populist alliance'. The 1950s, argues Anglade, are thus not only a cause of the crisis culminating in the 1964 coup but a forerunner of the difficulties and contradictions of the post-1964 model.

He then proceeds to a detailed analysis of the post-1964 experience. His main concern is with a more accurate characterisation of the functions of the state in accumulation, the extent to which they express and influence the composition and internal dynamics of the power bloc and the interaction between the two and the features of the political regime, notably party and election politics. He argues that the break that is usually postulated between the 'stabilisation' period of 1964–68 and the ensuing developmentalist and state-oriented period of 1968–74 is misleading: in both periods the overall objective of state policy is 'to make market capitalism work'. Further, the emphasis put on the post-1968 role of the state as producer and accumulator is also doubly misguided: firstly, because some of the major state instruments to 'make market capitalism work' did not entail the direct involvement of the state in production but rather the management of macroeconomic variables, notably the foreign debt; and secondly, because the presence of the state in direct production did not imply state accumulation, but rather a subsidisation of private capital involving losses for state enterprises. A reassessment is therefore called for of the common characterisation of the power bloc as a 'triple alliance' of MNCs, the state bourgeoisie and local private capital; the collapse of the alliance following the exhaustion of the miracle in 1974 has thus older and deeper causes in the contradictions of the model itself. Indeed, the role of the state increases when the model enters into crisis, as it must attempt to maintain a level of capital accumulation that private capital, whether foreign or local, is not sustaining. The result is a fiscal crisis and a crisis of balance of payments. Throughout, the ability of the state to face economic contradictions has been limited by the fact that the regime – while authoritarian and repressive – has never completely abandoned a pretence of legitimation through the popular will, and that therefore elections have taken place periodically. Each electoral

A Conceptual and Historical Introduction 43

period implied constraints on those among the state managers who felt a return to democratic procedures was a desirable long-term goal: measures of economic policy had to be tailored to the political necessities of doing well in the elections. The contradictions culminate when the social tensions calling for a return to democracy coincide with the exhaustion of the miracle, and the government is faced with the need to open up the political system at a time of recession rather than boom. As the 'external' autonomy of the government to decide on policy is also eroded, this leads to a fiscal and balance of payments crisis which the government appears incapable of handling.

Fortin's Chapter 3 on Chile takes an even longer term view, tracing the question of the state and capital accumulation back to the early forties, and discussing in some detail the ISI period with its 'compromise state' and the socialist experience of the Allende government. The latter is, of course, fundamental to understand the process following the September 1973 coup; the coup was as much a reaction of the bourgeoisie to the socio-political threat represented by the Allende experiment as a result of economic contradictions. Inasmuch as the Allende experience was linked by the new military rulers to the growth of industry, the proletariat and the state, the new model represents a deliberate break with the developmentalist emphasis of the preceding 30 years; the new power bloc is hegemonised by the financial and commercial rather than the industrial bourgeoisie, the 'state middle class' that provided most of the state managers is replaced by the military and the economic technocrats (the 'Chicago boys') and the productive apparatus of the state is drastically reduced. However, Fortin argues, the state does not wither away. Its role as guarantor of the conditions for private capital accumulation is dramatically increased through the repression of the working class and the popular sectors generally; its withdrawal from economic regulation is 'partial and selective', amounting in effect to a major intervention in favour of the financial and monopoly fractions of local capital and of international capital. Even in the area of direct involvement in production, the state retains a significant presence; what changes substantially is the dynamic of state activity. The state ceases to accumulate but it does not essentially subsidise private capital; state enterprises, operating at a profit, become sources of surplus for the fiscal budget, allowing more flexible taxation policies, compensating for the reduction in tariff duty revenues, etc. Fortin then attempts to link these features of state activity with the repressive nature of the regime, emphasising the extent to which, contrary to what Anglade observes for Brazil, it dispenses with forms of 'democratic' legitimation until the 1980s, and does not attempt to generate forms of ideological mobilisation in the shape of pro-government movements or parties. The economic crisis of the model is also entirely different from the Brazilian one, even though its outward appearance might be similar. While in Brazil the fiscal and balance of payments crisis is a function of the attempt by the state to step up capital accumulation by intervening to replace private accumulation, in the Chilean case the crisis of balance of payments and the general financial crisis is a function of the indiscriminate opening up of the economy, which was flooded with luxury imports, and the replacement of a productive dynamics with a financial and speculative one. There is little accumulation in Chile in this period; the 'Chilean miracle' is even more of a mirage than the 'Brazilian miracle' is.

Mexico appears to be closer to the Brazilian prototype than to the Chilean. FitzGerald's contribution deliberately emphasises the managerial and regulatory aspects of state intervention with preference to the involvement in direct production. He is also particularly concerned with the role of the 'state managers' and the extent to which they acquired increasing degrees of autonomy in the period of the 'Mexican miracle' (1950–65), when the role of the state was primarily to support a process of capital accumulation carried out by a private sector composed of large Mexican entrepreneurs and foreign capital. The process began to lose momentum in the mid-1960s. FitzGerald rejects the interpretation that the cause of the slowing down was a structural insufficiency of demand, and suggests instead that it was the pressure on industrial profits produced by increases in real wages – which the model used to legitimise itself – coupled with the emergence of more attractive rates of return in non-productive sectors such as tourism. At this stage, like in Brazil, the state attempts to step in to make up for the reduced private accumulation; it finds, though, that it lacks sufficient resources for intervention, since the tax base is restricted and the internal financial market is dominated by a small group of powerful local banking interests. It has therefore to resort to foreign indebtedness. The appearance of oil and natural gas as major sources of surplus does not fundamentally change the situation, since the surplus is also captured by the private banking system. A fiscal crisis of the state, in O'Connor's sense, develops, particularly under President Echeverría, who puts forward the most coherent and radical project of state intervention to date. The crisis deepens under Echeverría's successor, López Portillo, and culminates with the nationalisation of the banking system at the end of 1982 and the start of a period of profound uncertainty not only *vis-à-vis* the Mexican economy but – given the huge Mexican foreign debt – for the international financial system generally.

In the three countries covered in this first volume, it would appear that the path towards crisis and instability varies, as do the meaning of the crises in terms of the characteristics of the state and the forms of political regime, and their relation to capital accumulation. It would also appear that the model of integration in the world economy and the conflicts and tensions it has generated has had a contradictory effect on the relative autonomy of the state. In Brazil and Chile, it seems to have increased the autonomy of the state *vis-à-vis* its social bases and internal social forces generally. On the other hand, in Mexico, in the advanced stages of the crisis, the room for manoeuvre of the state managers in terms of internal social groups began to be reduced. In all three cases though, there was an increase in the degree of dependence of the state and the national economy on the world economy and the world financial system in particular. This highlights, again, the need for revision of the notion of dependency to address a situation in which the dominant process is the internationalisation of financial, rather than productive capital. The matter, in fact, has ceased to be solely of concern to the debtor countries The strenuous efforts of the world banking community with the support of the United States government and international financial institutions to prevent the default of Brazil and Mexico are essentially a self-preserving operation. The cost, however, is to be borne by the Latin American countries which embarked in the dubious path of mounting indebtedness. In some cases – notably Brazil – there is an emerging tendency among the policy makers who adopted the model in the first place to attempt to blame the IMF and world capital for the unpopular measures that are being implemented. Whether this heralds a more general response in the direction of self-reliance and de-linking or whether it is simply a temporary political tactic aimed for internal consumption remains to be seen.

NOTES

1. In the excellent collection of articles edited by Bianchi (1969), which encapsulates the major contributions by Latin American economists in the 1960s, the term capital accumulation in the sense referred to here is not used once. By contrast, major works published by two of those economists in the late 1970s make the concept of accumulation the focal point for the analysis (Furtado, 1976; Prebisch, 1981).

2. Furtado (1965b), (1966) and (1970); Pinto (1968) and (1971); Sunkel and Paz (1970). Furtado (1965b) pp. 108–12 actually uses the concept of capital accumulation in relation to inflation in Brazil in the post-1930 period.
3. Standard economic histories of individual Latin American countries devote a good deal of attention to the role of the state in early import-substituting industrialisation, income redistribution, etc. For references see Furtado (1970) and Glade (1969).
4. For a good summary of CEPAL's theses, see CEPAL (1969). For a critical analysis, Rodríguez (1972).
5. Rostow (1960).
6. Lewis (1970) p. 409.
7. Hirschman (1958).
8. See, for example, *World Financial Markets* (1983).
9. *World Financial Markets* (1983) p. 11.
10. Nurkse (1953); Strassman (1956); Furtado (1965).
11. Chenery *et al.* (1974).
12. Baran (1957); Baran and Sweezy (1970).
13. Amin (1977); Frank (1967), (1972); Wallerstein (1979); Wallerstein and Hopkins (1981). For a good analysis of 'dependency theory' see Palma (1978).
14. Emmanuel (1972) and (1974).
15. Warren (1973) and (1980).
16. Mandle (1980) p. 871.
17. Mandle (1980) pp. 869–70. Kay (1975) is an attempt at building a theory of development based on *Das Kapital*; interestingly, its analysis is closer to that of the 'dependency' writers than to Warren's. See especially pp. 124–30.
18. Vaitsos (1974); Lall and Streeten (1977); Hymer (1980); Murray (ed.) (1981). At a more popular level, see Barnet and Müller (1974).
19. Cardoso (1972).
20. Cardoso (1975); see also Cardoso (1980).
21. Such an essentially optimistic view of the dynamism of 'dependent development' in Brazil was presented in Evans (1979), but see Chapter 2, note 103.
22. For a recent, encyclopaedic survey, see Jessop (1982).
23. The basic texts on the 'bureaucratic-authoritarian state' are O'Donnell (1973), (1978) and (1979). A good assessment of the approach with an extensive bibliography is contained in Collier (1979).
24. The distinction originates in the political writings of Marx, Engels and Lenin through the concepts of 'state power' and 'state apparatuses'; see the further elaboration and the classical textual references in Poulantzas (1978a) pp. 115–17 and 331–6 and (1978b) pp. 11–14 and *passim*. Cardoso (1977) proposes a similar distinction between the state as a 'pact of domination' and the state as organisation, or the 'regime'. The differences among the various conceptualisations will be briefly discussed below. For applications of the fundamental distinction to Latin America see Cardoso and Faletto (1979); Cardoso (1979); and Fortin (1983).
25. Block (1980).
26. Cardoso (1975) pp. 40–3.
27. Garretón (1979).
28. Cardoso (1979) p. 39.

29. Poulantzas (1978a) pp. 147–56 and 234–52.
30. Poulantzas (1978a) pp. 151ff. and 242.
31. Compare the quote in note 28 above with his discussion of the variability of both the 'pact of domination' – 'made up of permanent tension and struggle' – and the 'possible alliances among the dominant sectors and between them and the dominated sectors'. Cardoso (1977) pp. 24–5.
32. Poulantzas (1978a) p. 116.
33. Cardoso (1979) pp. 39–40.
34. Mandel (1978) pp. 475ff.
35. Poulantzas (1978a) pp. 50–6; (1978b) pp. 166ff.
36. Altvater (1978) p. 42.
37. O'Connor (1973).
38. Evers (1979).
39. Gough (1979).
40. Poulantzas (1978b) pp. 28–9.
41. Gough (1979) pp. 11–12.
42. Marx (1969) p. 398.
43. See Fortin (1982).
44. For a discussion of the concept of interdependence see Morse (1972) and references cited therein.
45. For bibliographical references see note 13; see also Chilcote (1974).
46. Mainly in Argentina, Brazil, Chile, and Mexico, and, to a lesser extent, in Colombia and Uruguay.
47. For an excellent summary of the economic history of Latin America in the 19th century, see Glade (1969).
48. This was achieved formally in most Spanish American countries by the constitutions that followed Independence. One should not, however, deduce from it that the *criollos* who designed those constitutions meant to implement the principles of liberty and equality that they were advocating. The treatment reserved to the Indians and Negroes and the confiscation of the Indian communal lands during the 19th century bear clear evidence to the contrary.
49. Rey (1976) p. 12.
50. See Laclau (1969).
51. Again, in the case of Chile, for example, through their control over both Congress and Senate, the landowning sectors could – in spite of their constantly decreasing participation in GNP – maintain an 'over representation' of their interests which was only partially affected in the 1920s under the administration of Alessandri.
52. See, for example, Diaz Alejandro (1970) pp. 38–9; McGreevey (1971), pp. 129–32; Cumberland (1968) pp. 198–203.
53. See Glade (1969) pp. 240–41.
54. On the last four points, see Randall (1977).
55. This section is based on Anglade (1975) from which a few sections will be used.
56. See Mauro Marini (1971) pp. 14–15.
57. See Lewis (1970).
58. Macario (1964) p. 74.
59. Hirschman (1971) p. 107.
60. Fortin (1983).

REFERENCES

Altvater, E. (1978), 'Some Problems of State Interventionism', in Holloway and Picciotto (eds), pp. 40–2.
Amin, S. (1977), *Unequal Development* (Brighton: Harvester Press).
Anglade, C. (1975), 'System adaptation in Latin America in the "forced" import substitution industrialization period', *European Journal of Political Research*, 3, pp. 47–67.
Baran, P. (1957), *The Political Economy of Growth* (New York: Monthly Review Press).
Baran, P. and Sweezy, P. (1970), *Monopoly Capital* (Harmondsworth: Penguin Books).
Barnet, R. J. and Müller, R. E. (1974), *Global Reach: the Power of the Multinational Corporations* (New York: Simon & Schuster).
Bianchi, A. (ed.), (1969), *América Latina: ensayos de interpretación económica* (Santiago de Chile: Editorial Universitaria).
Block, F. (1980), 'Beyond Relative Autonomy: State Managers as Historical Subjects', *The Socialist Register 1980* (London: Merlin Press) pp. 227–42.
Cardoso, F. H. (1972), 'Dependency and Development in Latin America', *New Left Review*, no. 74, July–Aug., pp. 83–95.
—— (1975), *Autoritarismo e Democratização* (Rio: Paz e Terra).
—— (1977), 'Estado Capitalista e Marxismo', *Estudos CEBRAP*, 21, São Paulo, July–Sept., pp. 5–31.
—— (1979), 'On the Characterisation of Authoritarian Regimes in Latin America', in Collier (1979) pp. 33–57.
—— (1980), 'The Surprises of Development in Latin America', *IFDA Dossier*, Geneva, 16, Mar.–Apr., pp. 31–7.
—— and Faletto, E. (1979), *Dependency and Development in Latin America* (Berkeley: University of California Press).
CEPAL (1969), *El pensamiento de la CEPAL* (Santiago de Chile: Editorial Universitaria).
Chenery, H. *et al.* (1974), *Redistribution with Growth* (Oxford University Press).
Chilcote, R. (1974), 'Dependency: A Critical Synthesis of the Literature', *Latin American Perspectives*, vol. I, no. 1, pp. 4–29.
Collier, D. (ed.), (1979), *The New Authoritarianism in Latin America* (Princeton University Press).
Cumberland, C. (1968), *Mexico, The Struggle for Modernity* (Oxford University Press).
Díaz Alejandro, C. (1970), *Essays on the Economic History of the Argentine Republic* (New Haven, Conn.: Yale University Press).
Emmanuel, A. (1972), *Unequal Exchange* (New York: Monthly Review).
—— (1974), 'Myths of Development Versus Myths of Underdevelopment', *New Left Review*, 85, pp. 61–79.
Evans, P. B. (1979), *Dependent Development: the Alliance of Multinational, State and Local Capital in Brazil* (Princeton University Press).
Evers, T. (1979), *El Estado en la periferia capitalista* (México: Siglo XXI).
Fortin, C. (1982), 'The Relative Autonomy of the State and Capital Accumulation in Latin America: Some Conceptual Issues', in Tussie, D. (ed.), *Latin America and the World. New Perspectives* (London: Gower Press) pp. 195–210.

—— (1983), 'Latin America in the 1980s: Issues, Trends and Prospects', *Boletín de Estudios Latinoamericanos y del Caribe*, Amsterdam, no. 34, June, pp. 3–15.
Frank, A. G. (1967), *Capitalism and Underdevelopment in Latin America* (New York: Monthly Review Press).
—— (1972), *Lumpenbourgeoisie, Lumpendevelopment. Dependence, Class and Politics in Latin America* (New York: Monthly Review Press).
Furtado, C. (1965a), 'Development and Stagnation in Latin America: A Structuralist Approach', *Studies in Comparative International Development*, I, pp. 159–75.
—— (1965b), *Dialéctica del desarrollo* (México: Fondo de Cultura Económica).
—— (1966), *Subdesarrollo y estancamiento en América Latina* (Editorial Universitaria de Buenos Aires).
—— (1970), *Economic Development of Latin America: a Survey from Colonial Times to the Cuban Revolution* (Cambridge University Press).
—— (1976), *Prefácio a Nova Economia Política* (Rio de Janeiro: Paz e Terra).
Garretón, M. A. (1979), *En torno a la discusión de los nuevos regímenes autoritarios en América Latina* (Santiago de Chile: FLACSO).
Glade, W. P. (1969), *The Latin American Economies* (New York: Van Nostrand).
Gough, I. (1979), *The Political Economy of the Welfare State* (London: Macmillan).
Hirschman, A. O. (1958), *The Strategy of Economic Development* (New Haven, Conn.: Yale University Press).
—— (1971). *A Bias for Hope* (New Haven, Conn.: Yale University Press).
Holloway, J. and Picciotto, S. (eds) (1978), *The State and Capital: a Marxist Debate* (London: Edward Arnold).
Hymer, S. (1979), *The Multinational Corporation: a Radical Approach* (Cambridge University Press).
Jessop, B. (1982), *The Capitalist State: Marxist Theories and Methods* (Oxford: Martin Robertson).
Kay, G. (1975), *Development and Underdevelopment: a Marxist Analysis* (London: Macmillan).
Laclau, E. (1969), 'Modos de producción, sistemas económicos y producción excedente. Aproximación histórica a los casos argentino y chileno', *Revista Latinoamericana de Sociología*, 2, Buenos Aires, pp. 276–316.
Lall, S. and Streeten, P. (1977), *Foreign Investment, Transnationals and Developing Countries* (London: Macmillan).
Lewis, W. A. (1970), 'Economic Development with Unlimited Supplies of Labour', *Manchester School of Economics and Social Sciences*, 1954, 22, pp. 139–91; reprinted in Agarwala and Singh (eds), *The Economics of Underdevelopment* (Oxford University Press) pp. 400–49.
Macario, S. (1964), 'Protectionism and Industrialization in Latin America' *Economic Bulletin for Latin America*, vol. IX, 1, pp. 61–101.
McGreevey, W. P. (1971), *An Economic History of Colombia, 1845–1930* (Cambridge University Press).
Mandel, E. (1978), *Late Capitalism* (London: Verso Editions).
Mandle, J. (1980), 'Marxist Analyses and Capitalist Development in the Third World', *Theory and Society*, 9, pp. 865–76.
Marx, K. (1969), *The Eighteenth Brumaire of Louis Bonaparte*, in Marx, K. and

Engels, F., *Selected Works in Three Volumes* (Moscow: Progress Publishers) vol I.
Mauro Marini, R. (1971), *Subdesarrollo y revolución* (México: Siglo XXI).
Morse, E. L. (1972), 'Transnational Economic Relations', in Keohane, R. O. and Nye, J. S. (eds), *Transnational Relations and World Politics* (Cambridge, Mass.: Harvard University Press) pp. 23–47.
Murray, R. (ed.), (1981), *Multinationals Beyond the Market: Intrafirm Trade and the Control of Transfer Pricing* (Hassocks, Sussex: Harvester Press).
Nurkse, R. (1953), *Problems of Capital Formation in Underdeveloped Countries* (Oxford University Press).
O'Connor, J. (1973), *The Fiscal Crisis of the State* (New York: St Martin's Press).
O'Donnell, G. (1973), *Modernization and Bureaucratic–Authoritarianism: Studies in South American Politics* (Berkeley: University of California Institute of International Studies, Politics of Modernization Series no. 9).
—— (1978), 'Reflections on the Patterns of Change in the Bureaucratic–Authoritarian State', *Latin American Research Review*, vol. XIII, no. 1, Winter, pp. 3–38.
—— (1979), 'Tensions in the Bureaucratic–Authoritarian State and the Question of Democracy', in Collier (ed.), pp. 285–318.
Palma, G. (1978), 'Dependency: A Formal Theory of Underdevelopment or a Methodology for the Analysis of Concrete Situations of Underdevelopment', *World Development*, vol. 6, no. 7/8, July–Aug., pp. 881–924.
Pintó, A. (1968). *Política y desarrollo* (Santiago de Chile: Editorial Universitaria).
—— (1971), *Tres ensayos sobre Chile y América Latina* (Buenos Aires: Ediciones Solar).
Poulantzas, N. (1978a), *Political Power and Social Classes* (London: Verso Editions).
—— (1978b), *State, Power and Socialism* (London: New Left Books).
Prebisch, R. (1981), *Capitalismo periférico. Crisis y transformación* (México: Fondo de Cultura Económica).
Randall, L. (1977), *A Comparative Economic History of Latin America*: vol. I, *Mexico*; vol. II, *Argentina*; vol. III, *Brazil*; vol. IV, *Peru* (Ann Arbor, Mich.: University Microfilms International).
Rey, P. P. (1976), *Les alliances de classe* (Paris: Maspero).
Rodríguez, O. (1972), *Informe sobre las críticas a la concepción de la CEPAL* (Montevideo: CECEA).
Rostow, W. W. (1960), *The Stages of Economic Growth: A Non-Communist Manifesto* (Cambridge University Press).
Strassman, W. P. (1965), 'Economic Growth and Income Distribution', *Quarterly Journal of Economics*, vol. LXX, pp. 425–40.
Sunkel, O. and Paz, P. (1970), *El subdesarrollo latinoamericano y la teoría del desarrollo* (Santiago de Chile: Siglo XXI).
Vaitsos, C. (1974), *Intercountry Income Distribution and Transnational Enterprises* (Oxford: Clarendon Press).
Wallerstein, I. (1979), *The Capitalist World Economy* (Cambridge University Press).
—— and Hopkins, T. (1981), 'Structural Transformations of the World

Economy', in Rubinson, R. (ed.), *Dynamics of World Development* (Beverley Hills and London: Sage).

Warren, B. (1973), 'Imperialism and Capitalist Industrialization', *New Left Review*, 81, pp. 3–44.

—— (1980), *Imperialism: Pioneer of Capitalism* (London: Verso Editions).

World Financial Markets (1983), 'International Debt: Progress Report and the Task Ahead', Sept., pp. 1–13.

2 The State and Capital Accumulation in Contemporary Brazil

CHRISTIAN ANGLADE

INTRODUCTION

In the early 1970s, the remarkable performance of the Brazilian economy was hailed as the much awaited 'miracle' reversing a secular trend of underdevelopment. It was also taken as evidence that the Brazilian authorities had embarked on the 'right' policies to promote development. For the other industrialising countries of Latin America, this was far more significant than the earlier achievement of Japan, from which there were few meaningful lessons to be learnt. Similarly, and quite understandably, they had never been convinced of the relevance of the experiences of countries like Taiwan, Malaysia, or even South Korea, to an analysis of their own problems and for an evaluation of their own prospects. For them, the Brazilian 'miracle' was the example to be followed or envied.

Now that the success story of the 1970s has faded a little, the key question raised by the Brazilian economy concerns the causes of its rapid growth between 1968 and 1973 and of its slowdown after 1974. When a crisis began to appear (in 1974–75), was it – as the Brazilian government then argued – only the sort of crisis that periodically affects *all* capitalist economies and which, in the 1970s, was provoked by a sudden increase in oil prices? If we retained this hypothesis, the possibility of a renewed expansion of the Brazilian economy would be essentially related to the solution found to the energy crisis. Since oil prices are now coming down, since Brazil has considerably increased its productive capacity over the last 15 years, and since it continues to benefit from lower labour costs than any developed capitalist economy, the prospects of expansion picking up again would then seem to be very good. This is still the opinion of the Brazilian government, and it was shared until recently by large sectors of the international banking community which, at an early stage of the Brazilian 'miracle', considered Brazil to be one of the most creditworthy countries in the world.

But is it valid to make the assumption that the Brazilian crisis is identical to *any* other crisis affecting capitalist countries today? It was suggested earlier (in the introduction to this book) that it is not. To attribute these crises to the same causes fails to recognise a fundamental difference between them, namely the conditions that determine the continuing reproduction of capital in those different processes of capitalist industrialisation. In Western Europe, the USA, and Japan, the process of continuing reproduction of capital is – and has always been – based on domestic savings and on the domestic control of capital accumulation. What will be argued in this essay is that, in Brazil, the insufficiency of domestic savings and the absence of a domestic control over the process of capital accumulation are inherent in the model of growth which was adopted; as such, they are the ultimate causes of the crisis and a structural obstacle to the capitalist development of the country.

This raises two sets of issues. *The first* concerns the type of model of growth and accumulation adopted in Brazil after 1964. Why was a model based on export industrialisation chosen in the first instance? How has it been implemented? And with what results? Since the choices and the decisions which shape a process of growth and capital accumulation are political as well as economic, an attempt to answer these questions must involve an analysis of the conditions in which both the political and the economic models came into operation in Brazil after 1964.

The second issue relates to the extent of state participation in the Brazilian economy, which became more pronounced after 1964. By palliating one of the traditional deficiencies of underdeveloped countries in not having a strong private capitalist sector, the Brazilian state appears to act as a substitute in the process of capital accumulation. Does this mean that a process of state capital accumulation is under way, or that state intervention is supporting a process of capital accumulation by the private sector? And if so, *what* private sector? An analysis of the nature of the 'substitute role' played by the state in that process is thus essential for an assessment of the Brazilian experience and of its value as an example to other Latin American countries.

THE BRAZILIAN MIRACLE IN ITS POLITICAL AND ECONOMIC CONTEXT

What came to be referred to as the Brazilian 'economic miracle' occurred in the period from 1968 to 1973, when the Brazilian economy grew at rates of over 10% a year on average. A breakdown of GDP growth rates during that period shows that – apart from 1971, when agriculture grew at the same pace as industry – growth was always induced by industrial production.

Table 2.1 shows that, during the 'economic miracle', the Brazilian economy grew according to a pattern of unbalanced growth recommended by an influential current of neoclassical development theory in the 1960s, and which was discussed in the introduction to this book.[1]

TABLE 2.1 Brazil: growth rates, 1968–73

	1968	1969	1970	1971	1972	1973
GDP	11.2	9.9	8.3	12.0	11.1	14.0
Agriculture	4.5	3.8	1.5	11.3	4.1	3.6
Industry	13.3	12.1	10.5	11.8	12.7	16.0

SOURCE *Conjuntura econômica*, various issues.

However, in spite of the ecstatic reaction to the Brazilian performance which came from the Brazilian government and from foreign bankers, it was not the first time that a similar model of growth had been implemented in Brazil with comparable results. Between 1958 and 1961, the growth of the Brazilian economy had also been impressive (Table 2.2) and, as a rule, with the exception of the 1963–67 period, industrial production had been responsible for the growth of the economy since the 1930s.[2]

What was new in the 'miracle' was that – contrary to what had happened under the Kubitschek administration (1955–61) – growth this time seemed to be well administered by a government which had finally got inflation under control. Heavy emphasis was put by government officials and by many foreign observers alike on the low rates of inflation which were the result of the anti-inflationary policies implemented between 1964 and 1967. Making political capital of this success, the government was always keen on emphasising the novelty of its own model of development and the definite contribution that the regime

TABLE 2.2 Brazil: growth rates, 1958–61

	1958	1959	1960	1961
GDP	7.7	5.6	9.7	10.3
Agriculture	2.0	5.3	4.9	7.6
Industry	16.2	11.9	9.6	10.6

SOURCE *Conjunctura econômica*, various issues.

which emerged from the 'Revolution of 1964' had made to the eradication of inflation. In 1964, a military government had replaced a civilian government whose inability to control inflation had been one of the causes of the coup launched against it. But inflation was only a visible instance of a more general crisis which was then affecting the Brazilian economy and – beyond it – Brazilian society as a whole. Failure to control inflation was only one indication of the overall failure of a civilian regime which had gradually grown more entangled in its own contradictions. One can understand why the military government which came to power in 1964 wished to emphasise the novel aspects of the post-1964 model of growth, but, with John Wells, 'we would emphasise the elements of *continuity* [sic] in the development of Brazilian capitalism between the mid-1950s and the mid-1970s and would not accept that the stabilisation of the mid-1960s was responsible for a radical restructuring of the system, which laid the foundations for the 'miracle'.[3]

It is important to develop this argument further, for, if a certain continuity of the policy was combined with discontinuity in political institutions after 1964, this would have several implications for an evaluation of the successes of 1968–73, but also of the problems which unfold afterwards.

Continuity or Discontinuity? The Contradictions of Populism and the Coup of 1964.

The political system of Brazil before 1964 was very influenced by the populist measures introduced by Vargas in the 1930s and 1940s. After 1930, 'populism' was established as a political model designed to cope with the social and political changes which resulted from the adoption of a new model of capital accumulation, following the collapse of the primary export model.[4] The presence of a large labour surplus allowed for a relatively easy adaptation of the previous traditional system to take place in Brazil, and, owing to the very low wages prevailing in agriculture, industrial workers could be co-opted into the system at low cost. Their wages – although higher than those received by rural workers – were still low enough not to affect the process of capital accumulation in the sector of industrial production.[5] This meant that a process of capital transfer from agriculture into industry was not required, contrary to what happened in Argentina. With profits guaranteed in both sectors of production, what might otherwise have been a potential source of conflict between the landowners and the industrialists was avoided in Brazil. Instead, their alliance led to a populist pact first administered by Vargas, and maintained until 1964. The cornerstone of that pact was the existence of a large labour surplus on which were based both the alliance between the two sectors of the dominant class and their efficient and low cost control over the industrial labour force.

However, in spite of the easiness of its operation, the new system had a number of inbuilt contradictions which began to emerge as a result of the recession in export earnings which followed the boom in export prices of primary commodities caused by the Korean War. Between 1954 and 1955, coffee prices fell so sharply that the Brazilian government could not support them, thus causing discontent among the export sectors.[6] At the same time, the process of Import Substitution Industrialisation (ISI) which was under way was heavily focused on the production of outputs, and it required constantly massive imports of industrial inputs; with the problems caused to the balance of payments by the crisis of exports, these imports could no longer be guaranteed by domestic capital. The contradiction that emerged was that while the adoption of a new model of capital accumulation (ISI) had been imposed after 1930 by a crisis in the balance of payments provoked by a recession in export earnings, the new model of capital accumulation continued to depend entirely on the same export earnings for all its essential inputs. Over more than 20 years, very little was done to reduce the import coefficient in the economy and to channel domestic savings into productive investments. This situation reinforced the position of many banking, industrial and commercial groups which were increasingly concerned by the low rate of investment of domestic savings in industry. Since higher rates of investment were required for a rapid development of industrial production, foreign capital had to be called in.

The decisive move in that direction was made under the presidency of

Kubitschek (1956–61), when several measures were taken to attract foreign capital in industrial production. A decree issued by the previous administration of Café Filho was extensively used: Instruction 113 of SUMOC (the monetary and credit authority) 'allowed foreign firms to import capital equipment at tariff levels below those imposed on Brazilian firms',[7] and at favourable exchange rates which were not available to local entrepreneurs. As a result, between 1955 and 1961, 2180 million dollars entered the country, mostly concentrated in manufacturing industry.[8] Foreign capital was first welcomed by Brazilian entrepreneurs, who anticipated its multiplying effect on their own rate of profit. It did this for some of them, but it also began to reveal and accelerate several of the contradictions of the process of growth on which expansion was based.

1. The higher rates of productivity obtained by the firms which imported foreign capital goods soon made those firms dependent on foreign capital and foreign firms for new technology, and the rapid rate of obsolescence of that technology gradually transformed their dependence into absorption. On the other hand, the lower rates of productivity of the firms which did not rely so heavily on foreign technology made them increasingly non-competitive. The simultaneous consequence of both tendencies was to accelerate (i) the rate of 'mergers' or takeovers of Brazilian firms by foreign groups and (2) the rate of concentration of Brazilian industry, reinforcing the oligopolistic structures of its organisation. As an example of *the first*, the proportion of all US manufacturing affiliates established by acquisition of Brazilian firms grew from 9% between 1946 and 1950 to 22% between 1951 and 1955 and 33% between 1956 and 1960.[9] *Secondly*, the concentration of Brazilian industrial production was already well established in the early 1960s, and this pattern was particularly clear in the sectors of capital goods and consumer durables. In São Paulo, the market share of the three largest firms in most sectors producing domestic electrical goods and electrical and non-electrical equipment was above 80% or even 90%.[10] Concentration was also high in many traditional non durable consumer goods, such as tobacco, beverages and foodstuffs.[11]

2. The process of industrialisation became more and more capital using, that is, more and more labour saving. In the 1950s, manufacturing output was growing at an annual rate of about 9·8% while employment in manufacturing grew on average at 2·6%,[12] i.e. below the rate of growth of the population, which was of about 3%. In an

underdeveloped economy, a fall in the rate of employment in industry is not compensated for by a larger capacity of absorption of labour by the tertiary sector. In Brazil, the combined result of these different factors was an increase in the rate of disguised unemployment and underemployment which – contrary to the unemployment rates that are functional to the process of capital accumulation in industrial economies by putting pressure on wages – was, both by its nature and by its volume, dysfunctional to the continuing reproduction of capital. *By its nature*, as the different spheres of labour tended to become increasingly isolated from each other, because of the constantly increasing skill requirements of the capital intensive sector; as a result, unemployment affecting unskilled labour did not put any real pressure on the wage levels of skilled labour. *By its volume*, because the reduced rate of employment in industry compared with the higher rates of productivity of that sector was exercising a negative effect on the aggregate demand for consumer goods, thus reducing the potential rate of expansion of the economy.

These contradictions were reinforced by the mechanisms used to accelerate the rate of capital accumulation, which was one of the key objectives of the *Programa de Metas* (Target Plan) of the Kubitschek administration. For this, long-term capital investments had to be made by the government in infrastructures as well as in those 'empty spaces' in production which are usually unattractive to private capital because they yield a low rate of profit, but which are both essential to economic expansion and necessary to the maximisation of private capital accumulation. The economic role of the state was thus clearly defined: outside oil production, which was a politically sensitive area in which foreign capital could not be allowed, *state action was to be limited to creating the conditions favourable to the expansion of the private sector*.

With the *Programa de Metas*, the Kubitschek administration wanted to achieve rapid development (fifty years in five) through an acceleration of the rate of industrialisation. If we measure it by the rate of growth of the economy, the Plan was successful. But it also had many shortcomings. *Firstly* – and mainly for political reasons – it neglected agriculture and maintained an inadequate system of taxation. *Secondly*, it soon began to finance the mounting pressures that rising import costs and declining export earnings were putting on the balance of payments by enlarging the public deficit, expanding the money supply, and resorting to external credit. As a result, the external debt had reached 2·2 billion dollars in 1961,[13] and 'both the interest payments and amortization, combined with profit remittances of foreign firms produced increased balance of payments difficulties'.[14] Government savings and the financing of gross capital formation from public savings declined, and the budgetary deficit was enlarged to cover rising public expenditures. Inevitably, the money supply was further enlarged after 1958, and inflation went up (Table 2.3).

Inflation soon began to reveal and accelerate two of the underlying contradictions of the system.

1. The high rates of productivity obtained in industry by the adoption of capital intensive methods of production increased the rate of extraction of relative surplus value, while – at the same time – real wages showed some improvement before 1964;[15] not enough to keep demand in line with supply (due to the fall of the employment rate in industry), but enough to make wages the main target for anti-inflationary policies.
2. The fall in demand combined with the high rates of growth of industrial production to provoke a crisis of excess capacity which openly began to affect some sectors of production in 1961. This had an adverse effect on the rate of industrial expansion itself, since many firms had to operate with high rates of unused productive capacity. In 1965, excess capacity had reached 47% in capital goods and 35% in consumer goods.[16] The firms worst hit were those in which heavy investments had been made to increase productivity, and which needed a constantly expanding market. Thus the contraction of demand particularly affected the firms associated with – and increasingly controlled by – foreign capital.

TABLE 2.3: *Brazil: budget deficit, public savings and inflation, 1958–62*

	(1) Government savings as % of GDP	(2) Public savings as % of gross capital formation	(3) Budget deficit as % of GDP	(4) Money supply	(5) Inflation
1958	4.5	25.9	1.8	21.3	12.3
1959	4.6	21.2	2.7	41.9	37.7
1960	4.7	25.7	2.8	38.1	30.9
1961	1.3	6.9	3.4	50.6	38.1
1962	−0.2	−1.2	4.3	63.1	53.3

SOURCES (1) and (2): Baer and Kerstenetzky (1972) table 3, pp. 110–11.
(3) and (4): idem, table 4, p. 112.
(5): Lafer (1970) table III, 24, p. 213.

As can be seen from Table 2.3, the crisis developed rapidly after Kubitschek and, in 1962–63, the government introduced policies which were themselves contradictory, since they were meant both to stabilise the economy through a curbing of inflation and to create a larger volume of demand capable of bringing down the rate of idle capacity of production of the large firms, by enlarging consumer credit facilities. However, it would be wrong to interpret the crisis of excess capacity which spread to most sectors of industrial production in 1962–63 as a sudden and unexpected change in the rate of expansion. It is statistically true that a crisis did not openly affect production until 1962, but it is also true that the same crisis had been gradually generated by the contradictions of the populist regime.

Beyond a certain point of operation, it is easy to see how those different contradictions, which had not necessarily emerged related to each other, soon came to develop a dialectical relationship which multiplied their effects and accelerated the crisis. State expenditures undertaken to attract foreign capital, and necessary to maintain high rates of private capital accumulation, continued to grow while the contraction of demand resulting from inflation was reducing the rate of capital accumulation. Similarly, inflation was largely responsible for growing political mobilisation which was a threat to the stability of populist governments and which led to frequent wage re-adjustments, particularly under Goulart. But the rate of inflation was such that wage re-adjustments did not have any positive effect on demand and merely contributed to further accelerate the rate of inflation (73·5% in 1963).

Falling demand aggravated another contradiction which was a serious threat to the stability of the populist alliance, since it affected the relations between the two sectors of the dominant class. The stability of their alliance had already been shaken when the Brazilian government had not been able to guarantee the profits of the agricultural export sectors against the constantly declining tendency of export earnings after 1955. But a major threat against the stability of this alliance appeared after Kubitschek when, alarmed by rapidly falling demand, some groups of industrial entrepreneurs began to join with industrial trade unions and with the fast expanding peasant leagues of the North East to demand the urgent implementation of a programme of agrarian reform. This most divisive issue had always been avoided before, and the fact that the existing patterns of landownership had eventually come to be denounced by some influential entrepreneurial groups can be rightly interpreted as the decisive step against the stability of the populist alliance set up in the 1930s. This was – from the very beginning of their alliance – probably the most crucial contradiction that existed between the interests of the two sectors of the dominant class. That the emergence of such a contradiction was delayed for so long can be explained by the type of industrial policies implemented by the Brazilian government and which were shaped in a context of structures of supply and demand determined by the concern to leave the patterns of landownership intact. In turn, the success achieved in preventing the emergence of this contradiction for about thirty years goes a long way towards explaining the limitations of the process of industrial development based on ISI, since the low level of wages in agriculture maintained an insufficient overall demand for industrial goods.

In spite of the ever growing scope of its action, the state issued from the populist alliance was limited in its policies by the lack of any 'significant' autonomy *vis-à-vis* the dominant sectors of civil society and by the contradictions of the intra-class alliance of which it was the institutional expression.

This cluster of contradictions was already apparent under Kubitschek, both *within* the dominant class and *between* it and the urban middle and working classes that it co-opted because it had to rely on a new model of capital accumulation after the crisis of 1930. Under Quadros – and even more under Goulart – the dialectical relationship between these contradictions dangerously weakened the efficiency of the state action, political as well as economic, since both popular mobilisation and inflation were getting out of control. More importantly, these contradictions were also rapidly affecting the internal stability of the state institutions.

It was under the presidencies of Quadros (1961) and of Goulart (1961–64) that the institutional crisis developed. The anti-Vargas political forces that had brought Quadros to the presidency thought that they could succeed in bringing down inflation through the implementation of austerity measures which could still salvage the stability of the populist alliance. But the sudden departure of Quadros, who left the presidency after only 7 months in office, revealed the depth of the crisis. Through what was obviously an anomaly of the Brazilian constitution, which allowed for two separate elections to be run for president and vice-president, the successor of Quadros was Goulart, who represented the Vargas heritage, and who – in conjunction with his brother-in-law Brizzola – was known to want to reactivate 'populism' by adopting redistribution policies. His access to the presidency precipitated the crisis, which then appeared irreversible, and it is still unclear why a military coup was delayed until 1964. This anomaly of the Brazilian constitution which allowed Goulart to become president was added evidence of an institutional crisis which threatened directly and, since it was backed by the authority of the Executive, decisively, the basic stability of the system of domination. The new contradiction was that the threat against the system of domination then began to come precisely from those institutions which had been designed to guarantee its stability.

Less paradoxically than it might seem at first, it was the development of mass politics in the 1950s and early 1960s which made the election of a constitutionally powerful president increasingly difficult to control through the mechanisms of political participation which had been set up by the populist alliance. Created in 1945 with the clearly defined objective to perpetuate the system of domination, the Brazilian party system reproduced the contradictions of the populist alliance that had engendered it. It was originally based on a mere adaptation of the relations of clientelism which had prevailed in the traditional party system before 1930, but which had to be readjusted to the requirements of the changing socioeconomic conditions resulting from industrialisation and rapid urbanisation. However, the acceleration of both the rate of socioeconomic change and of the contradictions brought about by populism (namely the falling standards of living of wage earning sectors provoked by rising inflation) gradually eroded the clientelistic nature of those parties. They had been created to control and 'functionalise' the class cleavages of the Brazilian society, but they tended instead – since they were the main channel of political participation – to become increasingly used to express antagonistic class interests. From this point of view, it could be said that the institutional crisis which emerged in the early 1960s was not due – as is too often repeated – to the inability of a supposedly artificial party system to articulate interests, but on the contrary to the fact that the party system had ceased to perform the original function for which it had been created, and that it had become 'real', in the sense that it had started to articulate horizontally (i.e. as social groups) those interests which it was supposed to articulate only in vertical, clientelistic–particularistic structures.[17]

As a mechanism of control for the system of domination, the party system began to prove its inefficiency when it allowed the arrival to power of an unreliable presidential candidate, Quadros, who was eventually 'recuperated' by the dominant classes when it had become clear that public opinion was flowing his way. The blow was even more severe with Goulart. The large powers granted to the President by the Constitution and the growing difficulty to interfere between him and public opinion led to a situation in which the control that the dominant classes maintained over Congress began to be used against the President to monitor his action. Control over Congress had long been easy to maintain thanks to an electoral system which allowed for an efficient manipulation of the voter in the rural areas.[18] But this too was changing, due to a very rapid process of urbanisation which was itself accelerated by the economic policies of the populist governments. The growth of the urban centres soon presented an electoral challenge which the populist mechanisms of control were not always able to meet. On the other hand, the patterns of political participation were changing also in the rural areas, where the radical mobilisation engendered by the action of the newly created peasant leagues was particularly difficult to contain.[19] As a reliable control over the decision-making power of the Executive could no longer be guaranteed by Congress, there was practically no other option for the dominant classes but to intervene against the institutional order they had originally set up.

In the Latin American context of the early 1960s, profoundly marked by the impact of the Cuban revolution, Goulart was held responsible for the fast developing urban working class mobilisation in the South and South East and for the new peasant mobilisation in the North East. Opposed as they were to the growing influence of foreign capital and foreign firms, most Brazilian entrepreneurial sectors did not hesitate long however before aligning with them – and with the landowners – against the new 'revolutionary' danger that they saw coming up. Some of them thought (or hoped) that a more or less independent form of capitalist development was still possible. Most of them simply preferred to negotiate the terms of their absorption by foreign firms rather than – as they saw it – risk losing everything in a revolutionary process. Alarmed by a very conservative press, most sectors of the middle classes were relieved by the military coup of April 1964 which deposed President Goulart. The authoritarian political model set up in 1964 and the economic model started in 1968 after 3 years of stabilisation were for them the only political and economic way out, even if there was a price to pay for it in the interruption of the traditional system of compromise of a civilian regime, which was probably more in tune with the political culture of the country.

The 'New' Model and its Operation: from Miracle to Slow Down

The first concern of the government established by the 1964 coup was to reduce the high rates of inflation supposedly caused by excess demand. To bring the money supply back under control, the budgetary deficit, consumer credit and wages had to be cut down. Lower wages were particularly important to the new policy makers, since excessive wage readjustments were singled out as the main cause of inflation. The partiality of this explanation is demonstrated by the data available for the period 1956–64, showing that, in manufacturing, the rate of growth of productivity grew increasingly ahead of real wages.[20] On the other hand, as Fishlow points out, 'real bank loans to the private sector had also shown steady decline. Since inflation accelerated nevertheless, neither merits the importance the stabilisation plan attached to them as causal elements.'[21] At the same time, another potential source of inflation was neglected both by the government and by many observers of the Brazilian economy.

We have seen earlier that the oligopolistic tendencies of Brazilian industrial production were reinforced under Kubitschek as a consequence of the implementation of the *Programa de Metas*. Fajnzylber demonstrated that, in 1968, the concentration of manufacturing production had further increased and that, in industrial production as a whole, the sectors dominated by foreign firms presented the largest degree of concentration.[22] Excess capacity developed due to falling demand, and this tended to increase the costs per unit of production. In a competitive setting, these higher costs would have had to be absorbed by the firms. In an oligopolistic structure, by contrast, the market power enjoyed by the large firms allowed them to pass on the higher costs in terms of higher prices. Evidence of this is provided by the fact that 'price and quantity changes by sector in the periods 1955–58 and 1962–66 are correlated negatively in each ... that is, those industries growing most rapidly raised prices least ... This evidence is highly suggestive of deeply rooted and pervasive price inflexibility'[23] which partially cancelled the attempts to stabilise. For Fishlow, the contradictions of the stabilisation policy '[testify] to the true priorities of the government.... Even during the Castelo Branco period [1964–67], the principal aim was not stabilization; it was making market capitalism work.'[24]

If that was the true priority of state action in Brazil after 1964, we must expect that priority to be present at all the levels at which the state can act on capital accumulation.

The most general level of state action in that area concerns the conditions which set up the distribution of national income between profits and wages in a way that will tend to maximise the extraction of surplus value within the limits fixed by the market requirements of supply and by the need to maintain social peace. The wage policy of a government – and its labour policy as a whole – is a good indicator of its role in the process of capital accumulation. Since this aspect of state action is also potentially one which most easily gives rise to conflict, it is clear that an authoritarian government will be better equipped to perform it in a way which – at least in the short run – will maximise the extraction of surplus value from labour. Lower labour costs will benefit the producers, but they might also – by reducing the volume of aggregate demand – have recessionary consequences for the economy. How serious those consequences will be tends to vary with the degree to which the growth of output depends respectively on internal demand and on exports. It is therefore logical to expect that strict wage policies and labour control should be combined with export orientation. But, apart from being socially divisive, such a policy also makes growth more vulnerable, as there are no mechanisms capable of guaranteeing a steady flow of exports; these are always likely to be subjected to protectionism and/or falling external demand which cannot be controlled.

State action at the general level of surplus extraction (or of the distribution of national income between profits and wages) is part of the wide regulating intervention of the state in the economy, in which – to guarantee the continuous process of capital reproduction – the state intervenes through a whole range of instruments designed to allocate resources selectively and to promote specific forms of capital accumulation which are more favourable to some sectors of private capital than to others.

If it is the free operation of market capitalism that is desired, then the distinction between national and foreign private capital is to some extent irrelevant, since it is assumed that there are no inherent contradictions between the two. In this perspective, the possibility of a conflict can only come from an extension of state activity into production.

A distinction is traditionally made between the state acting as an entrepreneur (1) in the so-called 'empty spaces' of production and (2) in 'other' forms of production reputed to be profitable. The *first* correspond to those sectors of production which are unattractive to private producers because of the negative or low profit rates that they usually offer, but which are none the less essential to the continuous growth of the industrial output. Public investment in infrastructures and the production by public companies of cheap inputs and intermediary goods are considered to be part of the supporting role of the state in a private process of capital accumulation. The *second* derive from a tendency of the state to continuously expand its productive activities and – in that process – to begin to compete with private capital in profitable forms of production. While the first type of intervention is considered desirable by private capital, the second is not, and its expansion is denounced as being contrary to the most basic principles of capital accumulation in a market economy. To perform their supporting role, public companies should stick to the 'empty spaces' which do not attract private producers.

The trouble with this distinction is that it is based on the assumption of fixed rates of profitability for different sectors of production, which is itself the result of a practice rather than of an immutable profit logic. There is no inherent reason as to why the production of industrial inputs or of capital goods should be less profitable than that of consumer durables, particularly when the public firms producing them are large and can benefit from economies of scale and potentially strong market power. If it is less profitable, it is because, in supplying those goods cheaply, the state supports a process of private capital accumulation which it subsidises in different ways. This is however the result of a political decision and, as such, it is not permanent. State subsidies of this type do not necessarily always benefit the same private producers, and the changes which do occur tend to reflect the fluctuating relationship of different sectors of private capital with the state. A period of economic recession, or a public deficit getting out of control, can also affect a long standing policy of subsidised prices by the state companies. The whole area of their supporting role to the private sector is then likely to be questioned and the potential market power of the large state companies can even be seen as a possible source of profits.

It is therefore difficult to consider that there are some 'fixed' areas of production in which the state as entrepreneur always acts in a supporting role, while there would be other areas in which its action would always conflict with the interests of private capital. In other words, it seems artificial to establish fixed categories within the scope of state action in production, with areas earmarked for state companies and areas reserved for private firms.

In a more general way, a distinction between 'indirect' and 'direct' forms of state intervention can also be misleading. It is useful to retain it for the purpose of analysis, provided it is understood that the nature of the various instruments used to support private capital accumulation matters less than the extent to which their supporting capacity is used. Attention is often unduly focused on the 'direct' role of the state in production, when 'indirect' forms of intervention such as the manipulation of fiscal and credit policies can frequently have a greater impact on the overall level of subsidies to private capital. Wage, fiscal and credit policies, price controls, inflation, export incentives, import controls, exchange rates, etc. ..., as well as the price of the goods supplied by state companies, can all have a more or less decisive impact on private accumulation. Similarly, each of these, or any combination of them, can have drawback effects on accumulation. Wage, fiscal and credit policies can, if they are too liberal, create an excess demand which might 'overheat' the economy and fuel inflation, but they can also have recessionary consequences if they are too restrictive. Import controls, implemented to reduce a growing current account deficit, can have the same effects. Fiscal and export subsidies will put a strain on public expenditure which – unless compensated by extra revenues elsewhere – will result in a growing public deficit; this might force the government to raise the cost of its services to the private sector. All the forms of the supporting role of the state are potentially contradictory to each other, and the least contradictory combination of them is the measure of the relative autonomy of the capitalist state.

What the Brazilian experience suggests is that – at least in the industrialising countries of Latin America – the combinations of different policy mechanisms and their impact on capital accumulation vary, not with the goal of state action (to make market capitalism work) which is constant, but with the contradictions of the model of capital accumulation which is adopted. If measured by a number of conventional indicators of economic performance, the operation of market capitalism in Brazil might look very impressive at times. However, because the goal is constant, the policy alternatives are limited, and their different combinations tend to reproduce constantly the same contradictions which – in a dialectical process – they accelerate. Ultimately, it is the autonomy of state action which is limited by the pursuit of a model of capital accumulation which has generated self-reproducing contradictions over which the state has lost control.

The policy orientations of the administrations of Costa e Silva (1967–69) and Medici (1969–74) confirmed the priority established by the administration of Castelo Branco, and they made market capitalism work. Between 1968 and 1973, annual average growth rates were impressive in manufacturing as a whole (13·3%), but they were particularly high in consumer durables (23·6%) and in capital goods (18·1%).[25] This was obtained through the utilization of the excess capacity accumulated during the period 1962–66; after 1967, it was also a result of the expansionist move of the first year of the Costa e Silva administration. That move was very selective. Because rising wages were considered as the main cause of inflation, and because the presence of a labour surplus was one of the comparative advantages of the Brazilian economy in that it allowed to keep labour costs low, the same strict wage policy was pursued as under Castelo Branco. But the wage squeeze did not seem to be incompatible with industrial growth:

1. The changing patterns of income distribution show that the real income of those middle and high income urban groups – whose demand was relevant to the growth of production of consumer durables – was enlarged, while 80% of the working population saw their share of national income further reduced from the already low levels of 1960. This is shown even by the most conservative calculations, as in Table 2.4.
2. The boom in the demand for consumer durables was also activated by a new expansion of consumer credit.
3. Credit facilities were also offered in the construction industry, to both producers and consumers. Stimulated by public sector investments, the industry grew by over 11% per year in real terms between 1967 and 1974,[26] with an impact on the production of capital goods and other inputs.
4. Fiscal incentives and subsidised credit were used to promote exports. However, in spite of the heavy official emphasis on their significance to the economy, the weight of manufactured exports on the growth of manufacturing production was modest (8% between 1968 and 1972),[27] and the distribution of exports during the period of the 'miracle' showed a pattern in which primary commodities and

TABLE 2.4 *Brazil: income distribution in Brazil, 1960, 1970*

% of economically active population	% of national income	
	1960	1970
Bottom 50	17.71	14.91
Next 30	27.92	22.85
Next 15	26.66	27.38
Top 5	27.69	34.86

SOURCE   Langoni (1973).

traditional non durables continued to dominate. Together, they still accounted for 86·6% of exports in 1972.[28]

5. The rate of fixed capital formation grew from 19·6% of GDP in 1966 to 23% in 1973.[29] The investment boom was particularly noticeable in the capital goods industry, which grew by 18·1% a year between 1968 and 1973.

6. The growth of the economy was helped by a favourable international environment. The rapid development of world trade boosted Brazilian exports which grew by approximately 25% per year,[30] while the liquidity of the international capital markets in the early 1970s allowed Brazil to borrow a large share of the foreign savings made available through commercial banks, with low spreads and long terms of maturity. As a result, the external debt grew rapidly, from 3332 million dollars in 1967 (11·08% of GDP) to 12 572 million in 1973 (17·30% of GDP).[31] That the debt was growing faster than GDP was not seen as a problem in the euphoria of the 'miracle', since exports were growing by 25% per year, and it seemed certain that the service of that growing debt would be easily met by the continuing success of the export policy.

7. Another source of optimism was that domestic savings were rising as well, from 21·1% of GNP on average between 1960–64 to 23·8% between 1970 and 1974.[32] Combined with a stricter control over government current expenditures and with improved tax and social security revenues, which increased the government current savings (from 2·7% of GNP in 1970 to 4·6% in 1973),[33] this helped to maintain the contribution of domestic savings to the financing of investment at 88·8% on average between 1970–74.[34] That represented a drop of nearly 10% from the previous 4 years period, but, with a rate of gross domestic investment which grew from 22·2% to 26·9% of GNP between the two periods,[35] the drop would have been much larger if domestic savings had not shown an upward trend.

One could continue to add to this list of indicators of the success story of the Brazilian economic 'miracle'. It seemed that the only area in which the success of the model could be challenged was that of the social distribution of income. Real minimum wages were falling steadily (in 1974 they were down to 78·8% of their 1963 level in Rio, according to the FGV, and 63·2% in São Paulo, according to DIEESE)[36] and social inequalities were increasing, due to the government savings in social expenditures. However, the government did not consider that the fall in minimum wages was a true indicator of the real evolution of wages; its standard response was that more and more wage earners were receiving earnings above the minimum wage, which thus tended to lose its significance as a concrete income category.

The euphoria was only partially tempered in 1974 by a sudden increase of the rate of inflation (from 15·7% in 1973 to 34·5%)[37] and by the large deficit in the trade account of the balance of payments (from +7 million dollars in 1973 to −4690 million). Both were seen to be consequences (1) of the very success of the economy, which had grown so fast that it had caused an overheating of industrial production, whose signs could already be seen in 1972–73;[38] and (2) of the increase in oil prices unilaterally decided by the OPEC countries. To counteract the upward trends of inflation and of the deficit in the trade balance – which were considered to be temporary – the new Geisel administration (1974–79) adopted in 1974 the Second National Development Plan (II PND). The main objectives of the Plan were at one and the same time to maintain expansion, slow down inflation, and reduce the deficit of the balance of payments. The obvious contradictions between these objectives were to determine the 'stop and go' character of policy making over the following five years. These 5 years were also to reveal the basic contradictions of the Brazilian model of capital accumulation and the impact of state intervention on that model. Nothing significantly new emerged in the early 1980s, and all the elements of the crisis that came into the open in 1981–82 had developed in the second half of the seventies. Afterwards, the crisis simply unfolded 'naturally', fed by contradictions which could no longer be controlled. The Geisel administration is thus the key period for an analysis of the contradictions generated by state intervention in the process of capital accumulation.

THE CONTRADICTIONS OF THE BRAZILIAN MODEL OF CAPITAL ACCUMULATION

The Effects of 'Indirect' State Intervention on Capital Accumulation: the Contradictions of Policy Making

In 1974, the first objective *seems to have been* to slow down. However, the measures that were taken to reduce the money supply (down from 47% in 1973 to 33·5% in 1974) were not very drastic, and consumer credit restrictions consisted mainly in repayment periods being temporarily reduced from 36 to 24 months. This seems hardly sufficient to explain the drop in the output of consumer durables, which grew by

8·3% in 1974 against 25·9% in 1973 (Table 2.5). The only sector that did not appear to be affected was that of capital goods, which grew by 22·3% in 1974 (27·7% in 1973) as a result of import substituting government investments.

As can be seen from Table 2.5, the 'crisis' affecting the growth of industrial production was a crisis only by Brazilian standards and, with few exceptions, most of the indicators of its performance would have satisfied any industrial country. The crisis was largely elsewhere, that is in the rate of inflation and in the performance of the balance of payments, but it was also in the expectations of growth which were contradicted by the erratic pattern of manufacturing growth after 1974.

TABLE 2.5 Brazil: rate of growth of industrial production, 1972–79

	1972	1973	1974	1975	1976	1977	1978	1979
Consumer durables	25.2	25.9	8.3	−4.2	14.6	0.6	16.4	7.5
Consumer non-durables	9.4	11.2	3.9	2.9	11.2	−0.5	7.3	4.7
Capital goods	25.7	27.7	22.3	4.7	14.9	−4.4	6.8	5.7
Intermediary goods	14.8	18.3	9.3	6.4	12.8	7.5	6.8	9.2
Total manufacturing	14.0	16.6	7.8	3.8	12.8	2.7	7.6	7.0

SOURCE Fundação Instituto Brasileiro de Geografia e Estatística (FIBGE).

This pattern somewhat reflected the indecision of the government and the contradictions of its policy making. The yearly succession of ups and downs until 1979 showed a clear downward tendency: the fall was deeper in 1977 than in 1975 and the recovery lower in 1978 than in 1976. (As we will see later, the apparent interruption of the cycle in 1979 was due to a temporary expansionist bluff which did not alter the pattern.)

The real slow down came in 1975, in spite of a relaxation of both monetary and fiscal policies. The government was *politically* worried by the poor performance of the economy that year and concerned by the consequences of this on the results of the municipal elections of November 1976. Politically, the worst aspect of the 1975 slow down concerned the sector of consumer durables, which had been the leading sector of growth in the early 1970s, and which dropped to −4·2%.

The political liberalisation ('*abertura*') to which the Geisel administration appeared to be committed had already been shaken by the results of the general election held in November 1974, when the opposition party MDB had made substantial gains, both in Congress and in Senate. Coming after the partial defeat of 1974, both hardliners and *Medicistas*, who were against '*abertura*' – and *Geiselistas*, who were for it – considered that the 1976 elections would be an important test. The government thus decided to adopt expansionist measures to boost consumer demand again. Wages were re-adjusted and the minimum wage went up by 4·4% in real terms, consumer credit facilities were enlarged and government expenditures were stepped up.

What was important in those measures were the political motivations behind them. This added a new dimension to the contradictory policy making of the government, which started oscillating between the 'economic' need to fight inflation and to reduce the deficit of the balance of payments, and the increasingly 'political' need to maintain expansion at a level compatible with social peace and with the demands of private capital. Those two contradictory objectives were now to be pursued consecutively ('stop-go') or sometimes even simultaneously ('stop *and* go'). Ironically, it is perhaps to its desire to maintain some formal democratic appearances – and to the obligation of electoral success that this imposed on the government party ARENA – that the Geisel administration owed part of its indecision in the conduct of economic policy. A stricter authoritarian line would probably have allowed for greater orthodoxy in the implementation of a recessionary policy.

But the importance of '*abertura*' in this respect should not be overstated.

Firstly, in 1976, the decision to liberalise did not entirely depend on the government any longer. In the mid-1970s, strikes continued to be illegal, but the extent of the discontent provoked among the lower paid by a combination of repressed wages and growing inflation had led to a degree of mobilisation which seemed already beyond the reach of the repressive capacity that the regime had demonstrated in the early seventies. This discontent had been expressed in the 1974 elections, and the government did not want to repeat the same experience in 1976. On the other hand, private domestic capital wanted nothing less than recession, and the employers' organisations were constantly pressing for measures to reactivate the economy. For them too, the economic but also the political price of an economic crisis could be serious, as the memories of the early 1960s were still present.

Secondly, the impact of '*abertura*' on the relaxation of the restrictions imposed since 1964 should not be exaggerated. Inspired by the economic success of the previous period, '*abertura*' was an attempt to capitalise on the political advantages that economic expansion could have for the regime. Economic success had been rather triumphantly presented by the previous government as a justification of their authoritarian line. The exponents of *'abertura'* considered this to be a rather crude and typically military attitude. For them, the idea was to relate economic expansion more closely to some form of legitimacy of political institutions. In the absence of other nationalist issues which could act as a catalyst, it was an attempt to utilize the political potential of 'Brazilian development' to increase the popularity of the regime and to reduce opposition. It was thought that a more 'liberal' (or less repressive) government which could maintain expansion should be able to achieve this objective.

In more general terms, this was an attempt to find a solution to the crucial legitimacy challenge which faces all military governments whenever they try to find a way out of repression but to stay in power. The timing was probably wrong however, since the key element on which the strategy was based, i.e. economic success, was fading away. There is an obvious contradiction in trying to liberalise at a time of a growing economic crisis. It can be productive for an authoritarian government to introduce measures of political liberalisation and to reopen some formal channels of participation when economic expansion goes on. When it does not, those moves can be counter productive and improve the chances of the opposition. This explains the anxiety of the Geisel government to reactivate the miracle, which – in turn – explains its increasing weakness, since, in order to avoid recession, it started using policies which had little impact on expansion, but which added to the two visible conditions which had started the crisis in 1974, i.e. *inflation* and *the deficit of the balance of payments.*

As it happened, the economic recovery of 1976 was not enough to spare the government another political setback at the municipal elections that year. On the other hand, *inflation*, which had been kept down at 29·2% in 1975, went up to 46·3% in 1976. The fact that this had happened after only one year of a minor reflation of the economy strengthened the position of those who – like the Finance Minister M. H. Simonsen – saw the main source of inflation in oil prices and in excess demand. To cut down the inflationary oil import bill, the government was now to encourage the development of alternative energy sources. To cut down excess demand, it decided to impose a strict wage policy and to restrict credit.

The formula by which wage adjustments were calculated every year had grown more complex since 1964. As a result of the implementation of the original formula, 'real wages ... were systematically reduced between 1964 and 1967'.[39] By 1976, the calculation started including also a 'terms of trade' factor which had yet another negative impact on real wages.[40] In general, it was widely recognised that the official wage adjustment factors by which the government calculated wage increases fell regularly below the cost of living indexes. In parallel, the restrictions imposed on credit were regularly stepped up until 1979 to slow down the growth of the money supply. Cuts were imposed on public spending and interest rates were freed in all sectors of domestic credit in 1977, in the hope that rising interest rates would reduce the demand for credit both from firms and from consumers, and that it would induce firms to get credit abroad, which would increase the volume of foreign reserves. It was thought that these measures would have a positive effect on an overheated economy which would pick up again later once the excess of demand had been cooled down.

The other problem was *the deficit in the balance of payments*. The measures taken since 1974 to reduce the deficit of the trade account had been so effective that the trade account deficit had gone down from 4690 million dollars in 1974 to 2254 million in 1976. The pursuit of the same policies even produced a surplus of 96 million in 1977.

Import controls were reinforced and incentives to import substitution were set in motion after 1975, particularly in the sector of capital goods. The argument behind this decision was that the cost of capital goods tends to grow faster than that of any other imports in a period of ISI, and thus contributes to widen the deficit of the current account, which has to be financed through more public borrowing abroad. This in turn leads to an increased outflow of capital which ruins the possibility of domestic capital accumulation. From 1974 onwards, numerous incentives and subsidies were offered by the government to promote the domestic production of capital goods.[41]

This action on imports was complemented by an aggressive export policy which was the cornerstone of the government strategy and which represented the means to keep economic expansion going. An improved export performance would not only mean a better trade account but a generally healthier economy with larger foreign reserves, as well as a policy of tight consumer credit at home easier to enforce. A lesser reliance on the domestic market would also help to maintain a stricter wage policy and would hopefully add to the docility of a labour force already worried by the prospects of unemployment which were growing fast in 1977.[42]

Several measures already existed to promote exports, such as an exemption from payment of IPI (*Imposto sobre Produtos Industrializa-*

dos), a federal value added tax, and of ICM (*Imposto sobre Circulação de Mercadorias*), a state tax on exports; tax credits for the purchase of inputs used in manufacturing exports; and a whole range of credit incentives and marketing services offered by the government Special Export Programme, BEFIEX, and the Foreign Trade Department of the *Banco do Brasil*, CACEX. For most of the products exported, these subsidies amounted to between 30% and 50% of their value. The obvious way in which this contravened GATT regulations provoked strong reactions in the USA and the EEC which, in 1978, started imposing non-tariff barriers and 'voluntary' curbs on Brazilian exports. But the worst aspects of these massive export subsidies were that:

1. They were a further evidence of the contradictory policy making of the government which – at the time it was multiplying its subsidies to exports – was maintaining an overvalued exchange rate (to reduce import costs) which discriminated against exports.[43]
2. They put a considerable drain on government resources, by contributing to enlarge the public deficit. As we will see later, the nominal positive contribution that exports made to the trade account of the balance of payments were more than negatively compensated by the impact they had on the growing fiscal deficit of the government.

Caught in the contradictions of its different objectives, government policy postponed recession instead of re-activating expansion, while the mechanisms designed to curb inflation and to reduce the deficit of the balance of payments did not prevent both from running high, in spite of numerous accounting tricks which helped to continue to underestimate both the official inflation index and the deficit of the balance of payments. With some accounting ingeniousness, inflation was temporarily reduced to 38·3% in 1977 and 40·8% in 1978, but it reached 77·2% in 1979. The current account deficit, also reduced to 4037 million in 1977, went up to 6015 million in 1978, and 10 021 million in 1979. There were probably other causes accounting for both problems, which differed from the diagnosis made by the government. In view of the significance of both inflation and the deficit of the balance of payments for an understanding of the true nature of the Brazilian crisis, we must examine in some detail what these *other* causes were.

Inflation

It is useful to start by looking at the evidence available to support the thesis of 'demand pull' inflation which was behind the decision to cool down the economy in 1977, after inflation had reached 46·3% in 1976. Too much re-activation of an economy which continued to be overheated was blamed for this.

It seems that serious doubts should be raised as to the validity of this interpretation. Already in 1974, 'the major factor responsible for the slower growth of loans ... to the private sector ... was the sharp reduction in the demand for hire purchase finance',[44] rather than the restrictions imposed on credit by the government. This drop in the demand for credit was caused not by a saturation of consumer demand but by the fact that the limits on household indebtedness had been reached for most middle income urban groups, particularly as a result of the acceleration of inflation in 1974.

As to the argument that excess consumer demand had added pressure on a fully used productive capacity, resulting in overheating and in inflation, it does not appear to be supported by empirical evidence on capacity utilisation in manufacturing. Based on the broadly accepted assumption that productive capacity was more or less fully utilised in manufacturing in 1972–73, and taking 100 as the basis of a relation of equality between production output and productive capacity in 1972–73, Bonelli and Malan demonstrated that this relation fell to 94 in 1974 and to 84 in 1975.[45] Although their research did not extend beyond 1975, the same tendency was maintained in 1976 and further, since the idle capacity of production continued to expand, as a result of heavy government financed investments in the capital goods industry and of the constant introduction of new technology in the consumer durables industry being increasingly unmatched by demand. (As we will see later, these were also two of the most critical aspects of the recession which unfold in the early 1980s.)

The other official cause of inflation was the increase in oil prices, from 2·8 dollars for a barrel of crude oil in 1973 to 11·1 dollars in 1974. The commodity structure of Brazilian imports began to change in 1974 as a result of these higher oil prices. From 11·4% of the value of all imports in 1973, oil imports moved up to 22·4% in 1974 and 30·6% in 1978.[46] The exact impact this had on inflation is difficult to calculate, but that impact was probably greater in the late 1970s (particularly after the new increases in the price of crude oil in 1979 and 1980) than in 1974–75, when the consumer price of oil had relatively little to do with the price of crude oil, due to the incidence of taxes. Imported inflation in general had some effect on the higher inflation of 1976, but the overemphasis put by the government on the bearing of oil prices both on the balance of payments and on inflation was politically motivated; it helped to distract attention from both the capital and the services accounts of the balance of payments, and to maintain the illusion that an atypical, externally induced, 'cost push' factor was, together with a conjunctural one (excess demand), responsible for inflation. The implication was that such a combination could in no way be taken to mean that the model of growth was wrong. As soon as that temporary aberration could be sorted out, the economy would start expanding again.[47]

Given the lack of empirical evidence to support the argument of an 'overheating' resulting from excess demand on manufacturing production and the partiality of the argument of oil prices, let us see how a combination of different other factors neglected by the official explanation contributed to inflation in the 1970s.

1. A reading of the cost of living index in Rio and São Paulo shows that – since 1974, when inflation picked up again – the largest single contribution to the increase in the cost of living has always been *food prices*.[48] The rise was partly due to widespread speculative practices, but also to an inadequate supply of foodstuffs which resulted from the traditional duality of Brazilian agriculture between export and home market production. The export drive of the Brazilian government in the 1970s accentuated the duality by offering subsidies to the producers of export staples. This in turn provoked a further relative fall in the supply of foodstuffs for the home market which pushed prices up.[49] The consequence for the lower income groups was a decline in food expenditures both in relative and in absolute terms. The middle income groups were hit as well, not in their food consumption, which fell only marginally, but through 'large cutbacks in housing outlays'[50] which help to explain at least partially the slow down in demand for consumer credit that we noted earlier.

High food prices were a new, destabilising factor in the Brazilian economy, in which low food prices had previously helped both to enlarge the consumption capacity for manufactured goods among urban middle income groups and – by allowing relatively low wages to be paid to industrial workers – to increase profits as well, hence capital accumulation. The explanation for rising food prices in the 1970s is simple: there was 'excess demand' for foodstuffs. However, falling basic nutritional levels among the lower paid was a clear indication that consumer demand was already too compressed, and that 'overheating' was due to a gross inadequacy of supply. In spite of this, the government – which was constantly enlarging credit to export agriculture and to manufacturing – neglected the production of foodstuffs for the home market. Through its policy of subsidies for export crops, it even managed to make the situation worse by encouraging the larger producers to switch away from home foodstuffs like rice and beans into export crops like soya beans; this pushed up the price of the former, while world overproduction in the latter soon pushed international prices downwards.

The causes for such a neglect came from the government obsession for exports but also – outside some limited pre-electoral periods – from its lack of concern for the social inequalities which its policies were accentuating. This was due to the belief that, since the lower paid do not save, a further deterioration in their standards of living is 'economically' irrelevant. However, since food prices were also gradually reducing the savings capacity of higher income groups, the government policy was contradictory with its overall objective in at least two ways, by contributing both to fuel inflation and to reduce the aggregate level of domestic savings.

The Brazilian inflation in that period offers no empirical evidence to support the neoclassical argument that inflation tends to act as an indirect form of taxation favourable to capital accumulation by transferring income from low income 'non-saving' groups to those high income groups whose income is mostly derived from profits (and from very high earnings in employment), and which are alleged to save. We can see from Table 2.6 that the higher rates of savings of the lower inflation early seventies were maintained only in 1976 and began to decline afterwards as inflation continued to go up.[51]

Another aberrant consequence of the inadequacy of food supply was that Brazil had to start importing foodstuffs in which it had been self-sufficient before the economic 'miracle'. In 1979, imports of foodstuffs reached 1500 million dollars, and a growing propor-

TABLE 2.6 *Brazil: savings and inflation, 1971–79*

	1971	1972	1973	1974	1975	1976	1977	1978	1979
1. Inflation (%)	19.8	15.5	15.7	34.5	29.2	46.3	38.8	40.8	77.2
2. National savings (as % of GDP)	22.8	23.1	25.2	24.9	24.7	24.2	19.8	18.3	16.6

SOURCE 1. FGV.
 2. Inter-American Development Bank reports.

tion of these imports were made up of staples traditionally produced in Brazil, such as rice and beans. The drain of these imports on the trade account and on foreign reserves added yet another inflationary pressure on the economy.

2. The second important source of inflationary pressures – and of contradictions – was to be found in the way *the monetary and the financial policies* operated. The combination of *the freeing of interest rates* in the whole financial system in 1977 and of a policy of *deficit financed subsidies to 'priority' sectors*, implemented since 1974 as part of the development strategy of the II PND, introduced considerable inflationary pressures in the economy. Some of them are self-explanatory, like the policy of subsidised credit to private firms, whose consequences can only be to enlarge the budget deficit. This form of inflationary finance was constantly pursued by the Brazilian government, even after 1977, in spite of the strict control which was then allegedly imposed on the lending activities of the official financial institutions (Table 2.7).

TABLE 2.7 *Brazil: growth of loans to the private sector 1970–79* (%)

1970	1971	1972	1973	1974	1975	1976	1977	1978	1979
49.3	50.6	52.4	55.5	55.5	56.3	57.9	51.1	49.4	63.1

SOURCE Banco Central.

The most interesting contradictions were those which derived from the implementation of deficit financed subsidies combined with the decision taken in 1977 to free interest rates. The result expected from this last decision was that – in a general context of tighter credit – free interest rates would mean more expensive credit, thus less demand for credit, which would help to keep the money supply under control and to reduce inflation.

We have just seen (Table 2.7) that the policy of subsidised loans which was pursued after 1977 was in clear contradiction with the latter objective, as the contraction of these loans after 1977 was more modest than should have been expected.

Inevitably influencing each other, the two policies started operating in the context of both a money market and an organisation of production in which they fed inflation. At the same time, the imperfections of the domestic money market and the pursuit of the policy of subsidised loans contributed to accentuate the already imperfect competition in manufacturing production which had developed under Kubitschek and grown substantially after 1964.[52] The characteristics of this process were as follows:

1. Because they have always been considered 'higher risk customers', the rate of interest charged has usually been higher for Brazilian firms than for foreign firms. On the other hand, the latter – through their easier access to international money markets – could, when credit became too expensive in Brazil, turn to foreign credit and use it to speculate on the Brazilian money market, particularly on the more loosely organised market to which most smaller Brazilian firms had to resort to obtain a credit which their reduced credit worthiness made very expensive.
2. Because of their privileged access to subsidised finance, the large foreign firms could also use official loans – on the utilisation of which there was little effective control by the government – to speculate in the same way. As examples of this, Pirelli made about 4 million dollars profit on the Brazilian money market in 1976, and Fiat 2 million dollars in 1974, 'some eighteen months before its manufacturing plant came on stream!'[53]
3. The government itself added directly to the prevailing financial perversion. In its forceful attempt to develop a money market after a short-lived stock exchange boom had come to an abrupt end earlier, the government decided in 1975 to flood the financial market with excess money in order to encourage speculation. The situation eventually went out of control and, to bail out several overexposed operators, the government intervened by expanding the money supply.[54]
4. When interest rates were freed, the largest firms started using their market power to pass on the higher costs of the marginal producers, which became equivalent to a monopoly rent for the large firms.
5. In a situation of rising inflation and market power of the large firms, the mere expectation of inflation induced the firms to put their prices up in anticipation of inflation, which again added to inflation.

Altogether, the way in which monetary and financial policies operated reinforced the oligopolistic tendency of production, *regardless of production efficiency criteria*,[55] while the financial backing and the market power of the foreign firms combined to put inflationary pressures on the economy.

Committed as most government officials were to make market capitalism work, it was rather unlikely that this should be their analysis of inflation. Even if it had been, it would have been politically difficult for them to admit it. In the meantime, they could see the effects of their policies on the money supply and on inflation: in spite of the government's intention to bring them under control, both went up in the late 1970s (Table 2.8).

The data in Table 2.8 also reveal some curious discrepancies between the expansion of the money supply and the growth of inflation, particularly during the years of the miracle, and again in 1975. The government's anxiety to do well in the 1976 elections might at least partially explain the low inflation data published for 1975; but it was also revealed in 1977 that the low inflation figures of the early 1970s (and particularly of 1972–73) had been considerably underestimated by the then Finance Minister Delfim Neto.

TABLE 2.8 *Brazil: rate of growth of the money supply and of inflation*

	1970	1971	1972	1973	1974	1975	1976	1977	1978	1979
1. Money supply	25.8	32.3	38.3	47.0	33.5	42.8	37.2	37.5	42.2	73.7
2. Inflation	19.2	19.8	15.5	15.7	34.5	29.2	46.3	38.8	40.8	77.2

SOURCE 1. Banco Central.
2. FGV.

If it is reasonable to show some scepticism *vis-à-vis* the inflation data published by the government, the same reservation should probably apply to the 'decisive' impact on inflation officially attributed to higher oil prices after 1973. While not denying that oil prices played a role in Brazilian inflation, it does not seem that their impact was as 'decisive' as the government claimed. An analysis of the deficit in the balance of payments, which was the other major concern of the government, should allow us to appreciate the extent of that impact and, beyond, to pursue our analysis of the contradictions of policy making and of their effects on capital accumulation.

The Deficit of the Balance of Payments

The deficit of the balance of payments can first be seen through the deficit of the current account (Table 2.9). From 1970 to 1979, the trade balance oscillated from small surpluses (in 1973 and 1977) to a deficit which – after the big jump of 1974 when it accounted for 66% of the total current account deficit – was contained afterwards to within 17% in 1978 and 28% in 1979. At the same time, the deficit on the services account was constantly enlarging, to reach 72% of the current account deficit in 1979. Its regular progression was the result of the growing volume of interest payments that had to be made on a fast expanding external debt. These interest payments – covering only the medium and long term debt – which represented 28·7% of the services account deficit in 1970, had gone up to over 58% in 1979.

If we move to the capital account, we can get a more comprehensive picture of the impact of the growing external debt on the overall deficit of the balance of payments and on the financing requirements imposed by the current account deficit plus the amortisation of the external debt. While the trade deficit had been brought down from an equivalent of 52% of all financing requirements in 1974 to 17% in 1979, the service of the debt (interests + amortisation) had moved up from 28% of those requirements in 1974 to 65% in 1979. In the most contradictory way, it was becoming increasingly obvious that Brazil's need to obtain credit abroad was growing with the financing requirements imposed by the service of the debt. In other words, the debt was expanding not to finance development, but to meet the costs of the debt itself.

This had not been the objective of the government when it had deliberately embarked on a policy of external indebtedness in the 1970s. The liquidity of the international capital markets which resulted from the rapid growth of the Eurocurrency market in the early 1970s was extensively used by Brazil, as it offered a much larger and easier credit than the traditional official credit sources of foreign governments and international aid agencies. In the heyday of the early 1970s, Brazil – with its impressive industry-based growth rates – was the ideal borrower for the large foreign commercial banks which administered rapidly growing deposits.[56] After 1974, the slow down of the Brazilian economy was compensated in the bankers' mind by the orthodoxy of Finance Minister Simonsen's policies to solve what he and they considered to be only a temporary crisis. Helped by the ongoing liquidity of the international capital markets due to the recycling of OPEC funds, the creditworthiness of Brazil continued almost unquestioned. During that period, the external debt grew fast, and its profile changed (Table 2.10).

TABLE 2.9 Brazil: balance of payments deficit: summary accounts, 1971–79 (in million dollars)

	1971	1972	1973	1974	1975	1976	1977	1978	1979
Trade balance	−341	−244	7	−4 690	−3 540	−2 255	97	−1 024	−2 840
Exports	2 904	3 991	6 199	7 951	8 670	10 128	12 120	12 659	15 244
Imports	3 245	4 235	6 192	12 641	12 210	12 383	12 023	13 683	18 084
Balance of services	−980	−1 250	−1 722	−2 433	−3 162	−3 763	−4 134	−5 062	−7 199
Net interest payments	−302	−359	−514	−652	−1 498	−1 810	−2 103	−2 696	−4 185
Current Account balance	−1 307	−1 489	−1 688	−7 122	−6 700	−6 013	−4 037	−6 015	−10 021
Capital Account	1 846	3 492	3 512	6 254	6 189	6 651	5 278	10 916	6 936
Amortisation of long- and medium-term loans	−850	−1 202	−1 672	−1 920	−2 172	−2 992	−4 060	−5 323	−6 540
Financing requirements (current account + amortisation of long- and medium-term loans)	2 157	2 691	3 360	9 042	8 872	9 005	8 097	11 338	16 561

SOURCE Banco Central.

TABLE 2.10　*Brazil: growth and profile of the external debt, 1970–79*

		1970	1971	1972	1973	1974	1975	1976	1977	1978	1979
Volume of debt (medium & long term credit only) (in $ million)	(1)	5295	6622	9521	12572	17166	21171	25985	32037	43511	49904
% of external debt to GDP	(2)	11.7	12.6	15.5	15.4	16.2	17.0	17.8	19.5	22.5	23.1
% of financial credit to external debt	(3)	43.1	48.2	58.0	62.4	65.3	68.8	70.0	67.2	67.8	69.4

SOURCE　1. Banco Central.
2. and 3. calculated from Banco Central data.

A few doubts were raised in 1978, when some foreign banks began to realise that they had broken a basic rule of commercial lending in becoming overexposed in their credit to Brazil. This had been partly due to their confidence in the Brazilian economy in general and in Simonsen in particular, and partly to the willingness of Brazil to accept to pay higher spreads than most other countries over the basic 8% lending rate fixed by the London Inter Bank Offered Rate (LIBOR) until 1978.[57] The doubtful advantage that a policy of such exaggerated goodwill could have was presented by the Government as the best possible guarantee of the country's credit-worthiness and of the extent of its self-confidence; supposedly, those high interest payments were to be compensated by the endless availability of funds that Brazil's reliability and self-confidence were presumed to secure.

Foreign commercial credit continued to grow in 1978 and 1979, but with higher basic interest rates, because LIBOR had gone up from 8 to 12% in 1978. To obtain money from increasingly concerned foreign banks, the Brazilian government was already gambling and bluffing its way through by submitting reassuring projections of its exports and by raising large loans on the Euromarket for prestigious development purposes (such as the alcohol programme or a major mining project), and then using them instead to cover balance of payments deficits. More generally, it seemed that Brazil was resorting to a modern version of a long standing tradition of '*para inglês ver*' measures (i.e. measures meant to impress the English), which date back to the 19th century, and whose ultimate aim had always been to present an 'improved' picture of the real situation of the country to the international financial community in order to raise credit more easily. In the late-1970s, this meant behaving in a manner designed to maintain the support Brazil had secured earlier from its commercial lenders. And yet it is not easy to understand what could still impress the bankers, since the debt service ratio (i.e. the proportion of export revenues used up for servicing the debt) was deteriorating rapidly, from 33% in 1970 to 70% in 1979 for the servicing of the medium and long term debt alone. Furthermore, the real cost of external credit was under-estimated in at least two ways:

1. By leaving a fast developing short term debt (loans with a maturity of up to one year) absent from any official account of the external debt. Precisely for that reason, it is difficult to make any reasonably accurate estimate of the volume of the short-term debt. It seems however well established that it developed massively from 1979 onwards, not only to cover normal commercial transactions but more and more to cover balance of payments deficits and immediate cash problems. An estimate of its volume – and of its impact on the balance of payments – can be obtained by looking at the difference it makes to the debt service ratio when service payments on the short term debt are included. For the year 1978 (i.e. before the expansion of short term debt), when medium and long term debt service payments only are included, the debt service ratio was 63%. When short term debt service payments are added, the total debt service ratio was 84%.[58]

2. The real cost of external credit was also underestimated through constant accounting tricks, the mechanisms of which were not always apparent, but which are revealed by the inconsistency of many of the official statistics. For example, the rise of LIBOR from 8% to 12% between 1977 and 1978 necessarily affected the bulk of Brazilian commercial borrowing which, since 1970, was on a floating rate 'recalculated every three or six months to match the rate London banks pay for Eurocurrency deposits'.[59] However, that rise of 4% was not at all reflected in the data on interest payments published by the *Banco Central* for 1978 and 1979. In 1978, commercial credit represented 29 500 million dollars. A 12% interest on that credit was equivalent to 3540 million dollars, i.e. more than the total amount of interest payments on the whole external debt of 43 511 million dollars declared by the *Banco Central* for that year (2696 million dollars). Similarly, in 1979, the interest that Brazil paid to commercial banks alone went up to 4155 million dollars, while interest payments on the whole external debt apparently totalled only 4185 million dollars according to the *Banco Central*.

This leaves 30 million dollars interest payments for the remaining credit of 15 279 million dollars, which would represent an interest rate of 0·2%.

Altogether, detailed and rectified accounts of the balance of payments indicate that the crisis affecting the Brazilian economy at the end of the 1970s was much deeper than was admitted by the government. The policies pursued to reduce their disequilibrium had not only failed, but they had also enlarged the external deficit and increased the vulnerability of the economy, with constantly larger capital outflows provoked by the growing burden of an external debt which was self generating. Added to the failure of the anti-inflationary policies to control inflation and to the impact of those policies on the concentration of manufacturing production and on accumulation, the contradictions engendered by policy making in trying to make market capitalism work had a strong negative effect not only for the Brazilian wage earners but also for domestic capital accumulation. Moreover, these negative effects were reinforced by the entrepreneurial action of the state.

The Effects of 'Direct' State Intervention on Capital Accumulation: the State as Entrepreneur

The direct intervention of the state in production has a long history in Brazil.[60] Although it dates back to the 19th century, its most significant developments took place after 1930 under Vargas; they were scaled up in the 1950s and 1960s in the mining and petrochemicals sectors and, after 1974, in the capital goods sector, which was one of the priorities of the II PND. In 1974, state enterprises were already prominent in mining production (62%), public utilities (88%), petrochemicals (55%), and they were expanding fast in the steel industry.[61] At the same time, the largest public firms like *Petrobrás* and *Companhia Vale do Rio Doce* (CVRD) were branching out from their original activities in oil and in mining into the whole range of petrochemicals and in the production of ferrous and non ferrous metals, creating wide ranging consulting, engineering and transport services.

The dynamism of the expansion of state intervention in production led several authors to the conclusion that a process of development of 'state capitalism' was taking place in Brazil.[62] At the political level, it was that 'aggressive state expansion at the expense of the private sector'[63] which was denounced by a powerful 'anti-statism' campaign mobilised by the private sector in 1975–76. Implied in the criticism of the state role in production was the idea that – by accumulating capital through its productive activities – the state was switching away from its supporting role in capital accumulation by the private sector. However, in spite of the political opposition that it generated among some entrepreneurial sectors, that argument seems to be unfounded. Evidence suggests on the contrary that, during the 1970s, rather than working against private capital accumulation, the entrepreneurial action of the state was perfectly congruent with the objective of its 'indirect' forms of intervention in capital accumulation, which was to make market capitalism work.

The supporting – or complementary – role of the entrepreneurial state in private capital accumulation has been extensively argued, both at the theoretical level[64] and in the particular case of Brazil as well.[65] The main mechanism through which such support operates in Brazil is the system of subsidised prices, by which the public sector offers cheap services and inputs to the private sector. This is so in the sector of public utilities, in which the deficit of the public sector is usually considered to be part of a process of 'socialising the costs'. It does not mean that these activities can never be made profitable, but that they are traditionally the areas *par excellence* in which the state performs its supporting role in private capital accumulation.

Given the quasi-monopolistic presence of public firms in that sector (88%), the expansion of the entrepreneurial activity of the state after 1974 could only take place in mining and in the whole range of manufacturing production. Here, the particular sectors in which the state chose to intervene are in themselves revealing. It is interesting to note that, in Brazil, there appears to be a division of labour between state and private firms, with the latter producing consumer goods while the former concentrate on producing basic inputs. This is already significant of the supporting role that public firms are meant to perform in the economy. However, since the public firms which produce those industrial inputs are large, often larger than the foreign (or multinational) private firms which dominate oligopolistically the production of high value added consumer goods, they too should be able to take advantage of their size to benefit from the same market power which allows the large private firms to fix prices. But they do not. *Downstream*, the conditions which prevent public firms from using their potential market power to ensure their financial autonomy are determined by the organisation of the sectors of production to which they sell their products. (i) If these sectors were composed mainly of small and medium size firms with little control over prices (which then tend to be fixed by market mechanisms), public firms could practice a policy of higher prices; these would not be transmitted to the final consumer, but they would result instead in lower profit rates for the firms producing outputs. (ii) But when the production of outputs is dominated by a few large private firms, these – through their control over prices – can both transmit the higher cost of their inputs to the final consumer and increase the oligopolistic tendencies in the sector of production concerned. As a result, public firms must constantly lower their prices and reduce their profits to avoid a fall in the demand for consumer goods (and particularly for consumer durables), on which the overall rate of growth of the economy has always depended during the 'miracle'.[66]

The price of the industrial inputs that public firms sell to private firms is fixed by considerations other than direct profitability. By cutting down the production costs of the private sector, they make an essential contribution to the level of consumer demand at home, to the competitiveness of Brazilian manufactured exports (for which they are yet another source of subsidy), and eventually to capital accumulation by the private sector. This is why their own operational deficit has always been central to the Brazilian model of export-led industrial growth.

With the policy of subsidised credit that has already been analysed, the policy of subsidised prices to private firms has also greatly contributed in the 1970s to the growing concentration in many sectors of manufacturing production through the acquisition of domestic firms by multinational companies. As example of this, the percentage of new US manufacturing affiliates established by acquisition of Brazilian firms, which had grown from 9% before 1950 to 33% between 1956 and 1960, had reached 66% between 1973 and 1975,[67] with some sectors of production becoming both highly concentrated and entirely or almost entirely foreign owned.[68]

Upstream, the operational deficit of the public firms is the consequence of their continuous branching into capital-using forms of production, particularly in the sector of capital goods, in which it was hoped after 1964 that Brazil would become not only self-sufficient but competitive enough to export. This implied the use of high cost technology, often with rapid rates of obsolescence, which is not produced domestically but always supplied by a few large foreign firms. It is these which – through several transfer mechanisms[69] – eventually increase their own profits, while the high costs of technology transfer which the public firms have to incur tend to transform their occasional nominal profits into losses and deficit.

Constantly increasing in the 1970s, the global deficit of public firms reached 341·6 billion cruzeiros in 1979 (approximately 12·6 billion dollars), which represented 32·3% of their own resources and 5·5% of GDP.[70] Given their inability to self-finance their operations, their deficit had to be covered by Treasury transfers and by external and internal credit. Contrary to Trebat's assertion that public firms did not have to resort to public finance in Brazil,[71] Treasury transfers to public firms amounted to 135·2 billion cruzeiros in 1979 (approximately 5 billion dollars), which represented 26·5% of all federal government current revenues for 1979.[72] Mainly as a result of the growing burden of public firms on public finance, the proportion of total government expenditure spent on current transfers went up from 29·4% on average between 1971 and 1975 to 43·7% in 1979.[73] Since current transfers are only designed to cover current expenditures, their regular increase was taking place at the cost of a proportionately declining percentage of total government expenditures spent on fixed investment which, from 21·8% in 1975 had come down to 7% in 1979,[74] thus reducing capital formation in a massive way.

The negative contribution made by public firms to a domestic process of capital accumulation was further accentuated by their growing need to compensate for their losses through heavy foreign borrowing. 'In mid-1979, according to *Banco Central* statistics, state-owned firms were responsible for 29·9 billion dollars of the total foreign debt of 46·5 billion dollars.'[75]

All the evidence available suggests that the public firms' deficit was the inevitable consequence of the supporting role of the state for private capital. Every survey carried out in the 1970s confirms that the development of the entrepreneurial role of the state was not the result of planned action, but that it corresponded instead to the *ad hoc* requirements of private capital in a process of expansion of market capitalism. The findings of a survey undertaken in 1976 under the supervision of Planning Minister Reis Velloso (Table 2.11) confirmed the results of another survey organised by the *Instituto de Planejamento Econômico e Social* (IPEA) in 1974, showing that public firms employ on average twice as many people as private national and multinational firms and that they also have larger capital assets and lower profits. 'The typical pattern of the sectors in which public firms operate is thus characterized by a large volume of capital with long maturity rates . . .

TABLE 2.11 Brazil: distribution of assets and profits among firms, 1976

Net capital assets	Public firms (%)	Private domestic firms (%)	Private foreign firms (%)
Net capital assets	52.2	27.7	20.1
Revenues from sales	24.3	37.4	38.3

SOURCE Almeida Magalhães (1979) p. 121.

and low levels of direct profitability.'[76] Against the argument that a process of state capitalism was under way in Brazil in the 1970s, we can argue that the multiplication of public firms is not equivalent to the development of state capitalism. The minimum requirement for a process of state capitalism is that the public sector should accumulate capital through its productive activities. Instead, a policy of subsidised prices to the private sector of production can only generate losses for the public sector. By branching into the production of new industrial inputs, the Brazilian public firms were merely extending their supporting role and thus increasing the global losses of the public sector and the drain on public finance.

The 'multiplying' or 'accelerating' effects that the government argued the public firms had on the economy were more than compensated negatively by their impact on inflation and on the deficit of the balance of payments. Moreover, from the point of view of domestic capital accumulation, their deficit was not justified as it could have been if it had supported accumulation by the private *domestic* sector. Instead, it made a heavy contribution to the rapidly growing *foreign* control over capital accumulation. This was achieved (i) through the profit returns of the foreign (or multinational) firms, which were the main beneficiaries of the supporting role of the state; (ii) through an acceleration of the foreign takeovers of private domestic firms; and (iii) through the interest payments on an ever-increasing foreign debt in which they participated massively and without any control by the government.

These trends could already be observed under the Geisel administration, when the growing involvement of the state in the economy helped to maintain the illusion that the 'miracle' of the early 1970s was but momentarily detained. By trying to hide the seriousness of the crisis, the stepping up of state action was accelerating the contradictions which it had engendered since the beginning. The panglossian belief that all was for the best would quickly disappear under the next administration of Figueiredo. But, before we move on to that period, two questions remain, to assess the effects on both 'direct' and 'indirect' state intervention on capital accumulation under Geisel: *firstly*, we must look at the consequences of state intervention on the fiscal deficit of the state, in order to measure the impact of a growing deficit on capital formation; *secondly*, we must examine the extent to which the supporting role of the state in private capital accumulation was 'generally' favourable to private capital or more favourable to some sectors of private capital than to others.

THE CONSEQUENCES OF STATE INTERVENTION IN CAPITAL ACCUMULATION

The Growing Fiscal Deficit of the State and Capital Formation

The combination of the different forms of intervention used by the state to guarantee the conditions of private accumulation generated a constantly growing public deficit. In 1979, the public deficit reached 8·3% of GDP and, together, the various credit and fiscal subsidies to private firms plus the Treasury transfers to public firms amounted to 81·6% of that deficit.[77] At the same time as public deficit was growing, the tax revenue of the government was declining, both as a percentage of total government revenues (from 87·5% on average in 1971–75 to 80·1% in 1979), and as a percentage of GDP (from 8·9% on average in 1971–75 to 7·1% in 1979).[78] This meant that the government was forced to expand the money supply and to resort to external credit to compensate for both the relative fall in its tax revenue and the growth of public deficit. As a result, the external public debt went up from 11·7% of GDP in 1970 to 23·1% in 1979 (see Table 2.10). The so-called debt trap which followed is a multi-faceted phenomenon in that public deficit was calling for an extended external credit which, by adding to the deficit of the balance of payments through debt servicing, was also adding to the global fiscal deficit of the state by enlarging the volume of its financial requirements which had to be met from external credit (see Tables 2.9 and 2.10). Instead of being used for investment purposes, the external public debt was absorbed to cover a fiscal deficit which it contributed to build up every year by regularly raising the cost of the debt service.

An ever-increasing fiscal deficit could only have negative consequences on gross domestic investment. The government's attempts to maintain a rate of capital formation compatible with its overall expansionist strategy led to an aggravation of both the deficit of the current account and the volume of the external debt between 1974 and 1976. After 1975, government expenditures on fixed investment began to drop rapidly as a percentage of total government expenditures. The level of gross national savings was maintained until 1976 and it contributed to domestic investment until 1977. But – contrary to orthodox expectations – inflation was pushing consumption up as a proportion of disposable income, and thus pushing savings down. Since foreign credit, which continued to be raised for investment purposes, was increasingly used to cover both the public deficit and the deficit of the balance of payments, the rate of capital formation went down after 1976 (Table 2.12).

TABLE 2.12 Brazil: domestic savings and capital formation, 1971–79

	1971–75	1976	1977	1978	1979
Gross national savings as a % of GDP	24.1	24.2	19.8	18.3	16.6
Gross domestic investment as a % of GDP	27.9	28.3	22.2	22.0	21.5
Gross national savings as a % of Gross domestic investment	86.7	85.5	89.0	83.4	76.9
Government expenditure on fixed investment as a % of total government expenditure	18.7	16.4	14.7	7.5	7.0

SOURCE IDB (1980–81).

The Selective Impact of State Intervention on Private Capital Accumulation

State intervention stepped up market concentration in the private sector and, because market concentration and profits are strongly correlated in manufacturing production, the high profits of the large private firms further reinforced the oligopolistic structures of production, thus the profits, and so on.

The report of a parliamentary enquiry requested by the opposition party MDB and conducted in the late-1960s on the degree of concentration and 'denationalisation' of the Brazilian industry, gave valuable information on the problem and showed that the trend started in 1954 by Instruction 113 of SUMOC was accelerated by the legislative action undertaken after 1964. This action consisted of the implementation of several measures which all contributed to make credit more difficult to obtain and more expensive for local firms, at a time when foreign firms had easy access to cheap international sources of credit not available to Brazilian firms.[79] As a result, foreign firms entered the Brazilian market by acquiring local firms, which were not taken over through inefficiency in production, but because of the imperfection of the financial market surrounding them.[80]

In a situation of increasing market concentration, foreign firms could count on rates of *real operational profit* much higher than those of domestic firms:

1. By benefiting from fiscal and credit export and import subsidies allocated to firms engaged in manufacturing exports. These subsidies – which amounted to between 30% and 50% of the value of the goods exported – had a considerable impact on real profits, but they did not appear in the profits declared by the firms, which were calculated by the relation of sales revenues to equity. Such subsidies were not earmarked for foreign firms, but since they varied with value added and since most sectors of export production which qualified for the highest subsidies had come to be dominated by foreign firms, these were in practice the major beneficiaries of export subsidies, which became a 'quasi-rent' transferred abroad through the mechanism of transfer pricing.
2. By using several more or less legal mechanisms to bypass the controls set up by the Brazilian law on profits remittance abroad.
   (i) Through *transfer pricing* (i.e. the practice of underbilling exports and overbilling imports), intra-firm commercial relations are used to transfer profits. Artificially lower revenues from exports reduce profits, and thus income tax paid on profits, while artificially higher import payments result in the Brazilian subsidiary making a disguised profit remittance to the parent company abroad. There are definite indications that these practices are commonly used by most foreign firms in Brazil. 'A confidential study commissioned by the government revealed a clear tendency for transnationals to incur larger

trade deficits (in 1976) than either state or Brazilian private companies';[81] data from CACEX also revealed that, in 1977, some foreign firms had accumulated a trade deficit much too large to be explained only by orthodox import-export patterns.

(ii) Apart from incurring the largest trade deficits, the subsidiaries of foreign firms also contracted the largest debts in the 1970s, particularly under *law 4131* which allowed foreign firms to substitute direct investments by loans from the parent company. According to the *Gazeta Mercantil*, these *intra-firm loans* represented 16·3 billion dollars at the end of 1977, which was equivalent to half the total external debt of Brazil. The considerable attraction that these loans seemed to have for foreign firms can be explained in two ways: (a) while profits on direct investments were taxed and could be remitted abroad only at the rate of 12% of the capital invested per year, the payments made by the subsidiary to the parent company on the amortisation and interests of these loans were not taxed; (b) foreign firms were using their subsidiaries to speculate on the Brazilian money market by transferring to them capital resources which were far in excess of their real investment needs.

(iii) The third major mechanism used to bypass the law on profits remittance abroad consists of the *payment for technical assistance and royalties*. Since these payments are considered to be part of the costs of the firms, they are exempted from income tax up to the value of 5% of sales revenues. Since – on the other hand – it is impossible to keep an effective control on these payments, they are normally used to remit profits abroad. To test their impact on profits, Von Doellinger and Cavalcanti calculated that, in four sectors of production in which the participation of foreign firms was already high in 1972, the estimated rate of remittance for technical assistance varied between 13 and 27% per year. The data shows that in the transport, electrical and pharmaceutical industries, the capital invested could be amortised in more or less four years without having to resort to any other form of remittance (such as profits, royalties, or interest payments).[82]

In addition, foreign firms could also count on the *high non-operational profits* resulting from their speculative operations on the so-called 'open' financial market. Being lower risk customers than domestic firms, they could obtain cheaper commercial credit in Brazil; as we have seen earlier, the existence of a *de facto* two tier financial market, which resulted from the government decision in 1977 to free interest rates, had the consequence of making credit easier and cheaper for foreign firms. Through their access to government-subsidised credit and to a very liquid international capital market, they stepped up their operations on the 'open' money market on which small and medium Brazilian firms had to turn more frequently to raise an expensive credit.[83]

Able to count on high rates of real profits, tax exemptions, export and import subsidies, cheap capital, cheap and controlled labour, subsidised inputs provided by public firms, and a congenial political framework which guaranteed adequate patterns of income distribution and made strikes illegal, it is not surprising that foreign capital and foreign firms were attracted by the Brazilian package offered to them. Further motivated by the liquidity of the international capital market and by the size of the domestic market open to them and which – in spite of the concentration of income distribution – represented 15% to 20% of the population, i.e. about 20 million potential consumers, they responded positively to these incentives and flowed into the Brazilian market.

For Brazil, however, the advantages of that policy were more doubtful, and the consequences of government action were denounced at all levels of society.

THE QUESTIONING OF THE BRAZILIAN MODEL OF ACCUMULATION

Open opposition to the principles on which the model was founded first came from within the government. As early as in 1974, confronted with signs of a slow down of the miracle and concerned both by the external deficit of the Brazilian economy and by the growing influence of foreign capital, several members of the government began to push for the adoption of a different strategy based on the ISI policies contained in the II PND.[84] Their objective was to develop the internal market and to change the supply structure of the economy. A more equal distribution of personal income was to be matched by heavy investments in public firms and by subsidies to private firms willing to shift production away from consumer durables and into wage goods.

Rallying around Finance Minister Simonsen, a campaign was soon organised against them under the banner of free enterprise. In it was the mainstream of interests which had been behind the adoption of the policies of the 'miracle'.[85] Their campaign was against '*estatização*' (statism), i.e. against the expansion of public firms, which was supposedly taking place at the cost of private firms. It was fought by various commercial and industrial associations, but – significantly – the leading national entrepreneurs kept a low profile in it.[86] This was suggestive in at least two ways: (1) contrary to the central argument of the campaign, there was a relative decrease in the expansion of the largest public firms after 1970, which – as Diniz and Boschi demonstrated[87] – was particularly visible between 1973 and 1974; (2) the argument that the development of public firms runs necessarily against the interests of private firms does not hold any axiomatic truth, as we have seen earlier. By 1975–76 – within the context of a tighter credit and of reduced activity – it was already apparent to many of the largest domestic groups that, although they too had benefited from the 'miracle', they had perhaps less to fear from the state than from foreign capital.

What the campaigners argued was that a cut in public expenditures would reduce inflation, and that the only solution to the external deficit was to further boost exports. For them, the expansion of the export policy had the advantage that it required changes neither in the distribution of personal income nor in the process of capital accumulation. The most interested party in the latter were the foreign firms but, since it was politically difficult for them to oppose too openly the proposed changes, they orchestrated the 'anti-statism' campaign through some of their powerful local supporters. Helped by the poor results obtained by the government in the 1976 elections and by the new inflation record of that year (46·3%), they won the battle in the government. Minister Severo Gomes resigned and the plan was abandoned.

It is not easy to speculate on what could have been its most likely results. Undeniably, it had some shortcomings, the most serious one being that it was not in tune with the interests of most sectors of private capital, both local and foreign. It was a realistic assessment of the problems of the Brazilian economy, but it was also an isolated attempt stemming from a momentary conjunction of forces within the government. Its defeat was 'an interesting example of the way in which a more self-reliant solution to the problems of external equilibrium has been partially thwarted by a coalition of private and international interest groups'.[88]

After successfully sweeping away the opposition within the government, the protagonists of the Brazilian model of accumulation were now to meet their most serious challenge in the growing social discontent provoked by the wage policy of the government. This policy and – more generally – the policy concerning the distribution of national income between profits and wages, dated back to the early years of the military regime and was inspired by two main considerations: (a) high wages were considered to have been the single most important source of inflation in the early sixties and (b) low wages increased the income received by the 'saving' social categories and thus contributed to capital accumulation.

At the same time – and rather contradictorily – whenever it was accused of making social inequalities worse through its minimum wage policy, the government replied that minimum wage was not a meaningful indicator of real wages, since the majority of wage earners were receiving wages above the minimum wage. Interestingly, this represented an implicit recognition (a) that real minimum wages were falling constantly behind inflation, in spite of the annual adjustments which were precisely supposed to compensate for inflation; (b) that rises in minimum wage had a lesser impact on inflation than was claimed by the government.

The discrepancy between the government's claims and the social reactions to its wage policy was not about the minimum wage, which was shown to be falling by different sets of data, ranging from the conservative Foundation Getulio Vargas (FGV) for Rio to the Trade Unions Research Institute (DIEESE) for São Paulo. Although the magnitude of the drop was larger in the latter's estimate, both coincided in showing a deterioration of real minimum wages after 1964. For the FGV, real minimum wage in Rio had fallen in 1978 to 86% of its 1963 level; for DIEESE, real minimum wage in São Paulo had fallen in 1978 to 69·8% of its 1963 level.[89]

The dispute was about the relevance of minimum wage as an indicator of real wage levels. Two surveys conducted in 1976 and 1977 by the Brazilian Institute of Geography and Statistics (IBGE) gave useful information on this matter.

The first, based on 1976 data, and known as the National Household Survey (PNAD), showed that, in 1976, 31% of the urban and 71% of the rural labour force of the country were earning one minimum wage or less,[90] i.e. the equivalent of about 70 dollars a month or less (at an official exchange rate which was constantly overvalued by at least $\frac{1}{3}$).

The second, conducted one year later, showed that the situation of the rural labour force had further deteriorated in 1977, since 75·6% were then earning one minimum wage or less (Table 2.13). However, if we bear in mind that the rural labour force was deliberately exploited

TABLE 2.13 *Brazil: wage distribution by sectors, 1977 (% of employed population)*

Monthly income	Agriculture	Industry	Construction	Commerce	Services	Total
nil	31.7	1.0	0.6	4.4	1.2	12.4
Up to 1 min. wage	43.9	23.7	21.0	27.7	55.2	35.9
1–3 min. wages	19.2	50.4	60.8	42.5	29.2	34.7
3–5 min. wages	2.6	12.3	11.1	11.8	7.0	8.3
Over 5 min. wages	2.5	12.5	6.4	13.4	7.2	8.6
Undeclared	0.1	0.1	0.1	0.1	0.3	0.1

SOURCE IBGE in *Latin America Regional Report Brazil* (1979).

by a model of capital accumulation which concentrated on industrial growth, it is more significant to look at the wage situation in those sectors directly associated with the model of growth and accumulation, i.e. industry and construction.

The situation of wage earners in industry was the same as in 1976 in respect of those at or below minimum wage (about 24%); but, if we put together those industrial workers who earned up to 3 minimum wages, we find that – even if we overestimate their real earnings by using the highest minimum wage for all of them – 75% of all industrial workers were earning less than 215 dollars a month. In the dynamic construction industry, which had been growing by 17% a year on average since 1970, 82% of the work force also earned less than three minimum wages.

The data also reveals the myth of high earnings for the employed middle class, which was supposed to be one of the main beneficiaries of the Brazilian miracle. Only 8·7% of the total employed population were earning over 350 dollars a month.

The overall pattern of income distribution had continued to deteriorate after 1970, with the self-employed and highest paid sectors of the middle class improving their share, while the middle income groups were losing out and half of the working population were falling still further behind (see Table 2.18), with social security benefits discriminating also against them.

The data on income distribution available for the 1970s justifies the criticisms made against the government for enforcing a wage squeeze which – in a situation of growing inflation – was affecting between 75 and 90% of the working population. With average monthly personal income of about or below 71 dollars, half the population lived in near-destitution and, in an average low income family, the number of people (including young children) who had to seek some form of employment multiplied, only to try (often unsuccessfully) to prevent very precarious standards of living from deteriorating yet further for the family as a whole. In these destitute social categories, infant mortality increased in many parts of the country during the 1970s. With food prices soaring up in the cities, the situation of 50–60% of the industrial labour force who earned between 71 and 215 dollars a month was also getting worse.

In 1977, both the general economic slow down and the growing capital intensiveness of industrial production began to add another dimension to the discontent of labour. The prospects of unemployment were developing fast in many industrial sectors, particularly since job security had been withdrawn in 1967 by the creation of the *Fundo de Garantia do Tempo de Serviço* (FGTS), a sort of pension scheme which abolished a 1940 law guaranteeing job security after 10 years of service. For most unskilled and semi-skilled workers, dismissals – made easier by the FGTS – doubled from pre-FGTS figures, with most of the dismissals taking place just before the annual wage review, after which workers were re-employed at lower wage levels. After 1977, the effects of the slow down were such that even the prospect of being re-employed at all was not guaranteed any longer.

Popular mobilisation developed around both wage levels and job security and it gained ground in 1978 when, following a long and peaceful strike in the car, engineering, and textile industries of São Paulo, the government, incapable of using force on the massive scale required against these 'illegal' strikes, appeared to give in. Wages were raised and workers on strike reinstated. For the government, this was a defeat which it tried to remedy by moving away from the crude repressive methods used in the early 1970s to a more legalistic form of repression, in which new laws were passed declaring strikes illegal in most sectors. The new legislation introduced in 1978 produced immediate results in that – within weeks – strikes were spreading exactly in those sectors in which they had been declared illegal. In 1979, a new labour code making no concessions to the growing importance of the labour movement was presented to Congress. It retained the power to prosecute strike leaders and it kept strikes illegal in all essential services. The irony of the situation was that – at the time the new code was presented to Congress – the government had just capitulated to the worst strike yet staged in São Paulo by 180 000 metal workers, by reinstating the union leaders and negotiating a pay agreement. This was the first real challenge to the government, and its first serious defeat so far. In July, 15 000 construction workers started a strike in support of a wage rise of 110%. Alarmed by the build up of social tensions in the country, the government tried to compromise. The strike lasted one month, it was declared legal by the local labour tribunal, and the workers' minimum wage was doubled.

Inspired by these successes, strikes developed throughout the country so that in 1979, with inflation out of control again and little prospect of expansion, all the elements of a social and economic crisis were in place. The real question was not about how and when expansion could restart, but when the government would officially recognise the existence of the crisis. On the other hand, opposition to the government had developed to such an extent that any further recessionary measures could only have negative consequences on the results of the elections which – sooner or later – the government knew it had to organise. The 1978–79 strikes had made it clear that the only way for the government to avoid defeat in any forthcoming election was to relax its wage policy, which might contribute to reduce the slump of internal demand, but which would also fuel inflation. At the same time, since its international credit-worthiness depended on its ability to control both inflation and the deficit of the balance of payments, the incompatibility between its economic and its political goals had never been so obvious.

THE ACCELERATION OF THE CONTRADICTIONS AND THE OPEN CRISIS

Caught in the web of its own contradictions and against all expectations, the Brazilian government surprisingly opted for an all-out expansion, designed to reassure the business community, and for a more liberal wage policy, intended to win over the opposition of the labour movement. But, behind the pretence to innovate, these policies were in fact the only ones left open to the ever narrowing scope of its policy making initiatives.

The Short-Lived Illusion of Renewed Expansion

The replacement of Geisel by Figueiredo as President in March 1979 was unfavourable to Simonsen – identified with monetarist orthodoxy – and favourable to Delfim Neto – identified with the 'miracle'. Delfim started rather modestly as Agriculture Minister in the new administration in which Simonsen was persuaded to stay as Planning Minister. But, as the latter never wanted to give in to the demands for wage increases and maintained the priority of anti-inflationary policies, the compromising attitude of the government *vis-à-vis* the strike wave of July–August forced him to resign. He was replaced as Planning Minister by Delfim in an attempt to find a solution to the growing economic and social crisis, within an expansionist framework.

Delfim's populist style was demonstrated by his handling of the strikes. To obtain social peace and in a show of strength and self-confidence, he granted a wage increase from 1 November to all unionised workers, with the highest increases going to the lower paid workers (those earning up to three minimum wages),[91] who represented three-quarters of the labour force; these were also to benefit from regular six-monthly adjustments above the cost of living. The higher paid categories (those who earned between three and ten minimum wages) were to receive six-monthly wage adjustments in line with the cost of living.

The net result of the new policy was a reduction in wage differentials which angered the middle income groups while having negative consequences on the aggregate level of demand for the consumer durables on which growth had always depended. This further depressed a market already suffering from an overproduction which had been made worse by the restrictions imposed on the entry of many Brazilian manufactured goods into the USA and the EEC. At the same time, the new wage policy predictably resulted in higher demand for food; this accelerated the inflationary pressures of food prices, which had been a characteristic of the Brazilian economy since 1973 and which – as in 1975–76 – were soon to have a strong negative effect on real wages. Again, as under Simonsen, the cost of living index (INPC) – by which the six-monthly wage adjustments were calculated – was always underestimated and started falling regularly below the rate of inflation.[92]

The inconsistency of the government's wage policy with its declared intention to renew expansion was manifest. A reflation of the economy would have required wage increases for the higher paid workers as well as a policy of price controls and subsidies for basic food commodities. Bearing in mind the immediate discontent of the higher paid and the erosion that inflation imposed (in particular through rising food prices) on the short-lived benefits of the lower paid, one can even wonder to what extent the political rationality of those measures ever went beyond a mere populist attempt to reduce temporarily popular dissatisfaction, i.e. without increasing support for the government. What is significant however is that from then onwards the contradictions of the model of growth and accumulation were going to be intensified by the impact of the new so-called 'social question'. This potential for popular mobilisation in defence of sectorial interests, which was reminiscent of the last two years of the previous populist regime, reappeared in 1978–79 and added to the confusion of policy-making. The major concern of the government was to prevent those sectorial interests from acquiring a political dimension which could damage yet further its electoral prospects. That the regime hardliners were then persuaded that the repressive response of the late-1960s and early 1970s should not be used again was perhaps only a temporary victory for the moderates. But inflation and the external deficit of the Brazilian economy were getting so much out of hand that it seemed difficult to postpone the adoption of deflationary measures any longer, particularly since the long lasting goodwill of foreign creditors was showing signs of running out.

Delfim first tried to gamble, or perhaps simply to bluff his way through the crisis, by repeating that the only solution was an expansionist policy based – once again – on an export boom. The business community welcomed what they saw as the end of recession, and an ambitious export plan was presented by the new Finance Minister, Rischbieter. But it soon became obvious that there was nothing new in that plan, apart from the fact that its targets were so clearly overambitious that it was never credible. From a 12·7 billion dollars export revenue in 1978, it aimed at reaching 40 billion by 1984. This figure had been obtained by simply projecting the 21% average annual growth in exports from 1970 to 1978. An annual breakdown of this data reveals the fragility of the projection: from an average of 31·5% between 1970 and 1973, the growth rate of exports had fallen to 12% between 1974 and 1978, and it fell to 4·4% that year. The oil crisis and world recession, but also the protectionist reaction prompted in the USA and the EEC by the extensive use of export incentives by Brazil, were all conditions over which Brazil had virtually no control. There was little doubt in 1979 that the most likely trend was one of continuity and even worsening of those adverse conditions.

Meanwhile, Delfim was multiplying contradictory measures. In his *Pacote do Natal* (Christmas package) of December 1979, he decided a 30% 'maxi-devaluation' of the cruzeiro, declared an end to export subsidies and generally reduced the volume of subsidies available to both industry and agriculture. Part of the same package was also to abolish the 'law of similarity' whereby import licences had not normally been granted until then for capital goods produced within the country. The idea behind the *pacote* was to stop the crisis without having to adopt stringent recessionary policies. The two essential targets were – again – inflation and the trade account of the balance of payments.

With the exception of the devaluation, the measures adopted seemed inspired by Simonsen's orthodoxy rather than by Delfim's expansionist plans. Their inconsistency with official declarations was also becoming a little too obvious and, with them, Delfim somehow managed to displease both the local business community and the foreign bankers. Local businessmen were less worried by the decision to end export subsidies than by the scrapping of the 'law of similarity' and by the scaling down of production subsidies. They knew that export subsidies would be reintroduced and they even suggested discrete ways of doing so to the government. A reduction of subsidies to industry was more serious for them, as it could only aggravate the difficulties of many entrepreneurs already affected by the slow down in demand.

In 1979, against Delfim's unshrinking optimism, the economic crisis emerged into the open, with the expansion of the money supply (73·7%), inflation (77·2%), and the deficit of the current account (10 billion dollars) all being new records. This situation led to a change in the attitude of the international banking community concerning Brazil's foreign debt, particularly since the debt service ratio had deteriorated yet again (from 63% in 1978 to 70% in 1979 for the medium- and long-term debt alone). As the image of Brazil as a debtor was getting worse, the conditions on which it would be able to obtain further credit were inevitably going to get tougher.

The urgency of the economic problems was such that Delfim had to change course before his expansionist bluff was called. In 1980 and 1981, a series of recessionary measures began to reverse the alleged 'developmentalist' drive of the previous year.

The Unsuccessful Attempts to Stabilise the Economy

In early 1980, the contradictions between the official expansionist discourse and the nature of the policies adopted led to speculation as to how far Delfim was prepared to extend a bluff which was becoming increasingly self-evident.

Although it is difficult to find a pattern in a policy making which was so erratic and contradictory, it seems that, for the first part of 1980, the main target was inflation, but that this took second place to the deficit of the balance of payments after November. It is also after that date that reference to growth as being the priority of government policy began to be dropped from the official discourse. This was the first half of the bluff gone. The other half (denying that the government ever intended to approach the IMF) was maintained until the end of 1982, just after the elections and well after negotiations on the external debt had started with the IMF.

From 'Expansion' to Stabilisation

The 1980 budget was the first official move towards recession. By imposing strict credit limits on public spending, Delfim was implicitly recognising that his policy of 'accelerated development' was part of an unrealistic rhetoric, and that inflation and the deficit of the balance of payments were the real determinants of his policy making. At the same time however, the municipal elections scheduled for November meant that the popular discontent of 1979 could not be risked again, so that the six-monthly wage increases were maintained. But Delfim's constantly repeated belief that the economy was healthy was challenged by the more pessimistic warnings of Finance Minister Rischbieter (who resigned in January) and Benedito Moreira – the director of CACEX – concerning both the balance of payments and the debt service ratio.

The widening of the trade gap and the growth of inflation during the first quarter of 1980 were an open denial of Delfim's optimism, and they reinforced the position of the hardliners in the government.

The ABC engineering workers' strike on 1 April marked a return to the previous hard line response, in spite (or perhaps because) of the wide support that the strike received among non-working class sectors of the population. By refusing to negotiate with the workers, the government made it clear that the economic crisis was more serious than was officially recognised, and that it was giving priority to those who wanted austerity and repression to replace the expansionist and populist orientations of Delfim.

The solution to the ongoing deterioration of the balance of payments was found in a further utilisation of Brazil's foreign reserves, which had the effect of reducing Brazil's international credit worthiness and of making future loans yet more expensive. On the other hand, inflation – fuelled by food prices – was rising faster than wages, casting doubt on the validity of the calculations by which wage increases were supposed to keep pace with inflation.

As a result of the growing unpopularity of the government, the municipal elections – originally scheduled for November – were cancelled in May. This was a desperate move. Elections were needed by the government, both for internal and external purposes, and Delfim's return to full economic power in 1979 had been largely inspired by a political strategy. But inflation was too high and it took precedence over the government's desire to increase its popularity.

In June 1980, the Economic Development Council (CDE) approved a new package of measures aimed at cutting down direct investment by public firms by a further 15% from the level established in the February budget. Imports were also cut and restrictions were imposed on the current expenditures of the public sector. Controls over retail prices were introduced and the money supply was reduced ($-2 \cdot 1$% in July). But – in spite of all this – the same expansionist ideology continued to prevail, although excess capacity was expanding, caused by insufficient internal demand and by growing export difficulties.

The rest of 1980 was marked by a constant deterioration of Brazil's credit worthiness, with most foreign bankers insisting that Brazil had reached its borrowing limit and that further credit would not be forthcoming unless an agreement was signed with the IMF. Faced with this reaction, Delfim continued to deny that he even intended to approach the IMF; but his bluff was made apparent when he suddenly changed course at the end of the year, in order to be able to obtain the 17–19 billion dollars which he had to borrow for 1981. In a policy entirely reminiscent of Simonsen's approach, he freed interest rates on the domestic money market, lifted both the price controls and the prefixed devaluation of the cruzeiro, and announced his intention of developing exports and giving priority to the balance of payments, the problems of which had always been denied by the government until then.

The attempt to curb inflation (which reached 110% at the end of the year) had been a complete failure; the price of food, consumer goods and rents had all gone up, while the anti-inflationary policy of the government had been yet another good example of the ineffectiveness of government policies and of its limited power over large companies. Through their control over market prices, these took advantage of the lifting of price controls to increase their profits in order to compensate for the fall in demand which continued to affect the economy in 1981.[93]

In view of the 1980 level of inflation, the 1981 budget was tough; with inflation expected to reach about 70%, it limited the expansion of both the money supply and bank credit to 50%, while the budget of the state companies was kept down to a 66% increase over their 1980 budget, and farm loans were raised by only 53·7%. The only sector to be spared the cuts was exports, earmarked to receive a 131·5% increase in loans.

The ISI policy pursued under Geisel suffered a setback, as it always does in Brazil, where – as soon as a recession appears – the ISI incentives are among the first type of subsidies to be withdrawn in order to allow for the pursuit of export subsidies. This attitude prevailed again in the 1981 budget and it was even reinforced in February when the funds made available to the capital goods industry through the BNDE were cut back.

There was an unavoidable impression of *déjà vu* in these measures, and a growing certainty that the problems already apparent under the previous administration were heading towards a crisis in which corrective state action had a more and more epiphenomenal impact. In a situation of clear stagflation, we will now see (i) how the government was almost surrealistically stepping up measures in those areas over which it was increasingly losing real control, i.e. *the balance of payments* and *public deficit*. (ii) As the scope of its effective action was gradually restricted to those home policy areas in which it continued to have a regulatory power, it used that power to make recession deeper, at a heavy political cost; its recessionary policies at home were insufficient to stabilise the economy, but decisive in precipitating a popular discontent which led to its political defeat in the November 1982 elections.

The Government Loses Control: the Ineffectiveness of State Action to Stabilise the Economy

(i) *The balance of payments*
For the government, the solution to the deficit of the balance of payments has been the same in the 1980s as it has always been since the late 60s: to export more and to import less. It is as if the equilibrium of the whole balance of payments depended on this formula. One can understand why so much emphasis has always been placed on the trade account by the governments stemming from the military coup of 1964: exports as a panacea to all the economic problems of the country is at the same time a justification of a repressive wage policy (always seen as a comparative advantage of Brazil), an attraction and a

guarantee to foreign credit, and a smokescreen over the real problems of the balance of payments, which are in its constantly deteriorating services account (Table 2.14). Since it had been admitted once and for all by the government that the trade account alone mattered, and that the only problem about foreign credit was that not enough of it was forthcoming, the export policy had become a focus of nationalist propaganda, and the real cost of servicing an evergrowing foreign debt was both played down and surrounded with secrecy.

TABLE 2.14 Brazil: balance of payments deficit summary accounts, 1979–82 (in billion dollars)*

	1979	1980	1981	1982
Trade balance	− 2.8	− 2.8	1.2	0.8
Exports	15.2	20.1	23.3	20.2
Imports	18.0	22.9	22.1	19.4
Balance of services	− 7.2	− 9.6	−12.2	−15.3
Net interest payments	− 4.2	− 6.3	− 9.2	−10.8
Current account balance	−10.0	−12.4	−11.0	−14.5
Capital account	7.5	9.4	11.4	10.5
Amortisation of long- and medium-term loans	− 6.5	− 6.7	− 7.3	− 7.8
Financing requirements (current account + amortisation of long- and medium-term loans)	16.5	19.1	18.3	22.3

* The data is given here in billion instead of in million dollars (as in Table 2.9) because the only Banco Central data available on 1982 at the time when this article was written was in billion dollars. However, the difference in the percentages calculated from this data is insignificant.

SOURCE Banco Central.

To reduce the trade account deficit of 1980, export incentives were reintroduced in April 1981, with manufactured exports being granted a 15% rebate on VAT. This was designed to offset partly a decision of the EEC Council of Ministers which, for 1981, had adopted a tougher set of quotas on imports from the more advanced developing countries than for 1980. Brazil's export trade success in 1981 was due both to those export subsidies and to a concentration on producing relatively simple consumer goods exported to less sophisticated markets and for which Brazil could take fuller advantage of its low labour costs. The 1·2 billion dollars trade surplus was however less significant than the

Brazilian authorities understandably wanted to portray it. *Firstly*, it was largely the result of renewed export incentives; *secondly*, many of the exports had gone to new but small markets in Latin America and Africa, where this initial success of Brazilian manufactured goods soon provoked protectionist reactions; *thirdly*, imports were held down below their 1980 value and – both in agriculture and in industry – many of the import cuts were short-sighted, as they affected essential inputs, which would inevitably bring about a drop in production in 1982.

Furthermore, as in 1977, when the trade account had shown a small surplus of 97 million dollars, the current account balance continued to show a large deficit, fuelled by the constantly rising deficit of the balance of services which resulted from the interest payments on the external debt. From 58% of the services account deficit in 1979, these payments – which referred only to the interest on the medium- and long-term debt – had risen to 70·6% in 1982. The servicing of the debt (interest + amortisation), which had absorbed 65% of the financing requirements of 1979, went up to 83·4% in 1982. The servicing of the debt is today a much greater burden on the financing requirements of Brazil than it was in the early 1970s (28% in 1974), and Brazil's foreign borrowing is now almost entirely used up by the servicing of the debt itself. In other words, the bulk of the credit raised in the 1970s has been used to meet balance of payments deficits which were themselves mostly caused by that credit. Similarly, the debt service ratio, which was 33% in 1970, had shot up to 70% in 1979 and 92% in 1982.

The picture is made even bleaker if we recall that short-term loans (i.e. with a maturity of up to one year) are excluded from foreign debt figures. When they are included, the debt service ratio is a serious blow to Brazil's credit worthiness. Although nobody seems to know exactly the size of that short-term debt, with estimates varying between 10 and 20 billion dollars for 1982, the estimate of the reliable Morgan Guaranty Trust Company puts the overall debt service ratio of Brazil at a staggering 122% in 1982 (84% in 1978).[94]

Several factors contributed to the deterioration of Brazil's credit worthiness in the early 1980s.

1. Only about one-third of its short-term debt can be considered to be normal trade credit. Since the late 1970s, the rest has regularly disappeared in the global debt, where it is used as an easier way to roll it over from year to year. But this roll over process itself, which – 'under normal circumstances' – is fairly smooth and automatic, tends to become a major problem when the credit markets are

State and Capital Accumulation: Brazil

affected by a liquidity crisis (as began to happen on the Euromarkets in the late-1970s) and/or when the creditors begin to question the ability of a particular country to service its debt. When that occurs, the credit worthiness of the country concerned is further reduced by the volume of its short-term credit.

2. In the early 1980s, the credit worthiness of Brazil began to be affected also by another factor, which was the falling level of its foreign reserves. In 1973, at 6·4 billion dollars, these represented 103·5% of its exports and 49% of its foreign debt. In 1979, at 10·2 billion, they had dropped to 63·6% of exports and 19·5% of the debt. They fell continuously afterwards, both in absolute and in relative terms, and in 1982, at 3·6 billion, they represented a mere 17% of exports and 5% of the medium- and long-term debt. In spite of the drastic cuts imposed on imports in 1982, foreign reserves were then equivalent to no more than two months' imports, when the minimum recommended by the IMF is three months. An urgent cash problem emerged as the country was simply running out of foreign currency to pay its creditors. This was the origin of the financial crisis which began in the autumn of 1982.

3. The success story of the export performance of the economy was increasingly questionable.

   (a) The much acclaimed growth of manufactured exports had been achieved through massive export subsidies which the USA and the EEC were no longer prepared to tolerate. Since Brazil's successive promises to phase them out were never fully implemented, retaliatory measures against Brazilian manufactured exports were stepped up. As a result, the export performance of 1981 was not repeated in 1982, when export earnings fell by 13·4% from their 1981 level. The traditional large export markets stood up better, but for primary products rather than for manufactured goods.

   (b) It then appeared that retaliation by the USA and the EEC were only in part responsible for the drop, and that many Brazilian manufactured exports were not in fact designed for sophisticated consumer markets. Since the Latin American and African markets on which they can find a demand have also a limited capacity of absorption, the growth of those exports is necessarily limited.

   (c) Some data was openly in contradiction to the official claim of an export-based expansion. Instead, exports remained more or less stable as a percentage of GNP since the late-1960s (6–8%) and –

what is more – the much praised performance of 1981 was becoming something of a myth when it was realised that Brazil had exported an even lower percentage of its GNP that year than before the oil crisis in 1973. The biggest myth was perhaps to have believed or made people believe for so long that both economic expansion and the balance of payments could rely on an unlimited export drive. The Brazilian experience shows that the promises of export-led growth have not been and cannot be fulfilled, since the growth of its exports does not depend only on policy decisions made by Brazil, but rather on the readiness of the potential importing countries to accept them. Even the revival of liberal economics today has not meant a return to 'free trade', particularly when the regulating of international trade has made it possible to monitor more closely the numerous infringements which countries like Brazil make constantly to the 'agreed practices' and which – in turn – set in motion the protectionist reactions against them.[95]

The consequence of a reduced credit worthiness is that credit becomes both more difficult to obtain and more expensive. The irony of the Brazilian situation is that even when its credit worthiness was good (during the Geisel administration), Brazil had always been prepared to pay higher spreads over basic lending rates than most of its competitors with a lower credit rating, in order to be in the good books of the bankers. As the profile of its total debt has continued to deteriorate, with 81% of its medium- and long-term debt being contracted at floating rates at the end of 1982, the Brazilian balance of payments is vulnerable to the slightest changes in international lending rates. Since its credit rating has also deteriorated rapidly in the 1980s, Brazil has combined the negative effects of high basic lending rates until 1983 and of high spreads (2·125%) over them. These high interest rates on its foreign debt have played a decisive role in its balance of payments deficit (see Table 2.14). The fall in basic lending rates in 1983 could, if it is not short-lived, help the Brazilian balance of payments; but it comes at a time when credit has practically dried up for Brazil, which has become a high risk customer for the banks. Many other less indebted countries might now take advantage of cheaper international credit, and the credit heydays of the 1970s do not look set to return easily to Brazil.

(ii) *The public deficit*
If we believe the Brazilian authorities, some success was achieved in

bringing down the public deficit from 8·3% of GDP in 1979 to 5·7% in 1982. But if we believe the IMF, the true figure for 1982 is not 5·7% but 16·9%. The accounting intricacies of the official Brazilian data have always been rather puzzling, but ingenuity in inventing new ways of disguising losses has been enhanced since Delfim took economic power again in 1979. In general terms, it is probably safe to assume that – compensating for the accounting tricks – the public deficit has not come down in 1982. To support the likelihood of the IMF data of 16·9%, the deficit of the public firms alone represented – on the basis of official Brazilian data – 5·5% of GDP in 1979 and 6·2% in 1982 (see Table 2.16), i.e. more than the total public deficit announced by Brazil that year (5·7%).

In the yet again intricate and highly unorthodox budgetary accounts used by Brazil – and bearing in mind the constant tendency to underestimate – we can however pick out a few interesting elements. The Brazilian total federal budget was considerably altered during the 1970s, and it is now composed of three separate yet related budgets which became 'consolidated' only in 1979. Of the three federal budgets, one, *the federal budget*, which – before 1964 – gave a reasonably accurate picture of the financial situation of the federal government, covers today less than 15% of its total expenditures (see Table 2.15). The other two budgets have developed as a result of the growing economic intervention of the state. Both have a constantly growing deficit. *The monetary budget* covers the revenues and expenditures which are under the responsibility of the monetary authorities, i.e. *Banco Central* and *Banco do Brasil*; it refers to the internal public debts, to subsidised credit and to exchange accounts. *The budget of the state companies* was already by far the largest one in 1979, and it has continued to grow ever since at the relative expense of the other two. It should be noted that only the first, i.e. the so-called federal budget, is debated at all in Congress, while the other two are exclusively under the responsibility of the government. The absence of any political debate on more than 85% of the funds spent by the government is a very significant limitation to the power of the political opposition in Congress, and it accounts also to a large extent for the unreliability of the data presented by the government on those two budgets on which no political control can be exercised.

However, unreliable as it is, the data available shows the importance of the State companies both to the total federal budget and to the Brazilian economy as a whole (Table 2.15). It also shows the contribution that public firms make to the total public deficit (Table 2.16).

TABLE 2.15 Brazil: global expenditure of the federal government, 1979–82

Type of budget	1979 (1) (%)	(2)	1980 (1) (%)	(2)	1981 (1) (%)	(2)	1982 (1) (%)	(2)
Federal	15.2	5.0	10.6	4.0	10.6	4.0	14.2	5.3
Monetary	13.8	4.6	17.1	6.5	13.1	4.9	9.4	3.5
State companies	71.0	23.7	72.3	27.7	76.3	28.7	76.4	28.2

Column 1 corresponds to the percentage of total federal expenditures for each individual budget.
Column 2 corresponds to the percentage of GDP.
SOURCE Von Doellinger (1982) p. 102, table 2.

TABLE 2.16 Brazil: operational deficit of state companies, 1979–82

	1979	1980	1981	1982
% of total public deficit*	52.2	54.0	70.7	72.0
% of GDP	5.5	5.1	6.5	6.2

* plus the Treasury Transfers to the State companies.

N.B. The figures in this table were calculated from data available in Von Doellinger (1982).

The data presented here was not available before 1979 and, until a special *Secretariat for the Control of the State Companies* (SEST) was created in that year, nobody – not even in the government – knew how many public firms there were, and much less how much they spent and how much they borrowed abroad. But mapping them out was not the same as controlling them, as can be seen from the data in Table 2.16. Since the early 1970s, the public firms had become almost independent entities, drawing heavily on the current revenues of the federal government and resorting also to internal and external credit in a massive way to cover their growing deficit. The volume of their deficit makes the measures undertaken by the government to control them ineffective. In 1982, the percentage of Treasury transfers earmarked for them was reduced in an attempt to reduce the public deficit, but the firms were encouraged at the same time to borrow more credit abroad. As a result, the debt of the state companies that year accounted for 70% of the foreign debt of Brazil,[96] and their operational deficit represented 72% of its public deficit.

We know that the heavy contribution that state companies make to both the public deficit and the foreign debt is the consequence of the role they came to play during the expansionist phase of export industrialisation in the 1970s. Because expansion gave way to recession in the early 1980s, we must now resume the analysis in this new context, to assess the impact that state companies have had on the Brazilian crisis.

Drawing from the experience of both periods, we can see that the deficit of the public firms which produce industrial inputs seems to be due to four main factors:

1. With overmanning and larger capital assets, their operational and administrative costs tend to be higher than those of the private industrial firms.[97] As a result, their exports have to be heavily subsidised in order to be competitive in the international markets. In steel production, which has been since the late 1970s one of the leading sectors in which the government hopes to boost exports, Brazil earned in 1982 196 dollars per tonne of steel exported while the mills' costs were about 320 dollars per tonne. BEFIEX, the government export agency, paid for the difference.[98]

   Being subsidised, Brazilian exports are exposed to protectionist reactions from the USA and EEC authorities who impose strict quotas or sometimes close their markets altogether to them, making excess capacity worse[99] and thus operational and administrative costs higher. The large iron ore public company *Vale do Rio Doce* has regular losses on its iron ore operations and, in spite of the BEFIEX export subsidies, it also depends heavily on Treasury transfers. In 1978, for example, with financial costs up by 130% from 912 million dollars in 1977 to 2·1 billion, the small profit of 1·3 million dollars which it announced was both dubious in itself and – if true at all – only the result of the non-operational profits of 5·5 million dollars made on the money markets.[100] In 1982–83, the slump in world steel making forced the company to cut the export price of iron ore by 10–12%, making its operational losses even larger.

2. The state companies sell at subsidised prices on the internal market as well. This policy was at the core of the overall economic strategy of the government during the expansionist phase, when it was intended to keep the price of consumer goods low and thus boost

internal demand further, and – at the same time – to contribute to capital accumulation by the private sector. When the economy slowed down in the second half of the 1970s, and when it went into recession in the early 1980s, subsidised inputs were used to maintain some manufacturing output. Moreover, since the late 1970s, the constantly high inflation rates have made the real level of the subsidies even higher than before. In 1980, for example, the giant public steel company *Siderbrás* was allowed to put the price of its steel up 60% while inflation was running at about 110%. In the same year, the oil company *Petrobrás* – the largest of all public firms – was not allowed to pass on the higher cost of crude oil, whose price per barrel had gone up from 18 dollars in 1979 to 28·5 dollars in 1980. As a result, its operational deficit had to be financed from public funds, which, only for the first four months of 1980, represented a 2 billion dollars transfer from the Treasury plus a 1 billion dollars transfer from the *Banco do Brasil*.

3. State companies are continuously expanding and diversifying their activities, and multiplying the number of their subsidiaries, both as a consequence of their own expanding drive and because the government frequently wants them to undertake new responsibilities in strategic export sectors. This growing branching out is rarely profitable, as it is usually associated with export activities which involve a scaling up of subsidies, thus a drain on the financial resources of the companies and, ultimately, a further deterioration of public deficit.

The three largest public companies which produce basic inputs have been transformed into conglomerates whose losses have grown with their size and complexity. The *Vale do Rio Doce* has invested in all kinds of mining projects, creating or absorbing in the 1970s many subsidiary companies supposed to contribute to the export drive which has always been seen as the solution to all the problems. Because of high production costs, most of them are unlikely to be competitive, even if international prices go up again. The company's attempts to sell some of its subsidiaries to the private sector in the last four years has not been successful since, with the exception of the big Carajás project, the buyers – whether national or foreign – have not been forthcoming. *Siderbrás* has been caught up in the vast excess capacity for steel production which has resulted from the II PND's objectives after 1974 to reverse capital goods imports into exports, particularly in steel products. Large steel mills were built in São Paulo (Cosipa), Minas Gerais (Açominas) and, together with other mills like Tubarão and Vibasa, they have large over-capacity, both because local and world demands are depressed and because Brazilian steel is too expensive to be competitive. Today, they are all facing solvency problems, with *Siderbrás*' foreign debt totalling 6·7 billion dollars in June 1983 (an almost 100% increase since 1980). *Petrobrás* – which has for long had the reputation of being efficient and profitable – has followed a similar pattern. It was drawn into the ambitious (and unprofitable) alcohol programme set up by the government and, made responsible for promoting alcohol exports, it had to start subsidising them as well, at the rate of 35% of the value of those exports. By selling fertilisers and petrochemical raw materials at below production costs on the internal market, and by bailing out charcoal and pig iron manufacturers, it has enlarged its losses to such an extent that – together with its oil operational costs – its official profits have become increasingly mythical. However, because of the political significance of the 'profitability' of *Petrobrás* for the government and because 'it would have a disastrous impact on public confidence if it were to record a loss', its profits for 1982 were 'artificially fixed at a meeting of the National Monetary Council'.[101] The accounting tricks through which this company was made to appear profitable have been multiplied, not only for *Petrobrás* but for the whole of the state sector, particularly since 1979. One of the latest discoveries in the 1980s – widely used by *Petrobrás* and other public firms ever since – has been leasing operations. For *Petrobrás* alone, the cost of the lease-back operations it has undertaken to disguise its deteriorating financial situation amounted in 1982 to 900 million dollars which it had to pay in foreign currency to lease or rent its equipment. In spite of this, its losses have been increasing so much that, pushed further by the higher cost of its foreign debt of 5·5 billion dollars provoked by the 'maxi-devaluation' of 23% in February 1983, the company declared for the first time a deficit of 200 billion cruzeiros (approximately 615 million dollars) on its account of the first term of 1983.

4. Another factor of the deficit of the public firms engaged in production is the accumulated debt which has developed within the public sector. Known in Brazil as the '*calote oficial*', it is – according to the dictionary – a debt which remains unpaid or which was contracted with the intention of not paying it back.[102] This *calote* involves all the levels of the public sector, from companies to federal, state and local governments. Within the public sector, the victims are the companies which sell their products – or their services – to other

companies or administrations and which are never paid for them. Consequently, their deficit goes up and so does the deficit of the National Bank of Economic Development (BNDE) and of the Treasury.

With the ever-increasing burden of the state companies on public funds, and with a tax revenue which continued to decline as a percentage of its total revenues (from 80·1% in 1979 to 72% in 1980), the government resorted to two inadvisable methods to finance a growing public deficit. One was the expansion of the public debt, both internal and external; the other one was the expansion of the money supply.

We have already seen how the external debt expanded and with what consequences for the balance of payments. The growth of the internal public debt was also considerable, and it doubled in one year as a percentage of GDP (from 6·8% in 1981 to 14·1% in 1982). With inflation running at about 100% a year since 1980 (officially 110·2% in 1980, 95·2% in 1981, and 99·7% in 1982), in order to be able to sell its bonds (ORTNs) on the money market, the government had first to index them, and then pay an interest of about 15% above inflation. By competing with the banks to attract private savings, the government was pushing up the cost of commercial credit (35–40% above inflation) and thus fuelling inflation.

The other method used to cover public deficit – expanding the money supply – was also generating inflation. In the early 1980s, the money supply continued to grow at the high rates which it had reached for the first time in 1979 (73·6%), and it remained 'stable' at a rate of expansion of about 70% a year.

To summarise the economic situation of the early 1980s, we could say that the loss of control over inflation after 1979 was largely the result of the loss of control over the public deficit, which was itself the result of the loss of control over public debt payments and over current transfers and subsidies. As a consequence, the two tendencies which could be observed in the second half of the 1970s were reinforced: both the rate of domestic savings and the rate of capital formation continued to decline (Table 2.17).[103]

In spite of its imaginative accountancy which managed to disguise the real extent of public deficit and of its constant denial concerning its intention of approaching the IMF, the government already knew in 1980 that there would be no other way out. In preparation, it began to introduce measures which were intended to reduce the size of the public deficit.

TABLE 2.17 *Brazil: domestic savings and capital formation (averages)*

	1974–78	1979–80
Private domestic savings as a % of total private income	14.2	9.4
Government savings as a % of total government revenues	29.5	22.9
Gross capital formation as a % of GNP	25.7	21.1
Government expenditures on fixed investment as a % of total government revenues	26.6	19.3

SOURCE *Centro de Contas Nacionais*, FGV, 1982.

The data compiled by the SEST on the contribution that state companies made to public deficit (see Table 2.16) and the pressures of the always powerful *anti-estatização* lobby combined to decide the government to start controlling the state companies. Their budgets were cut in 1981 and in 1982, but these cuts did not prevent them from continuing to account for an increasing share of both total government expenditures (over 75%) and public deficit (over 70%) (see Tables 2.15 and 2.16). They got around the attempts at controlling them by practising a policy of *fait accompli*: having spent their budget allocation after six months, they would simply ask for more funds, knowing that – in the end – the government would give in. They also began defaulting systematically on their foreign debt payments, knowing that the *Banco do Brasil* would eventually have to bail them out. In 1981 alone, according to the President of the *Banco Central*, this cost the *Banco do Brasil* about 1·5 billion dollars.

All this was made possible because there was an equally powerful political lobby behind the state companies. It was made up of those who – particularly among the military – had benefited from their development, and of those who had their eyes fixed on the November 1982 elections in which – after its previous electoral setbacks – it was crucial that the government should do well. For this to happen, economic policies had to soften the impact of recession, not to sharpen it. Caught yet again – but in a much more pressing way – in this contradiction between its short-term political objectives, which demanded some relaxation of its economic policies, and its equally short-term economic goals, which called for austerity measures, the government multiplied the contradictions of its own policy making.

These contradictions (i) made recession worse while failing to stabilise the economy, (ii) undermined the confidence of both foreign creditors and local entrepreneurs, and (iii) aggravated popular discontent to such an extent that the government could only be defeated in the 1982 elections.

We will now turn to a closer examination of these developments.

Recession and Political Disarray

Recession without Stabilisation

(i) *To reduce the deficit of the balance of payments,* since the optimistic official predictions concerning exports were always exposed by the real export performance, the government started cutting down imports. These were down from 22·9 billion dollars in 1980 to 22·1 billion in 1981, and 19·4 billion in 1982; the projected figure for 1983 is 16 billion. In 1981 and 1982, the cuts became so severe that they began to affect essential inputs, and thus production in both the public and the private sector. The 1981 import cuts were particularly hard on chemicals, whose stocks fell dangerously for industry, and fertilisers, which had the farmers worrying about a drop in production in 1982.

In spite of the drop in industrial production from 8% in 1980 to −8% in 1981, the squeeze was made even harder in 1982 when – instead of a 12% increase in imports which had been promised to businessmen – further import cuts were introduced throughout the year. This was done whenever it became clear during the year that the export target of 28 billion dollars was looking more and more unrealistic, and that import cuts were the only way open to the government to obtain the trade surplus that it needed. In September, CACEX, the *Banco do Brasil* export agency, banned the import of about 1300 products, among which there were some important industrial inputs. In October, a further squeeze was announced through an 'adjustment programme' for 1983 intended to reduce the current account deficit from 14·5 billion dollars in 1982 to 8–9 billion in 1983. Since little can be done to reduce the deficit of the services account, the reduction will have to come from an enormous trade surplus of 5–6 billion dollars. Since – on the other hand – everyone agrees that the export target of 22 billion dollars for 1983 is unrealistic, a trade surplus depends entirely on import cuts, which are constantly stepped up: in the first term of 1983, the value of imports went down by 20·7%,[104] making recession harder for both industry and agriculture; this tendency was reinforced in the following months, with further negative consequences on recession and on employment. In the meantime, while the 23% maxi-devaluation implemented in February 1983 in order to help exports has not fulfilled its goal, it has aggravated the balance of payments deficit by making debt servicing more expensive, it has increased the financial difficulties of the Brazilian firms indebted abroad, and it has contributed to further enlarge the public deficit.

Evidence of the growing panic and impotence of the authorities, the scaling up of import cuts has now replaced 'export-led growth' as the new 'model' designed to redress the disequilibrium of the balance of payments. However, it is unlikely to achieve much in this respect, in view of the impact of the services account deficit; the artificial way in which it can help to produce a trade surplus in 1983 is short-sighted as it increasingly affects the potential export performance.

(ii) *To reduce the public deficit,* which has been the single most important cause of inflation in the 1980s – the government introduced measures which *either* had a negative impact on the balance of payments *or* further contributed to push inflation up.

1. As we saw, to compensate for the cuts imposed on their budgets, the state companies were encouraged to borrow directly abroad, which increased their own deficit and – in the end – the deficit of the *Banco do Brasil* which has to bail them out when they default on their debt payments. On the other hand, a reduction in their level of spending could only make recession worse, not only for them but also for the private domestic firms which had come to depend heavily on them for their orders. This has accelerated the rate of takeovers of domestic firms by foreign firms subsidiaries, which have taken advantage of the high cost of domestic credit to increase their non-operational profits, and which – after reaching the legal limit of their profit remittances abroad – have used them to buy bankrupted Brazilian firms at bargain prices.
2. Because the government is effectively competing with banks for private savings through its ORTNs, local businessmen have to pay 35–40% interest above inflation for the money they borrow, making the Brazilian commercial credit the most expensive in the world, even accounting for indexation.[105] This constantly adds to inflation.
3. Because it was such a drain on public finance, the government

decided to cut most of its subsidies to consumer prices and to credit. These cuts affected the price of basic commodities (such as wheat and sugar) on the internal market as well as subsidised credit for agriculture, which had a further negative impact on food prices. By opting for 'corrective inflation' of this kind, the government inevitably provoked an increase in wages readjusted by the INPC which, even though it did not prevent real wages from falling (given the way the INPC is calculated), added yet another inflationary pressure on the economy. These cuts have also reduced the amount of disposable income available for the purchase of manufactured goods for about 90–95% of all wage earners. Here again, inflation – but also recession – have been made worse, while the private domestic savings rate was further squeezed.
4. The latter was achieved in obvious contradiction to the simultaneous move to encourage domestic savings in order to reduce foreign borrowing. To pursue this in a context of declining savings, high levels of indexation were necessary for savings accounts and ORTNs, which added to inflation both directly and also by raising yet further the cost of commercial credit.

The Economic and Political Impact of Recession on Brazilian Society

The recessionary policy of the government and its failure to control inflation have had a profound impact, both economic and political, on civil society. *Economically*, it has ruined many local business sectors, created massive unemployment and reduced the standard of living of two-thirds of the working population (those earning up to three minimum wages)[106] further below the already low levels of the 1970s. *Politically*, as the illusion of legitimacy was disappearing fast with recession, the conflict between the State and civil society was gathering momentum. It culminated in the November 1982 elections in which pre-electoral manipulations were not sufficient to assure the success of the government.

(i) *Business: the demise of the 'triple alliance'*

The Brazilian business community had greeted the replacement of Simonsen by Delfim in August 1979 with enthusiasm. Delfim promised them renewed expansion but – apart from reintroducing export subsidies, which helped foreign firms' subsidiaries more than local firms – he gave them very little. Local entrepreneurs wanted a reactivation of the economy through cheaper credit to producers and consumers alike; a scaling up of public investments to generate demand for the large capital goods industry which had been expanded since the mid-1970s; and, more generally, an expanding market. But instead, those local business groups which had managed to survive the aftermath of the 'miracle' and had not been taken over by foreign firms in the seventies, have been hit across the board by practically every measure implemented by the government in the 1980s.

1. Import controls – and the difficult export drive – have affected the utilisation of their productive capacity, which has fallen to 70–75% for manufacturing industry as a whole. The capital goods sector is the worst affected, with idle capacity running at about 50%; it has – more than any other – suffered from an overdimensioning made worse by the cuts imposed on the public firms from which it received three-quarters of all its orders.
2. The high cost of local credit has been an increasing burden for all domestic firms. Even the large local companies – which can benefit from the government guarantee when borrowing abroad – find it difficult to obtain foreign credit, as their own credit worthiness has been affected by the reduced credit worthiness of Brazil. With LIBOR down to 9·5% and the American prime-rate down to 10·25% in the first term of 1983, the cost of international credit has become more favourable than it was up to July 1982 (when LIBOR was at about 15% and the prime-rate at 16·5%). But the credit worthiness of Brazil has also gone down so much in the meantime that – even with high spreads over basic lending rates – Brazilian firms do not obtain credit easily on the international money markets. Foreign firms, on the other hand, have always been in a better position in this respect; throughout the years, they have been able to borrow abroad and then take advantage of the high cost of credit on the Brazilian money markets to make large non-operational profits; these take them through the crisis while allowing them at the same time to carry on with their take-over operations of Brazilian firms in financial difficulties.
3. Their difficulties were enhanced by the *calote* of the public sector, with most government bills remaining unpaid. Since private firms could not rely on being bailed out of their debts, bankruptcies multiplied.

With recession getting deeper in 1981, they came to realise that they could expect no help from a government which was acting more and more under the pressure of its foreign creditors. Leading industrialists like Antonio Ermirio de Moraes, Claudio Bardella, and Paulo Villares began to criticise openly the government for having encouraged the domestic companies to expand their productive capacity in the 1970s and then – through recessionary policies – leaving them with large debts and without a market, at the mercy of foreign firms and financial conglomerates.

In 1981–82, the *anti-estatização* campaign started again, and, more so than in 1976, many local businessmen expressed their preference for a development of the internal market while voicing their fear that a larger opening up of the economy would benefit foreign firms yet further. With the elections coming up, they thought that reflationary policies would be on their way. But recessionary measures were stepped up, and bankruptcies and takeovers followed.

Small and medium-sized domestic firms had been in financial trouble already in the 1970s. The largest ones resisted longer, but their own difficulties accelerated in the 1980s. In July 1981, the powerful Matarazzo group had to sell most sectors of its textile complex but also cement and mining plants to foreign firms at knock-down prices. The pace quickened in 1982, with 'ten big companies, including the steel mill Conferraz, Cimetal, Maeda (the largest cotton producer), Correa Ribeiro (the leading cocoa exporter), Ciferal (one of the biggest producers of bus chassis), and Bel Recanto (the main manufacturer of prefabricated housing) all [calling] in the receivers'.[107]

The capital goods industry was particularly critical of the government which – to obtain a momentary relief in the balance of payments – was accepting foreign 'financial packages' linking cash loans to suppliers' credit for the purchase of foreign equipment which could have been purchased locally.

Heavily in debt with local and foreign banks, the large private domestic firms find it increasingly difficult to roll over their debts, and the 'maxi-devaluation' of 23% decided in February 1983 to – once again – try to boost exports, has – in the short-run – made their position worse by raising the cost of servicing their foreign debt and by making new foreign credit virtually inaccessible for them.

With both recession and economic policies out of control in 1983, the producers of agricultural exports, whose subsidised credit the industrialists had envied for three years, suddenly became a target for the cuts as well. Cheap credit was no longer available and, immediately after the 23% devaluation 'to help exports', the government decided to impose a 30% tax on the exports of coffee, soya, cocoa and beef. With apparently greater success than the industrialists, the protests of these exporters brought about lower taxes, but – with higher import costs for fertilisers – their financial situation is becoming increasingly difficult as well.

For the industrialists, who were supposed to be partners in the 'Triple Alliance' in which they were alleged to share profits with the state and with foreign capital, the myth of this alliance is made even more evident than for the state.[108]

(ii) *Labour: from political opposition to social unrest*
The great majority of Brazilian wage earners were affected by the recessionary policies of the 1980s as they had been by the expansionist policies of the 1970s. In global terms, the patterns of inequality in the distribution of the national income were reinforced; according to the statistics of the official FIBGE, half of the population, which had been made to pay earlier for the cost of the miracle, was made to pay for the recession as well, while income was concentrated yet further at the top (Table 2.18).

TABLE 2.18 Brazil; income distribution, 1960, 1970, 1980

	1960 (%)	1970 (%)	1980 (%)
Bottom 50%	17.4	14.9	12.6
Top 10%	39.6	46.7	50.9
Top 5%	28.3	34.1	37.9
Top 1%	11.9	14.7	16.9

SOURCE FIBGE.

Inflation affected real wages and – inefficient though they were in achieving their goal – the measures undertaken to reduce the public deficit had a strong negative impact on the standard of living of most wage earners. Together with the wage policy, cuts in welfare expenditures and in subsidies have contributed to increase popular discontent in the 1980s and to enlarge the legitimacy gap of the regime.

1. The 1980s have been characterised by a constant reduction of the percentage of government expenditures spent on 'social programmes', i.e. on welfare. These had gone up in the late-1970s (from 42·9%

in 1977 to 48% in 1978 and 53·5% in 1979), but, one of the first victims of the cuts, they dropped to 21·6% in 1980, recovered a little in 1981 (29·2%), and fell again in 1982 (20·3%). 'Compared with 1977, 1982 shows a real drop of 55·9%; i.e., in 1982, the social expenditures of the government were less than half in real terms of those made in 1977.'[109] Inspired by a desperate urgency to cut down public expenditure where it seemed easier to do so – and in contradiction with its electoral objectives – this radical change of government policy in the 1980s has seriously reduced the social ('reconciliation') function of the state and increased the potential for open social conflict.

2. This trend was strengthened by the new wage policy established by Delfim in November 1979 following the wave of strikes which had contributed to Simonsen's dismissal. With wage adjustments benefiting the lower paid workers most, it soon failed in its objective to rally popular support around the government (because the INPC on which wage adjustments were calculated was always lower than inflation), and – as we saw earlier – it also antagonised the better paid workers by reducing wage differentials.

The wage structure was based on multiples of a minimum wage which had been unified for the whole country in May 1980 (Table 2.19).

TABLE 2.19 Brazil: the wage structure, 1980 (% of working population)

Number of minimum wages	less than ½	½–1	1–2	2–5	5–10	10–20	Over 20
% of working population	12.5	20.8	31.1	23.6	7.2	3.2	1.6

SOURCE FIBGE.

To appreciate the significance of these percentages, we must evaluate what the minimum wage represents in practical terms. In May 1980, when it was unified, it was readjusted up to 4149·60 cruzeiros on the basis of changes in the INPC (equivalent to 79 dollars at the overvalued official exchange rate). For February that year, DIEESE estimated that the monthly cost of a so-called 'minimum food ration'[110] for one person in São Paulo was 1870·54 cruzeiros. If we take an average family of three persons, a minimum food ration alone cost them 5611·62. In other words, the minimum wage, i.e. the maximum income available to 33·3% of wage earners nationally (21% in São Paulo),[111] was falling far below what was necessary to purchase a minimum survival diet for three people. Since DIEESE estimates that food represents about 48% of all expenses for low income families, the consumption of that minimum ration would have required a minimum wage of 11 690 cruzeiros (about 222 dollars), which was equivalent to almost three minimum wages in 1980. If – by whatever criteria – most of those who earn less than three minimum wages are thus either destitute or very poor, equally, those who earn less than five minimum wages have a very low standard of living. Since 88% of the total working population earned less than five minimum wages in 1980, two consequences follow:

1. In an average low income family, the trend already observed in the 1970s was reinforced, and wives and children have had to contribute to a family's income in conditions of growing unemployment.
2. The myth of the prosperous middle classes is exploded. To which wage category do they correspond? If they are the 7·2% who earn between five and ten minimum wages (395 to 790 dollars at the overvalued official rate), they can hardly be described as prosperous, further hit as they are by the way the INPC is calculated, which tends to discriminate against them.[112] On the other hand, if we have to move above ten minimum wages to find the 'middle classes', we are left with only the top 4·8% of all wage earners.

The situation changed relatively little in 1981 and 1982. According to DIEESE, the real minimum wage, which had improved slightly in 1980 and 1981 on its 1975 level, fell again in 1982. However – in view of the proximity of the elections – the six-monthly wage adjustments on the INPC were maintained, which did not prevent real wages from falling, but which somewhat cushioned their deterioration. Once the elections were passed and lost, wages were again in the forefront of government attacks at the end of 1982. Delfim – in yet another of his many U-turns – denounced the six-monthly wage increases as one of the main causes of inflation. But – a sign of his waning influence – they were maintained in early 1983, although in a scaled down version: the lower paid (up to three minimum wages) would continue to receive increases in line with changes in the INPC; those earning between three and twenty minimum wages would have readjustments of between 95% and 50%, which was a particularly heavy blow to skilled workers and to the 'middle classes'; only the small numbers of those who earn over twenty minimum wages would continue to depend on direct negotiations with their employers for any increases.

With no immediate elections in sight and with the IMF stepping up its pressures for both inflation and public deficit to be reduced, the government multiplied the cuts in food subsidies and reduced yet again the level of subsidised credit for the farmers. The consequence was immediate: in Rio, the general price index went up by 37·4% in the first quarter of 1983 (the highest increase since the first quarter of 1964, just before the coup), with the retail price of food products going up by 49·5%. But the most radical measure was implemented in May, when Delfim decided to eliminate new price increases from the calculation of the INPC and to restrict total wage increases to a maximum of 80% of the INPC. In a situation of fast growing inflation (127·2% in June), in which the cuts in food subsidies had a definite impact, the difference increased rapidly between the rate of inflation, calculated by the FGV, and the INPC, calculated by the government. There had always been a gap between the two, constantly pointed out by the trade unions and by the opposition. From June 1983, the distance grew between the new 'purged' INPC and inflation, and real wages fell accordingly (Table 2.20).

Social unrest inevitably began to accelerate a political crisis which was mobilising all sectors of Brazilian society against the government, and which the main opposition party PMDB was trying to organise. One would expect the virtual collapse of the Brazilian model to make this task easy.

TABLE 2.20 *Rate of growth of inflation and INPC, June–September 1983*

	Inflation (%)	INPC (%)
June	127.2	112.2
July	142.8	124.3
August	152.7	131.7
September	174.9	142.2

SOURCE FGV.

The Logical Collapse of the Brazilian Model

The data available for 1983 confirm the tendencies which had become apparent during the Geisel administration and which are the result of the contradictions inherent to the Brazilian model of growth and accumulation. Because of their multiplying effect on each other, and because of the peripheral nature of Brazilian capitalism, those contradictions could only exacerbate the crisis of the Brazilian model and eventually bring about its virtual collapse, instead of allowing accumulation to take place at a higher level.

GDP growth projections are negative both for 1983 (-3 to -4%) and 1984 (-5%). In July 1983, the output of capital goods had fallen by 22·7% on its July 1982 level. Excess capacity has risen higher than its critical levels of 1982 in all sectors of manufacturing production as a result of constantly falling demand. That internal demand for industrial goods is continuously falling is due to the way in which the new wage policy hits the already squeezed middle-income groups; as to exports, they had fallen in the first term to $-6\cdot2\%$ of their 1982 level, with manufacturing exports falling to $-10\cdot7\%$, due to the persistence of the same causes that had hindered their growth in previous years and to the additional impact of the import cuts. Bankruptcies of local firms have mounted up. Unemployment in industry is at 20–25% which, added to underemployment figures estimated at about 35% of the total labour force helps to understand why, between 1981 and 1982, the number of those who earn less than one minimum wage went up from 17 to 21 million; with neither social security nor unemployment benefits to reduce the impact of the crisis on the unemployed, strikes have developed and social unrest has intensified. As for inflation, from 99·7% in 1982, it will reach over 200% in 1983, and everyone in the government agrees that it has become uncontrollable.

At the same time, the revised 1982 balance of payments data published by *Banco Central* in mid-1983 showed an even bleaker picture than had been portrayed by the earlier set of data used in Table 2.14, with the balance of services (and thus the current account) presenting a further deficit of about 2 billion dollars, which were added to the already heavy financing requirements of the country for 1983. With forecasts of interest payments varying between 10·5 and 15 billion dollars for 1984, Brazil, which is trying to obtain a rescheduling on the principal in 1983, might also have to suspend interest payments as well and declare a much feared moratorium.

This is the logical outcome of a crisis which had been gathering momentum since 1979 to come finally into the open in November–December 1982 when, after losing the elections, the government had to make its talks with the IMF public. Its only real tactics during the previous three years had been to play for time, perhaps in the hope that a reasonably good electoral performance would make its international standing stronger and impress its creditors. In the event – as might have been expected – the opposite happened. The package imposed by the IMF could also have been anticipated, since it had the usual IMF emphasis on a reduction of both public sector and balance of payments deficits. Perhaps thinking that it could trick the IMF with some new accounting ideas, the government has multiplied *ad hoc* measures which have had inevitably adverse results both on the economy and on the IMF.

The latter was little impressed by the preliminary results of the Brazilian attempts to comply with its recommendations concerning the reduction of the public deficit which, instead of being held at 2800 billion cruzeiros, reached 4300 billion (9·9 billion dollars) in the first three months of 1983, when the limit fixed by the IMF for the whole year is 8800 billion.[113] It is this in particular which prompted the IMF decision in May not to extend any further credit to Brazil until the situation of public finance had improved.

Highlighted in July when it was refused a bridging loan by the Bank for International Settlements, the need to obtain IMF support has become the major concern of the government. In September, it sent a letter of intent to the IMF that contained new austerity measures which – in view of its record and of its present performance – appear very unrealistic. It pledged (a) to limit inflation to 160% in 1983 (it had already gone over that limit in September) and 60% in 1984; (b) to reduce the current account deficit to 7·6 billion dollars in 1983 and 6 billion in 1984, when it hopes to obtain a 9 billion dollars trade surplus (with imports already critically low and exports falling, this target is wholly unrealistic); (c) to eliminate public deficit in 1984 (this is patently out of reach).

It is probably safe to assume that this letter had little credibility for the IMF. However, before commenting on it, the IMF required the Brazilian government to have the most politically controversial of its proposals – i.e. its new wage legislation – accepted by Congress. After some initial difficulties, it eventually managed to do that in October, although in a scaled down version: instead of the original 80%, wage increases would, in total, be limited to 87% of the changes in the INPC.[114] The fact that this partial political success was apparently sufficient to secure IMF support in November is an indication that the IMF wanted (or had) to find some satisfaction in it because of the risks of a moratorium for the international banking community. However, IMF support given on so little evidence is also an implicit recognition that its own recommendations too lacked realism: to expect the Brazilian government to bring about a massive and rapid reduction in the public deficit, the deficit of the balance of payments, and inflation is unrealistic and contradictory; to ask for more wage restraint is politically irresponsible.

The Brazilian crisis is so deep and so 'structural' that the policy recommendations made by international creditors and by the domestic opposition alike are all unrealistic as well. *The first* endorse the IMF requests and see the way out of the crisis in an improved export performance based on the prospect of recovery in the OECD countries, but, at the same time, make projections of negative growth for Brazil in 1983 and 1984.[115] Devaluation is sometimes proposed, since the explanation of the inadequate export performance of Brazil is often attributed to an overvalued cruzeiro;[116] but, with the interest payments that Brazil has to pay on its foreign debt and with the imports needed after more than two years of drastic import cuts, the effects of a devaluation would be more negative than positive for the balance of payments.

The second, the domestic political opposition, wants Brazil to declare a 'negotiated' moratorium on its foreign debt which, since it would affect interest payments, is unlikely to be negotiable with the creditors and which would also rule out IMF support. Whether Brazil can and should do that anyway is very questionable, unless it can embark on a policy of self-reliance, which its structures of production do not make a viable alternative.

CONCLUDING REMARKS

The Brazilian model of growth and capital accumulation has managed, simultaneously, to bring the country to a point of insolvency while exhausting the limits of popular endurance at home and credibility abroad. This should make predicting easy, but it does not. Brazil is part of Latin America but – even at its worst – the military regime in power since 1964 has never gone as far as those of its Spanish-speaking neighbours in the use of repression. Admittedly, its wage policy has always been repressive, but, under the previous civilian governments, a majority of the labour force had also been excluded from the distribution of any benefits. Those who are feeling the pinch today probably more than they have ever done in the history of the country are the urban middle income groups, who had benefited from the 'miracle' less than is usually assumed, and who are now affected by recession in a way which they find intolerable. They might prove the real challenge for the continuity of a regime from which they have increasingly withdrawn their support, and the government might find it more difficult to cope with this kind of middle class opposition than it would with the more traditional spontaneous popular unrest.

Ironically, the political crisis brought about by its austerity measures might still give the government some room for manoeuvre. By pushing its unpopular wage policy through Congress, it was able to rally support from PMDB ranks, which increased the internal divisions of that party and helped the more radical PT to improve its score in opinion polls. Instead of uniting the opposition, the political crisis has created a very volatile political situation which will complicate rather than simplify future political developments. The 1984 successful campaign for direct presidential elections is no more evidence of a united opposition than it is a measure of its capacity to control popular dissent in the event of a return to civilian rule.

If it is not easy to predict the likely political consequences of widespread social discontent, it is easier to ascertain that the model of growth and capital accumulation based on export industrialisation has reached a point of crisis which confirms its underlying contradictions: massive State intervention has not produced higher rates of domestic savings and capital accumulation, but it has, on the contrary, accelerated the rate of capital transfers abroad and the takeovers of domestic firms, while increasing the country's public deficit and foreign indebtedness beyond any manageable proportions. The recent IMF support and the possible renewal of some international credit facilities will perhaps reinforce the government's conviction that its policy of continuously trying to expand its foreign debt was right. But such support can only be a temporary remission, since the basic contradictions of the Brazilian model will inevitably continue to operate.

For the other countries of the area, perhaps the main lesson to be learnt from the Brazilian experience is that state-supported export-led industrialisation increases the externality of the process of capital accumulation and causes more problems than it solves, even when it is pursued not as a means to achieve development, but in some sense as a substitute for it.

The implication of this is that, in underdeveloped countries, any general policy which seeks to avoid tackling the real cause of low aggregate domestic demand can only fail to promote sustained growth. This cause is – and has always been – the pattern of gross inequality in the distribution of wealth and income. The problems to which this is related are always bypassed because confronting them is *politically* too difficult; but to hope that these problems will somehow 'solve themselves' in the long run is wishful thinking.

To put it in other words, the Brazilian experience is a modern version of a well established pattern of policy making in Latin America. Indeed, *reformist* policies in the area have always been postponed or quickly abandoned to make room for those policies less likely to affect privileges and to produce a much talked about but also much feared social change. Those who are behind the current policies (including those outside who advise them today to step up the squeeze at home and to export more) might soon regret having for so long ignored the fact that to run away from problems does not solve them; it simply makes them worse.

NOTES

1. See 'The State and capital accumulation in Latin America: a conceptual and historical introduction', pp. 4–7.
2. See Suzigan (1975) p. 437, table 1.
3. Wells (1979) p. 227.
4. See Anglade (1975). See also Chapter 1 of this book, pp. 32–7.
5. See Lewis (1970).
6. Tavares (1972) p. 65 and Singer (1976) p. 44.
7. Connor and Mueller (1977) p. 19.
8. Leff (1968) pp. 42–3.
9. Newfarmer (1979) p. 27, table I.
10. Tavares *et al.* (1964) p. 52, table 38–III.
11. Fishlow (1973), p. 77.
12. Baer and Hervé (1973) p. 271, table 1.
13. Von Doellinger (1976) p. 422, table 1.
14. Baer and Kerstenetzky (1972) p. 113.
15. See Baer and Kerstenetzky (1972) p. 137, table 10.
16. See Baer and Kerstenetzky (1972) p. 138, table 11.
17. On the pre-1964 Brazilian party system, see in particular Campello de Souza (1976).
18. See Nunes Leal (1949). See also the collection of *Revista Brasileira de Estudos Políticos*.
19. See Alcántara de Camargo (1973).
20. See Baer and Kerstenetzky (1972) p. 137, table 10.
21. Fishlow (1973) p. 74.
22. See Fajnzylber (1971).
23. Fishlow (1973) pp. 77–9.
24. Fishlow (1973) p. 80.
25. Bonelli and Werneck (1978) p. 194, table V.9.
26. Bonelli and Façanha (1978) p. 312, note 9.

27. Bonelli and Malan (1976) p. 373.
28. Von Doellinger et al. (1974) p. 77, table V.3.
29. Bonelli and Façanha (1978) p. 317, table VIII.2.
30. Bonelli and Façanha (1978) p. 313, note 11.
31. Von Doellinger (1976) p. 427, table 4.
32. IDB (1979) p. 63, table III.2.
33. IDB (1979) p. 67, table III.4.
34. IDB (1979) p. 65, table III.3.
35. IDB (1979) p. 62, table III.1.
36. See Corrêa do Lago (1980) p. 65, table 2.
37. Unless otherwise stated, all data in this article come from *Banco Central.*
38. Bonelli and Malan (1976) p. 362, table 2.
39. Fishlow (1973) p. 85.
40. Wells (1979) p. 260.
41. See Suzigan (1976) pp. 119–23.
42. The government attitude was split on the significance of unemployment. For some, like Planning Minister Reis Velloso, it would increase worker militancy; for others, like Finance Minister Simonsen, job insecurity would be a further incentive to be quiescent.
43. See Tyler (1981).
44. Wells (1979) p. 250.
45. Bonelli and Malan (1976) p. 379, table 5.
46. Calculated from data in *Conjuntura Econômica* (Indicadores de conjuntura), various issues.
47. Bonelli and Malan (1976) pp. 359–61.
48. See *Conjuntura Econômica* (Indicadores de conjuntura), various issues.
49. See Barros and Graham (1978).
50. Oliveira Alves and Disch (1981) p. 101.
51. This corroborates the findings of Little, Scitovsky and Scott (1970) for the 1960s.
52. See, for example, Newfarmer (1979).
53. LAER (1977) p. 189.
54. LAER (1977) p. 189.
55. See Newfarmer (1979).
56. Financed by the large dollar deposits which followed the restrictions imposed by the US on capital exports in the 1960s (for balance of payments purposes), the London money market was further expanded after 1973 by the huge stocks of petrodollars resulting from OPEC countries' balance of payments surpluses. Operating from London, where all major world commercial banks had set up branches, the eurocurrency market soon came to be the main source of credit for all non-OPEC Third World countries which presented guarantees to the lenders.
57. LAER (1978) p. 382.
58. This is an estimate of the Morgan Guaranty Trust Co. See *World Financial Markets* (1982) p. 5, table 5.
59. Lipson (1981) p. 610.
60. See Suzigan (1976); Baer, Kerstenetzky and Villela (1973).
61. Almeida Magalhães (1979) p. 123, table V.5.
62. See Baer, Kerstenetzky and Villela (1973); Baer, Newfarmer and Trebat (1976); for a critical presentation of the arguments, see Fox (1980).

State and Capital Accumulation: Brazil

63. Baer, Newfarmer and Trebat (1976) p. 84.
64. For specific references, see Chapter 1 of this book, particularly pp. 17–24.
65. See Suzigan (1976); Dain (1977); Bresser Pereira (1977); Cipolla (1980); Mantega and Moraes (1979); Tavares (1980).
66. The apparent desire of the Brazilian government to reduce the inflationary pressures that excess demand put on a supposedly overheated economy in 1974–75 should logically have led to the adoption of a policy of higher prices for the various inputs supplied to private firms by public enterprises. By being passed on to the final consumers, these would have contributed to reduce excess demand while giving public enterprises the benefit of market prices. Instead, the same policy of subsidised prices to manufacturing industry was maintained, making it clear that the priority of government policies was not to accumulate but to make market capitalism work.
67. See Newfarmer (1979) p. 27, table 1.
68. See Newfarmer and Mueller (1975); Connor and Mueller (1977); Bandeira (1975). *Conjuntura econômica* (1976); (1978); (1979); (1980); (1981); *Exame* (1982).
69. See Fajnzylber (1974); Vaitsos (1973); Von Doellinger and Cavalcanti (1979).
70. Von Doellinger (1982), calculated from data in p. 101, table I.
71. Trebat (1980), in particular p. 842.
72. Von Doellinger (1982).
73. IDB (1980–81) p. 78, table III.8.
74. IDB (1980–81) p. 421, table 39.
75. *Latin America Regional Reports – Brazil* (1980) p. 8.
76. Translated from Suzigan (1976) p. 127.
77. Calculated from data in Von Doellinger (1982).
78. IDB (1980–81) p. 75, table III.7 and p. 72, table III.6.
79. See Gasparian (1966); Medina (1970); Bandeira (1975).
80. See Newfarmer (1979); Newfarmer and Mueller (1975); Connor and Mueller (1977).
81. LAER (1978) p. 114.
82. Von Doellinger and Cavalcanti (1979) pp. 94–5.
83. An idea of the level of profits made by foreign firms in that market was given by the business newspaper *Gazeta Mercantil* on the basis of the profits declared in 1977. Most of them, whether 'multinational' or not, had non-operational profits much in excess of their 'declared' operational profits. See *Gazeta Mercantil* (1977).
84. Among the most prominent protagonists of the new policy were the Planning Minister Reis Velloso, the Industry and Trade Minister Severo Gomes, and the President of the National Bank for Development, Pereira Vianna.
85. The leading 'visible' actors of the campaign were monetarist economists like Gudin and Gouveia de Bulhões, and the ex-Finance Ministers Roberto Campos and Delfim Neto.
86. Such as the Matarazzo and Votorantim groups, Paulo Villares, Claudio Bardella, Azevedo Antunes, Helio Beltrão.
87. Diniz and Boschi (1978) p. 134.
88. Wells (1979) p. 246.

89. Corrêa do Lago (1980) p. 65, table 2.
90. See Macedo (1981) p. 61, table 1.
91. At the overvalued official rate, three minimum wages were then equivalent to 246 dollars a month. (About ⅓ less on the 'parallel' market, i.e. approx. 164 dollars).
92. See *Latin America Regional Reports – Brazil* (1980) p. 6.
93. See *Latin America Weekly Report* (1981) p. 4.
94. *World Financial Markets* (1982).
95. The fact that South Korea and the industrialising countries of S. E. Asia manage to export 30–35% of GNP cannot be explained purely in terms of the genuine competitiveness of their exports. Their internal setting might help them to reduce production costs even more than Brazil can do, but their strategic international location also allows them to ignore many 'agreed practices' and get away with it. On the characteristics of the South East Asian model, see Fajnzlber (1981).
96. *Latin America Regional Reports – Brazil* (1982) p. 4.
97. See Suzigan (1976) pp. 126–7; see also Almeida Magalhães (1979).
98. *Latin America Regional Reports – Brazil* (1982a) p. 6.
99. Over 70 per cent in manufacturing industry as a whole and 50 per cent in the capital goods industry, according to *Conjuntura econômica*.
100. LAER (1978) p. 350.
101. *Latin America Regional Reports – Brazil* (1983) p. 7.
102. Buarque de Holanda (1961).
103. Data on domestic savings and on capital formation are not available for Brazil for any year after 1979 in the IDB 1982 report.
104. Data from CACEX reproduced in *Conjuntura econômica* (1983).
105. With inflation running at 95·2 per cent in 1981 and 99·7% in 1982, commercial bank lending rates were at 138% in December 1981 and 166·5% in December 1982. See *World Financial Markets*, statistical appendix, any 1983 issue.
106. Equivalent to 163 dollars at the official exchange rate in April 1983. (In spite of the maxi-devaluation of February, 1983, the cruzeiro continues to be overvalued *vis-à-vis* all major world currencies.)
107. *Latin America Weekly Report* (1982) p. 11.
108. The 'triple alliance' hypothesis was presented by Evans (1979). To be fair, the moderate optimism that he showed in this book concerning the advantages of the 'triple alliance' for Brazil was considerably watered down in a later article. See Gereffi and Evans (1981).
109. Von Doellinger (1983) p. 100.
110. As defined by Decree 399 of 30 Apr. 1938.
111. See Macedo (1981) table 1.
112. The INPC is supposed to reflect the increase in the cost of living for low-income families, who spend nearly half of their income on food. The 'middle classes' who spend only about 30 per cent of their income on food, lose whenever food price rises slow down, while other expenditures, like education and health, on which the 'middle classes' traditionally spend more, continue up.
113. *Latin America Weekly Report* (1983) p. 4.
114. If the INPC continues to fall below inflation at the same rate as it has

done so far in 1983 since it was 'purged', total wage increases will be adjusted up to increasingly underestimated rates of the real changes in the cost of living. As an example of the magnitude of the difference, if we take the last 1983 figures available at the time of writing – which were for September – it means that, by adding the gap between inflation and the INPC (see Table 2.20) to the 13% difference accepted by Congress in October, wage increases that month could only compensate for a maximum of 68·3% of real inflation. Although this will obviously affect all wage earners, it will also make recession worse in view of the way in which wage increases further discriminate against those who earn more than three minimum wages.
115. See *World Financial Markets* (1983).
116. See Tyler (1981).

REFERENCES

Alcántara de Camargo, A. (1973), *Brésil Nord-Est: mouvements paysans et crise populiste*, thèse pour le doctorat du 3° cycle, Paris.
Almeida Magalhães, J. P. (1979), *Modelos alternativos de desenvolvimento* (Rio: Paz e Terra).
Anglade, C. (1975), 'System Adaptation in Latin America in the "Forced" Import Substitution Industrialization Period', *European Journal of Political Research, 3*, pp. 47–67.
Baer, W. and Kerstenetzky, I. (1972), 'The Brazilian Economy', in Roett, R. (ed.), *Brazil in the Sixties* (Nashville: Vanderbilt University Press) pp. 105–45.
Baer, W., Kerstenetzky, I. and Villela, A. (1973), 'The Changing Role of the State in the Brazilian Economy', *World Development*, vol 1, 11, Nov., pp. 23–4.
Baer, W. and Hervé, M. E. (1973), 'Employment and Industrialisation in Developing Countries', in Jolly, R. *et al.* (eds), *Third World Employment* (Harmondsworth: Penguin Books) pp. 269–86.
Baer, W., Newfarmer, R. and Trebat, T. (1976), 'On State Capitalism in Brazil: Some New Issues and Questions', *Inter-American Economic Affairs*, vol. 30, 3, pp. 69–91.
Bandeira, M. (1975), *Cartéis e desnacionalização* (Rio: Civilização Brasileira).
Barros, J. R. and Graham, D. H. (1978), 'A agricultura brasileira e o problema da produção de alimentos', *Pesquisa e planejamento econômico*, vol 8, 3 (Rio) pp. 695–726.
Bonelli, R. and Malan, P. (1976), 'Os limites do possível: notas sobre balanço de pagamentos e indústria nos anos 70', *Pesquisa e planejamento econômico*, vol. 6, 2 (Rio) Aug. pp. 353–406.
Bonelli, R. and Façanha, L. O. (1978), 'A indústria de bens de capital no Brasil: desenvolvimento, problemas e perspectivas', in Suzigan, W. (ed.), *Indústria: política, instituições e desenvolvimento* (Rio: IPEA/INPES) pp. 309–72.
Bonelli, R. and Werneck, D. (1978), 'Desempenho industrial: auge e desaceleração nos anos 70', in Suzigan W. (ed.), *Indústria: política, instituições e desenvolvimento* (Rio: IPEA/INPES) pp. 167–225.

Bresser Pereira, L. C. (1977), *Estado e subdesenvolvimento industrializado* (São Paulo: Brasiliense).
Buarque de Holanda, A. (1961), *Pequeno dicionário brasileiro da língua portuguesa* (Rio: Civilização Brasileira).
Campello de Souza, M. C. (1976), *Estado e partidos políticos no Brasil* (São Paulo: Alfa-Omega).
Cipolla, F. P. (1980), 'Proporções do capitalismo de Estado no Brasil pós-64', *Estudos Cebrap* (São Paulo) 25, pp. 27–65.
Conjuntura Econômica (1976): Sept. (1978): Sept. (1979): Oct. (1980): Oct. (1981): Sept., 'As 500 maiores empresas'.
Conjuntura econômica (1983), 'Indicadores de conjuntura', (Rio), May.
Connor, J. M. and Mueller, W. F. (1977), *Market Power and Profitability of Multinational Corporations in Brazil and Mexico*, Report to the Sub-Committee on Foreign Economic Policy of the Committee on Foreign Relations, United States Senate, Washington.
Corrêa do Lago, L. Aranha (1980), 'Relações trabalhistas e salário real no Brasil', *Conjuntura econômica*, vol. 34, 4, (Rio), April, pp. 62–9.
Dain, S. (1977), 'Empresa estatal e política econômica no Brasil', in Martins, C. E. (ed.), *Estado e capitalismo no Brasil* (São Paulo: Hucitec-Cebrap) pp. 141–65.
Diniz, E. and Boschi, R. (1978), *Empresariado nacional e Estado no Brasil* (Rio: Forense).
Evans, P. (1979), *Dependent Development: the Alliance of Multinational, State and Local Capital in Brazil* (Princeton University Press).
Exame (1982), 'Melhores e maiores', Sept.
Fajnzylber, F. (1971), *Sistema industrial e exportação de manufaturados (Análise da experiencia brasileira)* (Rio: IPEA/INPES).
——(1974), 'La empresa internacional en la industrialización de América Latina', in Serra, J. (ed.), *Desarrollo Latinoamericano. Ensayos críticos*, México, Fondo de Cultura Económica, pp. 122–58.
——(1981), 'Some reflections on South East Asian export industrialisation', *CEPAL Review*, 15, Dec., pp. 111–32.
Fishlow, A. (1973), 'Some Reflections on Post-1964 Brazilian Economic Policy', in Stepan, A. (ed.), *Authoritarian Brazil* (New Haven: Yale University Press) pp. 69–118.
Fox, J. (1980), 'Has Brazil Moved Toward State Capitalism?', *Latin American Perspectives*, Issue 24, Winter, vol. VII, 1, pp. 64–86.
Gasparian, F. (1966), *Em defesa da economia nacional* (Rio: Saga).
Gazeta Mercantil (1977), *Balanço Anual*, Rio.
Gereffi, G. and Evans, P. (1980), 'Transnational Corporations, Dependent Development, and State Policy in the Semi-periphery: a Comparison of Brazil and Mexico', *Latin American Research Review*, vol. XVI, 3, pp. 31–64.
IDB (Inter-American Development Bank) (1979), *Economic and Social Progress in Latin America*, Washington.
IDB (1980–81), ibid.
LAER (1977), *Latin America Economic Report*, London.
——(1978), ibid.
Lafer, C. (1970), *The Planning Process and the Political System in Brazil: a Study of Kubitschek's Target Plan, 1956–1961*. Ph.D. Thesis, Cornell University.

Langoni, C. (1973), *Distribuição da renda e desenvolvimento econômico no Brasil* (Rio: Expressão e Cultura).
Latin America Regional Reports – Brazil (1979), no. 79–01, London, 9 Nov.
—— (1980), no. 80–03, London, 14 Mar.
—— (1980a), no. 80–08, London, 12 Sept.
—— (1982), no. 82–05, London, 28 May.
—— (1982a), no. 82–06, London, 2 July.
—— (1983), no. 83–01, London, 7 Jan.
Latin America Weekly Report (1981), no. 81–17, London, 1 May.
—— (1982), no. 82–30, London, 30 July.
—— (1983), no. 83–17, London, 6 May.
Leff, N. (1968), *Economic Policy-Making and Development in Brazil 1947–1964* (New York: Wiley).
Lewis, W. A. (1970), 'Economic Development with Unlimited Supplies of Labour', in Agarwala and Singh (eds), *The Economics of Underdevelopment* (Oxford University Press) pp. 400–49.
Lipson, C. (1981), 'The International Organisation of Third World Debt', *International Organisation*, vol. 35, 4, pp. 603–31.
Little, I. M. D., Scitovsky, T. and Scott, M. F. G. (1970), *Industry and Trade in some Developing Countries: a comparative study* (Oxford University Press).
Macedo, R. B. M. (1981), 'Minimum Wages and Income Distribution in Brazil', *Luso-Brazilian Review*, vol. 18, 1, pp. 59–75.
Mantega, G. and Moraes, M. (1979), *Acumulação monopolista e crises no Brasil* (Rio: Paz e Terra).
Medina, R. (1970), *Desnacionalização – Crime contra o Brasil* (Rio: Saga).
Newfarmer, R. and Mueller, W. (1975), *Multinational Corporations in Brazil and Mexico: Structural Sources of Economic and Non-economic Power*, Report to the Sub-committee on multinational corporations of the Committee on Foreign Relations, US Senate, Washington.
—— (1979), 'TNC Takeovers in Brazil: The Uneven Distribution of Benefits in the Market for Firms', *World Development*, vol. 7, pp. 25–43.
Nunes Leal, V. (1949), *Coronelismo, enxada e voto* (Rio: Forense).
Oliveira Alves, D. C. and Disch, A. (1981), 'Oil Prices, Agricultural Production and Changes in Real Income in Brazil', *Luso-Brazilian Review*, vol. 18, 1, pp. 77–116.
Singer, P. (1976), *A crise do milagre* (Rio: Paz e Terra).
Suzigan, W. (1975), 'Industrialização e política econômica: uma interpretação em perspectiva histórica', *Pesquisa e planejamento econômico*, vol. 5, no. 2 (Rio) Dec. pp. 433–74.
Suzigan, W. (1976), 'As empresas do governo e o papel do Estado na economia brasileira', in Rezende, F. et al., *Aspectos da participação do governo na economia* (Rio: IPEA/INPES) pp. 77–130.
Tavares, M. C. (1972), *Da substituição de importações ao capitalismo financeiro* (Rio: Zahar).
—— (1980), 'La dinámica cíclica de la industrialización reciente del Brasil', *El Trimestre Económico*, vol. XLVII (1), 185 (México) pp. 3–47.
—— et al. (1964), 'The Growth and Decline of Import Substitution in Brazil', *Economic Bulletin for Latin America*, vol. IX, 1, pp. 1–59.
Tyler, W. G. (1981), 'Advanced Developing Countries as Export Competitors in Third World Markets: the Brazilian Experience' in Center for Strategic

and International Studies (ed.), *World Trade Competition* (New York: Praeger) pp. 331–408.
Trebat, T. (1980), 'Uma avaliação do desempenho econômico de grandes empresas estatais no Brasil', *Pesquisa e planejamento econômico,* vol. 10, 3 (Rio) Dec. pp. 813–49.
Von Doellinger, C. (1976), 'Endividamento e desenvolvimento: algumas lições da história', *Pesquisa e planejamento econômico,* vol. 6, 2 (Rio) Aug. pp. 407–29.
—— (1982), 'Implicações da ação do Estado', *Conjuntura econômica,* (Rio), Oct. pp. 99–105.
—— (1983), 'As disfunções sociais do Estado', *Conjuntura econômica,* (Rio), Apr. pp. 97–103.
—— and Cavalcanti, L. (1979), *Empresas multinacionais na indústria brasileira* (Rio: IPEA/INPES).
—— et. al. (1974), *A politica brasileira de comercio exterior e seus efeitos: 1967/1973* (Rio: IPEA/INPES).
Vaitsos, C. V. (1973), 'Bargaining and the Distribution of Returns in the Purchase of Technology by Developing Countries', in Bernstein, H. (ed.), *Underdevelopment and Development* (Harmondsworth. Penguin Books) pp. 315–22.
Wells, J. (1979), 'Brazil and the post-1973 Crisis in the International Economy', in Thorp and Whitehead (eds), *Inflation and Stabilisation in Latin America* (London: Macmillan) pp. 227–63.
World Financial Markets (1982), Oct.
—— (1983), Sept.

3 The Political Economy of Repressive Monetarism: the State and Capital Accumulation in Post-1973 Chile

CARLOS FORTIN

INTRODUCTION

Chile under the military regime that was installed following the overthrow of the Allende government in September 1973 is an extreme instance of what can be termed the false paradox of the new authoritarian state in Latin America. Paradox in that a politically all-pervasive state which ruthlessly crushed any form of serious dissent purported at the same time to withdraw from the economic sphere in order to allow complete freedom to the individuals as economic agents. False in that, as the more astute analysts of the Chilean experience have observed, the two elements are not only compatible but arguably require each other: political repression might be necessary for the operation of the doctrinaire free market model adopted.[1]

The paradoxes, though, seem to go further. The withdrawal of the state from economic regulation was partial, selective and staggered; it amounted in effect to a major form of intervention, with a profound impact on the pattern of capital accumulation and on the distribution of economic and social power in Chilean society. At the same time, the state retained a substantial degree of control over direct production of goods and services, and transfers from state enterprises became a growing source of revenue for the government.

Thus, despite the anti-state bias of the model implemented, the state in Chile remained a central economic actor under the military regime, even though, to be sure, its role was dramatically redefined both in content and in direction. In what follows I will attempt to review the issues and the evidence concerning that redefinition.[2] The analysis will be organised in terms of the conceptual framework presented in Chapter 1 of this volume. It highlights, on the one hand, the issue of the form of the state, i.e. the composition of the power bloc and the roles the state is called upon to play in capital accumulation (guarantor of the fundamental conditions of accumulation *vis-à-vis* labour; interventor to affect the sharing of the surplus among capitals; accumulator in its own right); and on the other, the question of the form of the regime, and particularly its bases of domination (coercion, ideological appeals, the handing out of 'welfare').

It is suggested that the particular pattern of roles that prevails at any given time is a function of both the context of capital accumulation and the level of social and political conflict associated with it; and that the pattern of roles acts upon, and is affected by, the bases of domination of the regime. The discussion will specifically try to separate the underlying logic linking the redefined role of the state in accumulation in Chile and the main features of the regime, from the extent to which one and the others are the outcome of the concrete vicissitudes of the political struggle within and around the military government.

The next section of the chapter will provide a background to the post-1973 experience by briefly reviewing the changing character of the Chilean state and its involvement in the economy in the last half century; in particular, it will discuss the role of the state in capital accumulation in the period 1964–73, covering the reform government of Christian Democratic President Eduardo Frei and the socialist attempt of the government of President Salvador Allende. The chapter will then concentrate on the developments following the coup of 11 September 1973, and will try to trace the evolution of the political features of the regime and of its economic model, and the links and asynchronies between them. It will explore the question of the social bases of the military project for the restructuring of society and the economy, the contradictions it has generated and the crisis of accumulation to which they have led. It will conclude by proposing an overall interpretation of the meaning of the military attempt and an assessment of its future prospects.

THE STATE AND CAPITAL ACCUMULATION IN CHILE UNTIL THE 1970S

Background: the 'Compromise' State and Accumulation, 1940–64

The year 1938 is a landmark in the contemporary history of Chile. The election of Presidential candidate Pedro Aguirre Cerda signalled the final collapse of the oligarchical state with which Chile had emerged into the 20th century; a state in which, despite its being formally organised as a representative democracy, economic, social and political power was highly concentrated in a relatively small class of landowners linked to banking, commerce, mining and incipiently manufacturing industry. With Aguirre Cerda, supported by a Popular Front coalition composed of the Radical, Socialist and Communist parties, the middle classes and sectors of the working class acceded to state power to implement a programme whose central plank was the need to accelerate the development of the country by means of vigorous state involvement in the promotion of industrialisation.[3]

The quarter of a century or so following the election saw major structural changes in the Chilean economy. Between 1940 and 1945 the share of industry in GDP went up by one-third (Appendix, Table 3.A2). It then continued to rise more slowly reaching over one fourth of GDP in 1965. At the same time the share of agriculture declined from nearly 15% in 1940 to about 10% in 1965, while the share of mining declined between 1940 and 1955, reflecting difficulties in the operation of the US-owned large scale copper industry.

The big increase in the share of industry in GDP was initially a response to the reduction in the availability of imports of consumer non-durables brought about by the war. In addition, however, industrialisation was deliberately promoted through the creation in 1939 of the Chilean Development Corporation (*Corporación de Fomento de la Producción* – CORFO); while its immediate task was organising economic reconstruction following a major earthquake in January of that year, it had a much broader developmental brief in the medium and long term.[4] Through CORFO the state began to play a central role in promoting, financing and even directly undertaking industrial ventures. It is estimated that no less than one-half of total investment in the period 1940–60 was financed with public sector savings, either directly or indirectly.[5]

And yet this process of change was not set in motion by the state of a vigorous and dynamic industrial bourgeoisie, implementing its project for society at the expense of the oligarchy and the workers. It was started by what has been called a 'compromise' state, one that in some sense was responsive to the interests of all politically articulate classes in Chilean society; the only clear exclusion was the peasantry.[6]

In the 1940s the main component of the new groups in charge of the state were the middle sectors of professionals and state white-collar employees that had grown in numbers and influence under the nitrate economy of the turn of the century and who saw in the growth of the state the chance of improving their own relative position in society. Alongside them there was the emerging industrial bourgeoisie, not as yet hegemonic but already a powerful political as well as economic actor; with the growth of industrialisation, this sector would be able to stake an increasingly credible claim to hegemony. The middle sectors were also supported by the workers – the miners and the industrial proletariat – and by the urban masses of relatively recent rural migrants without a definite insertion in the production system. The old landowning class and their financial and commercial allies, who had lost the power to rule the country by themselves and were initially excluded from the group in power, had nevertheless retained their economic and social hold, and remained a major actor in the ruling group and in coalition politics throughout the period. More importantly, they were in effect able to extract from the group in power the tacit commitment that industrialisation would not be carried out through interference with the structure of power and property in the countryside.[7]

This was, therefore, a transitional state. Between 1938 and 1952 the middle sectors in charge of the state apparatus oscillated between their working class and their bourgeois allies, the latter increasingly including sectors of the old oligarchy. As industrialisation proceeded, so did the recomposition of a new power bloc under the emerging hegemony of the industrial bourgeoisie; the trend was towards the exclusion of the working class parties from government and generally from political power. This culminated in 1948 when the government of radical President González Videla, elected with Communist support and which initially had Communist ministers, passed legislation outlawing the Communist Party. A populist interlude at the beginning of the government of Carlos Ibáñez (1952–58) was reversed in 1955 when policies of fiscal austerity and demand contraction were implemented; in its last year, the Ibáñez government moved again to the left, re-legalising the Communist Party, enacting legislation to eliminate electoral malpractices and reflating the economy. The government of Jorge Alessandri (1958–64) expressed the recomposition of the power bloc with all fractions of the dominant class – including the old landowning oligarchy – under the hegemony of the industrial bourgeoisie. By now, US capital in control of the copper industry was also firmly established as an important component of the power bloc; copper at that time was providing some 70% of the total export revenue of the country. The Alessandri government attempted a partial departure from the model of state-led industrialisation and a devolution of initiative to private enterprise.

The main contradiction of the 'compromise' state was the need to expand the resources available for investment for industrial growth while at the same time having to maintain the appearance that no major social group was paying for that expansion in a systematic manner. The way out of the contradiction was inflationary expansion of government borrowing (Appendix, Table 3.A5). This was supplemented at points with increased taxation of the copper industry and with external borrowing. The former was important in the 1940s and early 1950s, and again in the 1962–64 period; the latter was particularly important in the Alessandri administration generally (Appendix, Table 3.A6). The result, however, was a less than vigorous level of growth of total output, in turn due to low levels of accumulation (Appendix, Tables 3.A4 and 3.A1). By the mid-1960s the economy had effectively stagnated, as the easy phase of import substitution had been exhausted. At the same time, social and political unrest was growing. Salvador Allende, who had been very narrowly defeated by Alessandri in 1958, was again the candidate of Socialists and Communists in 1964. When the dominant sectors realised that he would be able to defeat the government-backed right wing candidate, they decided to throw their support in favour of the Christian Democratic candidate, Eduardo Frei, who promised reforms within a socially progressive neo-capitalist model. Frei was elected President in September 1964 and took office in November of that year.

The Reformist Model of Accumulation, 1964–70

The Frei government was elected on a programme aimed at both renewing the stimulus to import-substituting industrialisation and at expanding exports. The former was to be done by means of attracting foreign capital and increasing state intervention for the provision of infrastructure and for direct production; the latter, by means of an investment programme in the large scale copper sector, involving joint ventures with the US companies that controlled it. At the same time, the government promised to modernise the agrarian structure and the countryside, to redistribute income and to mobilise hitherto excluded sectors of the population, notably the peasants and the slum dwellers. The project followed closely the approach of the Alliance for Progress, and the Frei government received massive inflows of Alliance for Progress funds.[8]

In terms of the conceptual framework proposed in the Introductory chapter, the regime within which this attempt was made was one in which compliance from the popular sectors was secured not so much by coercion – though there were a few serious incidents of repression of workers – as by the legitimacy provided by the democratic ideology later supplemented by the ruling party's vigorous efforts at ideological mobilisation around notions derived from the social doctrine of the Catholic Church; and by a fair amount of 'welfare' handed out by the state. The role of the state in accumulation was conceived as 'interventionist' in favour of industrial capital, whether national or foreign, but with a non-negligible component of state accumulation, mostly in the form of joint ventures with foreign capital; in addition to copper mining, these were introduced in the petrochemical industry and others. Again, although the state did play, when necessary, the role of ultimate resort to secure workers' compliance with the basic conditions for private accumulation to take place, it was not in the nature of the model for the state to guarantee an increase in the absolute exploitation of labour.

In terms of its social bases, the central difference between the Christian Democratic attempt and the preceding situation was the extent to which, for the first time, the landowning sectors' interests were negatively affected. The agrarian reform introduced by Frei – although criticised by the left as insufficient and timid – and the concomitant mobilisation of the peasantry represented a shift in power and influence against the traditional agrarian dominant sectors, and as such were fiercely resisted by them. The share of income accruing to labour in agriculture, which in 1960–64 averaged 39·5% – as opposed to 49·2% in all sectors – went up to 42·6% in 1965–70; while not a spectacular increase, this was significantly more than the increase in the share of labour in manufacturing industry, which went up from 39·6% in 1960–64 to 40·3% in 1965–70.[9] At the end of the Frei government the agricultural workers were getting a considerably higher share of agricultural income than the workers in manufacturing industry were getting of manufacturing income. This affected the level of accumulation in agriculture; although no complete figures are available, figures for 1963–66 – the last two years of the Alessandri government and the first two of the Frei government – show that in the latter the share of agricultural investment over total investment went down from 17·8% to 15·9%, while the share of industrial investment went up from 13·8% to 17·6%.[10]

The model, however, had built in contradictions that conspired against a firm and sustained resumption of capital accumulation. The populist and redistributive element in the model prevented any significant increase in the share of the surplus accruing to capital as a whole. In fact, the overall share of labour shows a gradual increase from the historic low reached in the last year of the Alessandri administration (Appendix, Table 3.A3).

Thus, capital accumulation by private local capital did not grow from its own resources and the state had to step in both through direct investment and through transfers to the private sector via credit or capital transfers (indirect public investment which reached three quarters of total investment, as shown in Table 3.1).

The second factor making up for the insufficiency of private local capital accumulation was foreign investment. Although no detailed figures are available, Table 3.2 conveys an idea of the way in which this, together with the preceding factor, altered the composition of the ownership of Chilean industry in the period.

TABLE 3.1 *Chile: public investment in fixed capital, 1961–69*

	A	B	C	D
1961	39.0	7.6	46.6	12.5
1962	50.7	9.9	60.6	20.0
1963	43.9	7.2	51.1	12.8
1964	47.4	6.5	53.9	12.4
1965	50.4	10.5	60.9	21.2
1966	55.0	10.0	65.0	22.1
1967	50.7	18.5	69.2	37.5
1968	50.2	22.4	72.6	45.0
1969	49.3	25.5	74.8	50.3

A = direct public investment as percentage of gross domestic investment in fixed capital.
B = indirect public investment as a percentage of gross domestic investment in fixed capital.
C = A + B.
D = indirect public investment as percentage of total private investment.
SOURCE original data in ODEPLAN (1973) pp. 20 and 144–8.

TABLE 3.2 *Chile: distribution of the equity of industrial stock companies by type of shareholders, 1967–69*

	1967 (%)	1968 (%)	1969 (%)
Foreign shareholders	16.5	16.8	20.3
National shareholders	76.1	70.2	63.0
State	7.4	13.0	16.7

SOURCE Bitar (1973) p. 246.

Overall, however, the level of capital accumulation in the economy remained insufficient, being barely able to cope with the replacement and maintenance of plant and equipment and with the growing population. This is reflected in the modest rate of growth of the economy during the period, as shown in the Appendix, Table 3.A4.

Concomitant with this process of economic stagnation there developed a rapid process of social and political mobilisation, partly deliberately induced by the government in order to expand its basis of popular support, partly led by the left wing parties. The number of voters in presidential and congressional elections as a proportion of the number of eligible voters went up from 42·9% in 1961 to 75·9% in 1970, representing 17% and 30% of the total population respectively (the actual number of voters in 1970 was 2·9 million).[11] There was also a large increase in trade union membership. In industrial unions, membership as a percentage of the total labour force rose from 14·3% in 1960 to 19·4% in 1970. Peasant unions, introduced for the first time in 1967, reached 137 000 members in 476 organisations by 1970.[12] The percentage of the vote received by the Socialist and Communist parties in congressional elections went up from 10·7% in 1957 to 31·7% in 1969.[13]

The combination of the failure to generate and sustain an adequate rate of capital accumulation and the process of rapid mobilisation of popular sectors created contradictions that the model was not capable of withstanding. In the presidential election of 1970 the government-backed candidate ended in third place in a three-way race, with 28·1% of the vote. The election was won by Salvador Allende who, supported by a coalition of the Socialist, Communist and Radical parties plus three smaller groupings (the *Unidad Popular* coalition) received 36·6% of the vote against 35·2% polled by the right-wing candidate. Despite an attempt by the CIA to prevent Allende from taking office, which culminated in a failed military coup in October, Allende was inaugurated President of Chile in November 1970.[14]

The Socialist Model of Accumulation, 1971–73

The basic feature of the programme of the Allende government was the constitution of a vastly expanded sector of state ownership that would control the most dynamic parts of the economy.[15] The state would, in the short and medium term, become the prime motor of capital accumulation, although some sectors of the economy were excluded from the start from the nationalisation process and private capital was encouraged to expand there.

This central strategy was accompanied by redistribution of income in favour of the poor, thus in effect producing a transfer of surplus from capital to labour. This was to increase aggregate demand and therefore the mass of profits, as distinct from the rate of profit. Other elements of the programme included the completion of the agrarian reform begun by Frei and the nationalisation of the large scale mining sector. A crucial element of the experiment was that it was to be conducted within the legal and institutional framework of representative democracy; this meant dealing with a Congress elected in 1969 where the opposition parties held a majority of the seats in both Chambers. Approval in both was necessary for any new legislation, but the President, through his veto power, could block any legislation not supported by two-thirds of the members of both Chambers.

As a result of the government policies, the percentage of the domestic income corresponding to payments to labour went up dramatically in 1971 and further in 1972 (Appendix, Table 3.A3). The corresponding increase in aggregate demand triggered an increase in the use of industrial productive capacity; industrial output in 1971 grew rapidly and unemployment reached a historic low.

At the same time, the establishment of what was called the 'area of social ownership' proceeded apace during the first year of government. This was done through expropriations, through purchase of shares – particularly important in the banking sector – and through a legal procedure known as 'intervention', dating from a short-lived attempt at setting up a Socialist Republic in 1932 and which had never been struck off the statutes book. It allowed the government to take over the running of a private concern if the latter was essential for the economy and was undergoing difficulties preventing its normal operation, such as protracted strikes. The government interventor then ran the concern on behalf of the owners.

The US controlled large copper mines – which produced about 60% of the total export revenue of the country – were nationalised in July 1971 and by the end of the year the state had acquired a controlling interest in, or had 'intervened', 15 out of a total of 21 private banks.

In the industrial sector, the government target was the nationalisation of 76 companies; together with those already owned or controlled by the state, they would account for about 44% of total manufacturing industrial sales. The total number of companies to be put under state control was about 130 out of 30 500 existing industrial establishments.

In fact the expansion of the state industrial sector took place in ways very different from those envisaged, as indicated in Table 3.3. The continued expansion in the number of state controlled enterprises during the second half of 1972 was not accompanied by any significant increase in the economic importance of the state sector in terms of

TABLE 3.3 *Chile: state control over industrial enterprises, 1970–72*

	December 1970	June 1972	December 1972
Number of enterprises controlled by the state	45	140	202
% achievement of target of 76 enterprises			67
% of total manufacturing sales accounted for state-controlled enterprises	12.6	29.7	31.9
% achievement of target of control over sales			73

SOURCE Martínez (1979) pp. 265–9.

sales. The reason is that by that time the economic strategy of the government, which was based on the establishment of a sufficiently large and coherent state controlled area, was running into serious political difficulties. The Christian Democratic party had joined forces with the right-wing parties in Congress to block the government plans for the expansion of the public sector. As a result, 25 out of 76 enterprises that the government regarded as fundamental for a viable state controlled sector remained outside the nationalised area at the end of 1972. Conversely, a large number of economically unimportant enterprises had been taken over because of pressure from the workers, particularly after the 'bosses strike' of October 1972, when many business concerns were closed down in an attempt to paralyse the economy and were subsequently taken over and reopened by the workers. These additions only compounded the management and planning problems faced by the government; on the other hand the government could hardly refuse the workers' demands to take over these enterprises since in many cases they had been abandoned and the workers were running them in a show of political support for the government.

The problem with the nationalisation policy of the Allende government was not, therefore, that it was either too fast or too slow, as the debate between the right wing and the left wing critics of the *Unidad Popular* could misleadingly suggest. It was that, through a combination of factors, the government found itself in charge of a state industrial sector that was too large in terms of number of enterprises and too small in terms of economic importance.

Lacking in sufficient size and coherence, and plagued by management difficulties, the state controlled sector of the economy did not fulfil its task of capturing surpluses from the private sector and directing them to capital accumulation. Through control over strategic sectors of industry, private capital was in a position to channel surpluses to itself and away from the state enterprises. This was made possible by the government policy of freezing prices of state companies, again dictated by both economic design and political necessity. The public sector developed a large deficit (Table 3.4) and the combined forces of opposition in Congress denied the government the legal instruments to raise the needed additional revenue. Table 3.4 further shows that the group of companies nationalised by Allende did not in

TABLE 3.4 *Chile: financial deficit of state enterprises, 1971–73 (as percentages of gross domestic product)*

	1971	1972	1973
Enterprises owned by the state prior to 1970	4.3	5.4	8.4
Total state enterprises	*	4.7	6.2

* No data available.

SOURCE Martínez (1979) p. 270.

fact have a deficit; on the contrary, they contributed to reducing the deficit of the pre-existing traditional state sector, that producing electricity, fuels and other generalised inputs whose prices were kept particularly low. However, the capacity of the public sector as a whole to accumulate was very small.

Private capital, on the other hand, enjoyed relatively higher prices as it concentrated in the area of consumer goods, and was furthermore able to manipulate the distribution system, which was not nationalised. A black market developed in 1972 with much higher prices than the official ones. State enterprises increasingly began to serve as channels through which surplus was in effect directed towards private capital.

Capital accumulation, however, did not follow. Private capitalists, both local and international, were too fearful of the project of the coalition in power to decide to plough back their increased revenue into investment. On the contrary, as the mobilisation of the popular sectors and the polarisation of the political system intensified, business began to join in increasing numbers the activities of the militant anti-government groups – supported and financed by the CIA – whose purpose was not to influence policy but to overthrow the government. Hoarding and sabotage of production became major problems, and were later coordinated into national lock-outs and employers' strikes.

Gross domestic investment dropped in 1971 to 13·9% of GDP and in 1972 to 11·8% (Appendix, Table 3.A1). Production levels also declined in 1972 and particularly in 1973, although the negative figure shown in the Appendix, Table 3.A4 (as well as the high unemployment figure) reflect more the drastic depressive effects of the convulsed period immediately preceding the coup of September 1973 and of the economic policies introduced by the military than the situation in the first half of the year. Nevertheless the trend was to a decline of output, as unused capacity was exhausted and as balance of payment pressures intensified; the latter was due to low prices of copper, the increased need for agricultural imports to satisfy the expanded demand, and the drying up of foreign finance. While elements of economic mismanagement were present, the root of the economic difficulties faced by the model lay in the political conflict surrounding the government's project; those difficulties, in turn, complicated the political position of the government as they eroded support among the middle sectors and lent some credence to opposition claims that a breakdown of society was in fact taking place.

At that stage a rescuing of the model of state-led accumulation could only have proceeded through a political consolidation of the government, that could allow it to overcome the obstacles put by Congress in the path of state control over the economy, as well as to rationalise the existing state sector through devolution of all economically unimportant companies. The government made an attempt at such consolidation following the Congressional elections of March 1973, in which the government parties increased their share of the vote to 42·1% as compared to the 36·6% of the Presidential election of September 1970. It invited the main opposition party, the Christian Democrats, to talks aimed at finding some common ground to put an end to the growing economic and political crisis. The talks failed to produce agreement, and the government at that point concentrated on stepping up the mobilisation of popular sectors with a view to discouraging the groups within the armed forces that favoured a military coup. By the middle of 1973 the international price of copper was rising, and the government felt that if it could hold out until the higher prices produced an easing of the economic situation, it had a fighting chance of obtaining a clear mandate from the people to go ahead with its socialist programme – through a plebiscite, as envisaged by the constitution – and of proceeding to introduce new dynamism to the socialist model of accumulation. It may well be that such a perception was shared by the pro-coup elements among the military, who preferred to act rather than accept Allende's proposal to resolve the impasse by means of a plebiscite.[16]

The Allende experiment was an attempt at transforming the nature of the accumulation process in Chile through allocating the role of dynamic agent of accumulation to the state. This also entailed a considerable element of 'interventionism' in the more traditional sense in so far as the model contemplated the subsistence of a sector of private ownership of industry and commerce that was to be more tightly regulated. The regime within which the attempt took place was one in which the element of coercion remained marginal, although as polarisation intensified in 1972–73 violence from extremist groups of both right and left increased. In the last months before the coup the armed forces, by then operating largely outside the control of the government, started to apply increasing amounts of coercion against the workers under the pretext of controlling the spread of firearms and weapons among the civilian population. In the ideological front, the government tried to shift the basis of consensus by emphasising the egalitarian elements of the common democratic ideology. This was successful in consolidating support for the government among the working class and in attracting some sectors of the middle class to the notion of a socialist path of development. In fact, the main opposition party, the Christian Democrats, were also programmatically commited to a 'non-capitalist' path, and their rank and file were initially responsive to the government's orientation. However, as socialisation proceeded and with it the intensification of class and political conflict, the right wing opposition succeeded in raising the question of liberty and economic freedom to a central place in the ideological debate. Consensus on a common democratic ideology broke down and the regime became increasingly inoperative, with the government unable to implement its model through legal means and the opposition unable legally to overthrow the government. The vastly increased 'welfare' activity of the state – which resulted, for instance, in 1972 having the lowest recorded level of infant mortality in Chilean history – was not enough to make up for the loss of ideological legitimacy of the regime. The government, furthermore, was unwilling and unable to raise the level of coercion so as to restore effectiveness; this would have been tantamount in fact to a fundamental change in the regime.

ACCUMULATION AND THE MILITARY REGIME: OVERVIEW AND PERIODISATION

The military coup of September 1973 and its aftermath represent a fundamental break in the economic, social and political development of Chile. They introduce what is in fact a new form of state, as distinct from a change in regime. The broad features of this new form of state, of its presence in the economic process and of its accompanying political regime are by now well known. Immediately after the coup the new military rulers closed down Congress, banned political parties and the national trade union organisation, destroyed the national register of voters, introduced press censorship, eliminated freedom of assembly and association and imposed a 'state of internal war' which served as justification for the elimination, imprisonment and torture of thousands of political opponents. While some of the worst excesses of the first period were later mitigated, the basic features of a police state remained throughout.

In the economic front, the junta adopted an extreme free-market model whose central objective was the restoration of a 'normal' equilibrium in the economy in order to allow the forces of the market to make optimal allocations of resources. In this view the normal equilibrium is upset by state intervention in the sphere of prices and wages, of tariff protection, of discriminatory taxation, of subsidies to industry and of artificial rates of exchange, as well as by the state's direct participation in production. This on the one hand leads to inefficiency in the operation of the eonomy – competition is not allowed to eliminate the inefficient operators – and on the other expresses itself in an inordinate expansion of the supply of money, leading to inflation and to further distortions of efficient resource allocations. Employment and a given level of economic activity are maintained only by sacrificing efficiency and productivity. The policy, therefore, was dominated by the notion of eliminating state intervention in the economy and allowing the free operation of market forces both internally and in relation to the world's economy.

The preceding describes the overall features of the political and the economic models introduced by the military. In both fronts, however, there were developments and changes during the decade of military rule. Thus the implementation of the economic model exhibits distinguishable stages, which correspond to the varying and successive demands of the management of the economy and the relative strength of the diverse groups and interests influencing policy – including, of course, the perceptions of the new military rulers themselves.

The political model also went through stages, albeit somewhat less clearly identifiable than the economic ones. The two periodisations, though, do not coincide; there is a time lag between the introduction of changes in the implementation of the economic model and the move from one political stage to the next. The interaction between the two processes, their partial overlap and their asynchrony provide an important clue into the dynamics of the political economy of the military regime.

The Stages of Economic Policy

The economic policy of the Chilean military regime went through three stages,[17] leading to the crisis of the model in the second half of 1982:

Liberalisation with Contraction of Demand (September 1973–June 1976)

The central stated objective of economic policy was monetary stabilisation and the elimination of inflation; the main thrust of the measures adopted was directed towards 'freeing the economy from state intervention'. Price controls were eliminated, public expenditure was reduced, state productive activities were privatised. Measures were introduced to stimulate the emergence of a private capital market. Also, the process of opening up the economy to the rest of the world began, including devaluation and tariff reductions.

The freeing of prices was introduced very quickly during September and October 1973, leading to a staggering rate of inflation of 128·5% in the last quarter of 1973 and to a rate of 605·9% for the whole year. Subsequently, the rate decreased, but at a much slower pace than was anticipated: the rate for 1974 was 369·2%, and the rate for the first quarter of 1975, 46·5%. It was at this point, in April 1975, that the government abandoned the somewhat more gradualistic approach followed until then and adopted the so-called 'shock treatment', involving a drastic contraction of demand and of public expenditure, and precipitating the deepest recession known in recent times in the country (see Appendix, Table 3.A4). Until then there had been a conflict within the government between the orthodox monetarist approach proposed by the Chicago-trained economists operating as advisers in the Ministries of Finance and the Economy, and the more gradualist approach favoured by members of the government linked to industrial capital, such as Minister of the Economy Fernando Léniz. With the decision to embark in the 'shock treatment', the conflict was clearly resolved in favour of the orthodox technocrats; their alliance with Pinochet and the military elite was to define not only the economic but the overall approach of the government until the crisis. Why this should have been the case and how it relates to the question of the class nature of the state are points to which I shall come back below.

The shock treatment, however, still failed to produce a major impact on inflation, which reached 343·3% in 1975 and 89·3% in the first half of 1976, anticipating a rate for the year of 265%. At the same time, the depth and the duration of the recession seemingly exceeded the expectations of the economic policy makers. The result was a change in policy; in June 1976 the government announced the end of the shock treatment and a Programme of Economic Recovery. In effect, the central policy change had to do with the exchange rate, but it was to have profound impact in the economy as a whole.

Opening of the economy with partial recovery (June 1976–June 1979)

This stage was dominated by the management of the external sector.

Control of inflation and monetary stabilisation remained the central objectives in the official discourse, but they were pursued through an intensification of the process of elimination of tariffs and by an initial revaluation of the currency, followed by controlled devaluations. The way the opening proceeded was, in fact, as much an outcome of decisions concerning the internal rate of inflation as an opening *per se*. Still, it basically reflected the solution adopted by the dominant sectors to the issue of the management of dependence.

In the preceding period reductions in tariffs were compensated by devaluations to produce a more or less stable real exchange rate for imports. At the beginning of the second stage with the average nominal tariff still going down the government proceeded to revalue the Chilean peso against the dollar in July 1976; a further revaluation took place in March 1977, while small devaluations took place in-between and subsequently. The reason for the revaluation was the fact that the anti-inflationary policy based on reduction of public expenditure and control over the internal supply of money was not producing the desired effect; as indicated above, the rate of inflation was in fact going up in the first half of 1976. It was then assumed that a revaluation of the peso by reducing both inflationary expectations and the cost of imported goods, would reduce effective inflation. In the event the prediction proved basically correct; inflation for the second half of 1976 was about 60%; for 1977 it was 84·2; for 1978, 37·2 and for the first half of 1979, 15%.

The net result of this change, however, was an abrupt revaluation of the real exchange rate for imports, with the latter becoming increasingly cheaper as compared to domestic products; the import bill, particularly for items of luxurious consumption, began to rise at an accelerated pace. A deficit in current account ensued, which was covered by the inflow of short-term capital. The result was a fast growing foreign debt; the net external debt in dollars of each year went up by nearly 30% between 1976 and 1979. The inflow of foreign loan capital, in turn, became the fundamental factor influencing the money supply: in 1977 foreign exchange operations represented 52% of the additional money supply generated in the year; in 1978 they exceeded 100% (i.e. all internal sources of money supply contracted). At the same time, however, the economy began experiencing some recovery: GDP grew at an annual average rate of 8·8% in 1977–79. Given the large fall in 1975, this represented no more than a recovery of the levels preceding the 1973 coup; in fact, in 1979 GDP per capita was only 95·5% of that of 1971 (Appendix, Table 3.A4). Nevertheless, the figures were greeted with enthusiasm by government propagandists and by monetarist sympathisers the world over. The international financial press began to refer to the 'Chilean economic miracle'.

Integration in the world economy with emerging contradictions (June 1979–June 1982)

By the end of the preceding stage, the economy was almost fully opened to the rest of the world (the maximum tariff was 10%), the intervention of the state was said to be minimised, inflation was significantly reduced and there were signs of economic recovery. At this point the economic policy of the government abandoned the closed economy monetary approach followed until then, whereby the inflation is assumed to be a function of the internal money supply, and adopted the so-called monetary approach to the balance of payments.[18] This maintains that in an open economy variations in internal inflation are a function of variations in international inflation and variations in the exchange rate; with a fixed exchange rate, internal inflation should equal international inflation. Thus, the third period was marked by a significant devaluation, that took place in June 1979, and the subsequent establishment of a fixed rate of exchange *vis-à-vis* the dollar. Internal inflation indeed began to approximate international inflation, but there was no equalisation in the short run; internal inflation remained considerably higher than international inflation until the end of 1980. This was tantamount to a revaluation of the peso and a further reduction in the real rate of exchange for imports. Industry, which in the preceding period had benefited both from the revitalisation of demand induced by increases in real wages and by measures aimed at export promotion, began to fall again into deep recession. The index of industrial production first stagnated and then began to decline; the index of production for industries oriented towards the internal market dropped as early as 1980, the construction industry being particularly affected. The debt of industry with the banks grew, foreign indebtedness continued to mount and the willingness of international capital to bail out the model began to appear doubtful. The government then took – in June 1982 – the step it had consistently denied until then it would ever take: it devalued the peso by over 70% in 5 months. The crisis was by then officially acknowledged.

The Stages of the Political Regime

From a political viewpoint, it is also possible to distinguish three stages [19] followed, again, by a political crisis towards the end of 1982:

Stage of Unregulated Military Dictatorship (September 1973–July 1977)

The point has already been made that the paramount feature of the Chilean political regime in the period immediately following the 1973 coup was the abolition of all forms of democratic processes as well as of civil, political and human rights, and the concentration of total, unregulated power in the military rulers. Initially, the four-man junta that deposed Allende took over the executive as well as the legislative power, with the judiciary placed in a subordinate position. Soon after the coup, though, a process of personalisation of power around Pinochet began to take place, leading to his being made Head of State and then President of the Republic in June 1974; the junta at that point assumed the role of legislative power while executive power was vested in Pinochet.

The political parties of the left were dissolved and banned, and their assets were confiscated. The Christian Democratic and the National (right-wing) parties were declared 'in recess', and their activities forbidden; the latter disbanded voluntarily claiming that its ultimate political goal had been achieved with the installation of the military government. Thus, the historic forms of political mediation between civil society and the state in Chile were eliminated by the military; no other forms of organised mediation were set up instead.

Above all, this stage was characterised by physical repression. This was at first massive and uncoordinated, carried out by the security services of the various branches of the armed forces and the police. Later, it began to be replaced with a centralised, technically more advanced and more selective – though no less brutal – approach. The turning point was the creation in June 1974 of the National Intelligence Directorate (DINA), directly under the authority of Pinochet and which started to take over all repressive activities. DINA was also involved in the assassination or attempted assassination of major political opponents of Pinochet living in exile: General Carlos Prats, former Commander in Chief of the Army under Allende, murdered in Buenos Aires in September 1974; former Christian Democratic Vice-President of Chile Bernardo Leighton, who narrowly survived an assassination attempt in Rome in September 1975; and Allende's former Foreign Minister, Orlando Letelier, killed in Washington in September 1976.[20] The operation of DINA, which was outside any form of legal or other control, became the most visible expression of the arbitrary nature of the political regime imposed by the military at this stage.

Stage of Redefinition of the Political Regime (July 1977–March 1981)

Towards the middle of 1976 there was an attempt at institutionalising the form of military rule that existed until then, i.e. indefinite in time and fundamentally unregulated in scope and procedures. This attempt went as far as the issuing of a series of Constitutional Acts in September 1976. It reflected the view of the hard-liners within the government – a sector of the Army and some quasi-Fascist civilian groups – who were able to convince Pinochet that the form of regime as it existed was necessary not only to safeguard the political order but also to continue with the implementation of the economic model. The link between the harsh policies towards labour and the disciplining of local capital involved in the initial period of the economic policies and the repressive authoritarianism of the first stage of the political regime was not lost to them. The attempt failed basically because of external pressures, including those from the US government under Carter, which reinforced the position of the soft liners within and around the government. The result was the abandonment of the attempt at institutionalising the existing situation and a statement by Pinochet that the regime was approaching a stage of institutionalisation leading to a 'protected democracy'. This was the so-called Chacarillas speech of September 1977, named after the town where it was made. It was immediately denounced as meaningless by the opposition because of the absence of timetables. It did, however, open a period of more or less public debate among the groups supporting the government on what was to be institutionalised. The government set up a Constitutional Commission to prepare a draft of a new Constitution. This was completed in September 1978, but the debate continued and it was only in mid-1980 that a final draft was produced and a plebiscite called to approve it. It was duly approved – amid cries of fraud and manipulation from the opposition – and it came into force in March 1981.

It is important to specify the precise meaning of the position of the 'soft-liners'. It did not represent a revolt of the liberal wing of the bourgeoisie against the excesses of the military government. The soft-liners did not question the fundamental features of the regime nor the personalisation of power in Pinochet. They primarily wanted to pacify international opinion by offering some limitations to military power and some form of timetable for the reintroduction of – highly restricted – democratic procedures. This was in line with their general ideological preferences and further promised a more formalised role for themselves in decision-making. As repression had already taken a heavy toll in the opposition, they felt it could be relaxed. But none of those motivations were strong enough at that time to lead the more liberal oriented bourgeoisie into anything remotely resembling a challenge to the bases of the regime.

While the Chacarillas speech opened, as suggested, the undefined possibility of a transition to some form of restoration of democracy, it was however preceded by two moves that catered to the position of the hard-liners: the Christian Democratic party was dissolved – as the left parties had been in 1973 – and strict provisions for press censorship were introduced. Conversely, in what was perhaps the most significant development in this period, the National Intelligence Directorate was replaced by a Central Intelligence Agency supposed to be more accountable; the move was aimed at placating criticism of DINA's excesses in the international press. Repression of the opposition remained high, but some of its more extreme forms were phased out; the activities of the opposition groups – trade unions, left parties and increasingly the Christian Democratic party – became somewhat more visible and vocal.

Stage of Attempted Institutionalisation (March 1981–Late-1982)

The Constitution enacted in March 1981 steered something of a middle course between the hard line and the soft line described above. This, of course, was not very difficult since the two positions were not fundamentally different. It essentially retained paramount power in the hands of Pinochet, who was confirmed as President for a further 8 years. Temporary Article No. 24 allowed the President to suspend constitutional guarantees, including the right of habeas corpus, whenever he deems public order or internal peace are threatened. No provision was made for the election of representative political bodies during the first 8 years of operation of the Constitution; the Junta remained the Constituent and Legislative power. A timetable was introduced for a return to more democratic arrangements: a bicameral Congress is to be elected in 1989, and a relegalisation of political parties is envisaged. However, the election of President after Pinochet's term of 8 years was vested in the Junta, subject to confirmation by plebiscite; Pinochet can be nominated for a further period of 8 years. Throughout, the Constitution reflected an authoritarian view of society and the state in the political realm and a free market view in the economic realm.

Simultaneously with this process of political institutionalisation the government embarked in what has been described as a process of social institutionalisation through the so-called 'seven modernisations'. These were structural changes in various areas of social life primarily with a view to introducing a market principle of operation. Thus, education, health, social security should be privatised, and all of them as well as labour relations – as will be discussed below – should operate under market rules. The purpose was to fragment and atomise social life, making all forms of social relations an individualistic affair and discouraging collective forms of social behaviour. Together, the political and the social institutionalisation processes aimed at generating a form of legitimacy for the regime that would allow a reduction in the need for coercion. However, as the economic situation deteriorated, social and political unrest intensified. By mid-1983 the situation was one of open confrontation between the government and a growing opposition, and of overt political crisis of the regime.

I shall now attempt a more detailed discussion of the role and characteristics of the state in the various stages of the implementation of the economic model and the overlapping political stages in terms of the two sets of distinctions contained in the framework proposed in the Introductory chapter.

THE ECONOMIC ROLE OF THE STATE IN CHILE UNDER THE MILITARY

The State and Labour: the Role of Guarantor

The first task of the state in a capitalist society is to guarantee the conditions for the extraction of surplus value, i.e. for the continuing subordination of labour. This, as already suggested, is a contradictory task; it entails primarily the disciplining and, if necessary, the repression of the workers but might also require the provision of welfare to facilitate the reproduction of the labour force as well as some protection of the workers against excessive exploitation that could destroy the supply of labour. In the first stage, the policy of the Chilean military government towards labour was dominated by the repressive element.[21] The national peak trade union organisation (*Central Unica de Trabajadores*) was dissolved and banned, and many union leaders were persecuted, imprisoned, exiled, and in a number of cases, tortured and killed. While unions at the factory and sector level were allowed to remain in existence, their activities were drastically curtailed, and they were forbidden to elect their officers; any replacements were to be made by the government. By contrast, the organised interest groups of capital were allowed to renew their leadership through elections.[22] A brief attempt by Nicanor Díaz Estrada, an Air Force General occupying the Labour Ministry in 1975 to develop a more populist approach was quickly stopped by the hard-liners who felt that demobilisation of the workers was a first priority. The repression of the workers and their organisation made it possible to effect a dramatic reduction in their standards of living.

The repression continued during the second period of the economic policy of the government, but some of the harshest features of the economic exploitation of the workers began to be relaxed. In the third period the main feature of the labour policy of the state was the introduction of a legal regime governing collective bargaining. This happened in June 1979, slightly preceding the announcement that, the government having consolidated the economic position, it was to launch processes of modernisation of seven areas of social, economic and political life: labour policy, social security, education, health, regional decentralisation, agriculture and the judiciary. The implications of this announcement in terms of ideological discourse will be discussed below. The Labour Plan (*Plan Laboral*) accepted the existence of trade unions and allowed them a role in collective bargaining. A major factor explaining this was the level of international pressure on the Chilean government for some relaxation in the tight control over the workers, as articulated by the AFL-CIO of the United States and the Carter Administration. In addition, the new legislation guaranteed a minimum level of wage rises, as it linked them to the level of inflation in the preceding year. On the other hand, it encouraged the organisation of several trade unions in a given enterprise, as well as competition among them. No trade union organisation above the plant level was allowed to take part in collective bargaining. Workers in basic services and in the public sector could not bargain collectively or strike. For other workers the right to strike was recognised, but it was subject to severe restrictions, the most important being that strikes could not last longer than 60 days, after which the workers could be made redundant; on the other hand, the employer must accept their return to work in the same conditions as before the conflict.

The *Plan Laboral* was therefore an attempt at co-opting the working class in the system by means of introducing a pattern of behaviour – atomised and competitive – consistent with a 'market' view of society.[23] As indicated, it was part of a larger attempt at what has been called the 'social institutionalisation' of the economic model. It was as such a contradictory attempt, involving both the relegalisation of trade union activity – until then repressed, although never completely destroyed – and the setting of limits, constraints and restrictions to its exercise. Its results were equally contradictiory. The workers, while explicitly rejecting the Plan, nevertheless effectively took part in two rounds of national collective bargaining in 1979–80 and 1980–81.

The results in terms of wage increases were very meager, and more so in the second round than in the first. Strikes took place but they seldom led to any improvement in the final offer of the employers. In fact, workers demands went down significantly from one to the other, indicating an increasing level of frustration and defeatism. On the other hand, the number of strikes did not decrease importantly. The reason has to do with the extent to which the collective bargaining process and the strikes allowed a level of trade union activity, organisation and mobilisation that was regarded as essential by the leadership for purposes of reconstitution of the movement. This was all the more possible because the national federations and confederations, although not allowed to take part in the actual bargaining, could act as 'advisers', and did in fact participate actively in the process. The onset of the crisis of mid-1982 changed drastically the context in which the *Plan Laboral* was operating, and opened the door to a radicalisation of trade union demands, as will be seen below.

This is therefore an area in which the state, far from withdrawing, intervened strongly to make possible a drastic reduction in the share of labour in the social product in order to allow for an increase in the share of profits. This led to a massive fall in the standards of living of the workers and the poor. Poverty, in fact, emerged as an issue of a magnitude unprecedented in recent Chilean history. Table 3.5 on the evolution of real salaries and wages provides a first indication of the process of impoverishment of the workers.

The decline in real salaries and wages in 1974–76 is staggering: they lost on the average 35% of their purchasing power as compared to

TABLE 3.5 *Chile: real salaries and wages, 1970–82 (1970 = 100)*

1970	100
1974	65.1
1975	62.9
1976	64.8
1977	71.5
1978	76.0
1979	82.3
1980	89.3
1981	97.4
1982*	82.2

* December.

SOURCE 1974–81, Cortázar (1980), table 8, p. 20 and Ffrench-Davis (1982), table 5, p. 32; 1982 estimated on the basis of data contained in Banco Central de Chile (1983b) pp. 1663 and 1673.

1970. The index improved somewhat from 1977 onwards as inflation levels were brought down, but in 1981 it was still slightly below the level of 1970 and by December 1982 it had slipped back to 17·8% below that of 1970.

The actual loss in real income of the workers is not, however, fully captured in the figures in Table 3.5 since the restructuring of Chilean industry – to be discussed below – produced historically high levels of unemployment. Table 3.6 shows the levels of open unemployment for the period 1970–81, as well as the percentage of the labour force

TABLE 3.6 *Chile: unemployment, open and total, 1970–81 (as a percentage of the labour force)*

	open	MEP*	total
1970	5.7	—	5.7
1974	9.2	—	9.2
1975	14.5	2.0	16.5
1976	14.4	5.8	20.2
1977	12.7	5.9	18.6
1978	13.6	4.3	17.9
1979	13.8	3.5	17.3
1980	12.0	5.2	17.3
1981	10.8	4.8	15.6
1982†	21.9	6.4	28.3

* Minimum Employment Programme
† October–December
SOURCE Ffrench-Davis (1982) p. 32 and Economic and Financial Survey (1983b).

included in the so-called Minimum Employment Programme. This started in 1975 and provided part-time menial work at very low levels of remuneration; it was in effect a form of disguised unemployment. The average unemployment for the period 1974–81 was 16·6% of the labour force.

The combination of the decline in real income of the workers and unemployment produced a major fall in the share of labour in gross domestic product. Unfortunately, it is not possible to quantify the fall after 1976, since the military authorities released two different sets of figures whose relationship is unclear. The series issued by ODEPLAN in 1977 shows labour's share of GDP dropping from 62.8% in 1972 to 41.1% in 1976. The revised series issued in 1981, while identical with the former until 1973, shows significantly higher levels for the share of labour in GDP (over 50%), for the years 1974–76, i.e. the first 3 years of the military government. No explanation of the change was given. The levels shown for the period after 1976 remain around 50%, with the exception of 1979 (See Table 3.A3). Even so, the average share of labour in GDP in the period 1977–81 is below the comparable figure for 1970.

The one aspect of the labour policy of the government where there was a withdrawal was the expenditure of the state in the social services. Reliable figures only exist until 1979, and they show a large fall in per capita social expenditure in 1975 and 1976, followed by some recuperation after 1977. Still, in 1979 it was only 83% of what it had been in 1970. The variation in the different components of the social expenditure of the state will be discussed below.

The State and Capital: the Role of Interventor

It has also been suggested in the Introductory chapter that the state can play a role in the sharing of surplus value among various capitals, and thus direct the process of accumulation in given ways. Instruments of intervention in this sense include the conventional array of economic policy measures, whether regulatory or promotional, and also the provision of basic goods and services for private accumulation (infrastructure). While in all cases such interventions will be justified by reference to capital in general ('the national interest', 'the development of the economy') their concrete impact will be to favour a given fraction of capital – and, indeed, specific individual capitalists – with preference to others. By the same token, a reduction of the levels of intervention can be a way of allowing the interests of some sections of capital to prevail. A discussion of the areas in which intervention is attempted, of its levels and of its direction is therefore required to characterise the role of the state in this sense and the impact on the distribution of economic and social power within the power bloc. In Chile under the military the fundamental impact of the intervention of the state has taken place in three areas: public revenue and expenditure, the reorganisation of the financial system and the management of the external sector. I shall now discuss them in order.

State Expenditure and Revenue

Table 3.7 shows the evolution of public expenditure for the period 1969–82.[24] Overall public expenditure as a percentage of GDP went down by over one-fourth between 1970 and 1976 and then stabilised around the 1976 level (27–8%) until 1980. It then went up to above 31% in 1981, and in 1982 reached 35% of GDP. This was the year of the crisis, and the state – as we shall see below – stepped up its intervention to try and face it.

The absolute real level of public expenditure also went down in the period 1970–79, but to a lesser extent. Its evolution through time had some unexpected features (Table 3.8). In the first place, it is clear that during the 'gradualist' phase of the first stage of the economic policy,

TABLE 3.7 *Chile: public expenditure excluding debt as a percentage of GDP, 1969–70 and 1974–82*

Year	%
1969	34.0
1970	38.0
...	...
1974	36.1
1975	33.1
1976	27.9
1977	28.7
1978	28.2
1979	26.7
1980	28.3
1981	31.3
1982	34.9

SOURCE Marshall (1981), table I, p. 55 and Banco Central de Chile (1983a) pp. 1406–7.

TABLE 3.8 Chile: evolution of public expenditure, 1970–79 (1969=100)

	Operational expenditure (1)	Transfer payments (2)	Investment (3)	Total (4)
1970	109.4	124.1	106.2	114.4
1974	149.1	122.5	121.1	130.6
1975	122.8	93.5	67.5	95.5
1976	122.2	88.9	56.8	90.5
1977	132.7	91.2	59.7	95.6
1978	139.7	112.1	50.9	103.8
1979	135.8	118.3	59.0	107.3

SOURCE Marshall (1981), table 6, p. 67.

i.e. until 1975, overall public expenditure not only did not decrease but in fact showed a significant increase as compared to the last full year of the Frei government. The second is that the most significant reduction in 1975 and 1976 is that of investment expenditure, which went down by 53·1%; operational expenditure went down by 18% and transfer payments by 27·4%. The meaning of the data becomes clearer if one recalls that operational expenditure refers basically to wages and salaries of public employees, including the military and the police. In fact, a disaggregation of operational expenditures by main sectors shows that in 1976 expenditure in general services – which includes the police – and defence, was 79·5% higher than in 1969 in constant currency. Operational expenditures in education also increased between 1969 and 1976, and all other sectors, including health, went down slightly.

What we have then is a policy of reducing the role of the state in investment; this may well have been the result of conflicting pressures, on the one hand, to reduce expenditure and on the other to maintain the military and police establishment and more generally the level of public employment and of social transfers.[25] The objective impact of the policy, however, was to reduce the level of support to productive capital, both industrial and agricultural, which were the main beneficiaries of public investment expenditure. It is likely that the initial reluctance to reduce expenditure was a function of pressures from industrial capital, which began to be disregarded in 1975. The partial recovery in the level of public expenditure in 1978 and 1979 is almost entirely due to an expansion of operational and transfer expenditures; investment remained low throughout the period.

The military government also introduced significant changes in the pattern of fiscal revenue. They essentially consisted in a reduction of taxes on capital – wealth, capital gains and profits tax – and an increase in indirect taxes, notably VAT, where the exemption of necessities was terminated.

The changes in the taxation system were presented as aimed at making the system 'neutral' and non-discriminatory, inasmuch as they removed differentiation by categories of income or goods to be taxed. It is, however, evident that the increased incidence of indirect taxes was an additional factor making for a regressive redistribution of income and a reduction in the standards of living of the workers. The alleged withdrawal of the state was, again, an intervention on behalf of capital and against labour.

The Restructuring of the Financial System

One central tenet of the philosophy of the economic advisers to the military government was the need to develop an internal capital market. In this they were perhaps less followers of Milton Friedman and the Chicago brand of monetarism than of R. I. McKinnon and the 'Stanford' brand,[26] although, as we shall see below, the issues at stake had more to do with concrete class interests than with abstract economic theories. Still, McKinnon's concept of 'financial repression', i.e. the constraints on the development of a private financial system in underdeveloped countries, provided a theoretical rationale for a fundamental restructuring of the Chilean financial sector, with profound implications for the distribution of economic power in the economy as a whole.

Early in the process, it was decided that the means towards the expansion and development of the internal capital market would be the elimination of controls on interest rates. Here, however, the notion that this should help the consolidation of a financial bourgeoisie was quite explicit, and was further expressed in the timing of the relevant measures. When the military took over, the majority of banks had been nationalised by the Allende government, and while the new regime vowed to return them to private ownership, this was in fact not done until late 1975. In April 1974, however, the government decreed the freeing of interest rates charged by private finance companies (*Sociedades Financieras*) while retaining a maximum interest rate for banks. The *Financieras* thus became a focal point for the reconstitution and consolidation of finance capital; when the banks were privatised later, it was the groups organised around the *Financieras* that took them over.[27] The banking interest rate had also been freed by then, and it shot up to a mind-boggling 178% (annual equivalent of the 30-day interest rate in *real* terms) in the third quarter of 1975.[28] Although with fluctuations, it remained very high throughout the period (Table 3.9), thus setting the bases for the process of indebtedness of industrial capital *vis-à-vis* finance capital which is at the root of the crisis of 1982–3.

TABLE 3.9 *Chile: real internal interest rate and interest rate for external credit, 1975–81*

	real internal rate (%)	external credit (%)
1975	127.2	n/a
1976	64.2	8.9
1977	57.1	8.9
1978	42.3	11.1
1979	16.9	14.3
1980	15.4	12.2
1981	39.8	n/a

SOURCE Ffrench-Davis and Arellano (1981), table 10, p. 27; Foxley (1982), table 8, p. 45.

The imbalances were intensified by the impact of foreign indebtedness, itself a function of the management of the external sector to be discussed below. Large amounts of monetary resources were made available to selected borrowers in Chile at international rates of interest and medium term repayment periods. The favoured borrowers were the economic groups that grew as a result of the first stages of the financial restructuring.[29] The difference between the rates of interests paid by them to their foreign lenders and the rates charged by them to their national borrowers is also shown in Table 3.9.

In addition, two other measures of the government contributed to distortions in the financial market. One was the elimination of restrictions on the uses of financial loans, which until then had been steered towards productive uses by a combination of regulations on quantitative controls and on loan/reserves ratios; the other was the abolition of minimum periods for bank loans. Together, these measures created the conditions for the development of a highly volatile market, directed towards speculation and consumption rather than productive purposes, highly discriminatory against local productive capital without access to the international financial markets and highly lucrative to the financial groups enjoying such access.[30] The implications of this state of affairs both for the relative position of the various fractions of capital and for the accumulation process will be discussed below.

The Management of the External Sector[31]

The aim of the policy of the military government in relation to the external sector was the complete opening of the Chilean economy and its full integration into the world capitalist economy. A programme of reduction of tariffs on imports was announced in early 1974, and was carried out at a faster than anticipated pace to reach a point in June 1979 where maximum tariff was 10%, except for automobiles. In the first stage of the economic policy the reduction in tariffs was accompanied by a devaluation of the Chilean peso. There was a major devaluation in 1974 (651% in annual average), followed by small but steady further devaluations and including a somewhat larger one in March 1975. The average nominal tariff in this period went down from 94% in 1973 to 45% in December 1975. The two processes, however, operated opposite effects on the real rate of exchange for imports, and the latter remained relatively stable (Table 3.10). However, in 1976 and

TABLE 3.10 *Chile: index of real dollar rate of exchange for imports, 1973–81 (October–December each year; 1973 = 100)*

	Index
1973	100
1974	106
1975	111
1976	77.4
1977	64.4
1978	66.3
1979	59.9
1980	49.3
1981*	44.3

* July–September.
SOURCE Foxley (1982), table 8, pp. 44–45.

again in 1977 the peso was revalued as part of the anti-inflationary policy. The index of the real rate of exchange for imports – i.e. the real rate of exchange adjusted by variations in tariff rates, in pesos per US dollars – went down from 1974 = 100 to 76·5 in July–September 1976 and to 64·6 in April–June 1979;[32] the establishment of a fixed rate of exchange in July 1979 – while internal inflation exceeded international inflation – meant a further revaluation. The result of this process was an enormous expansion of imports, particularly of consumption items.

The other aspect of the foreign trade policy of the government was the promotion of exports. Copper exports increased significantly as a result of increases in output; by 1976 the nationalised copper industry was producing at full rated capacity. In addition, a policy of diversification of exports was introduced, which led to the rapid growth of such exports as fruit and vegetables, fishmeal, timber, pulp and paper, and some mineral products such as molybdenum. In 1981 non-copper exports accounted for 56% of total export revenue, as against 25% in 1970.

The fact is, however, that the growth of imports far exceeded that of exports, a situation compounded by the low price of copper (Table 3.11); the balance of trade developed a mounting deficit which was covered with flows of foreign finance (Table 3.12). The government's

TABLE 3.11 *Chile: copper prices, 1970–82 (annual averages, US cents per pound)*

	current c	1982 c
1970	64.1	195
1971	49.3	138
1972	48.6	125
1973	80.8	173
1974	93.3	159
1975	55.9	84
1976	63.6	95
1977	59.3	81
1978	61.9	72
1979	89.8	93
1980	99.2	95
1981	79.0	79
1982	67.1	67

SOURCE Banco Central de Chile (1974) p. 628, (1980) p. 188, (1980a) p. 1212 and (1983b) p. 1670; 1982 values estimated using World Bank Manufacturing Unit Value Index.

TABLE 3.12 Chile: balance of payments, 1974–81 (millions of current US dollars)

	1974	1975	1976	1977	1978	1979	1980	1981	1982
Current account	−211	−491	148	−551	−1088	−1189	−1971	−4814	−2382
Balance of trade	357	70	643	34	−426	−355	−764	−2598	218
exports	(2151)	(1590)	(2116)	(2185)	(2460)	(3835)	(4705)	(3960)	(3798)
imports	(−1794)	(−1520)	(−1473)	(−2151)	(−2886)	(−4190)	(−5409)	(−6558)	(−3580)
Services	−579	−571	−523	−660	−732	−914	−1320	−2316	−2700
Capital account	218	240	199	572	1946	2247	3165	4769	1304
Direct foreign investment	−17	−4	−1	16	177	233	170	376	365
Autonomous capital	235	244	200	556	1769	2014	2995	4393	939
Balance of payments	−55	−344	414	113	712	1047	1244	70	−1165

SOURCE Banco Central de Chile (1983b) p. 1596. Figures for 1981 and 1982 are provisional.

policy *vis-à-vis* capital movements was considerably more restrictive than its policy on external trade.[33] It included minimum periods and compulsory deposits in the Central Bank of a percentage of the loan, which varied inversely with the period of the loan. Those two restrictions varied through time, the second showing a declining tendency. In addition, the banking system was initially subject to restrictions concerning maximum lending and borrowing levels in foreign currency; they were later relaxed and by 1979 they had been removed. While the rationale for maintaining restrictions on capital movements was the need to have control over the inflow of foreign loans given their impact on internal inflation, the maintenance of those restrictions and the timing of their relaxation had the effect of further facilitating the concentration of access to foreign credit in a few large borrowers.[34]

Finally, a determined attempt was made by the military government to attract foreign investment by offering it a generous regime of taxation and other privileges. Decree-Law 600 of 1974 amended by Decree-Law 1748 of 1977 offered the foreign investors, among other benefits, a guarantee that the rate of taxation of 49·5% of gross profits could not be changed for the first 10 years of the life of the investment, and a guarantee that there would be no restrictions for the repatriation of profits. In addition, specific mining investment agreements with foreign companies entered into in 1977 included such concessions as exemptions from most other taxes, accelerated depreciation of equipment, machinery and installations in three years, and the investor's right to deduce from profits any losses incurred in a period up to 5 years prior to the tax year in question.[35]

Despite this exceptionally favourable regime, the inflow of foreign direct investment was disappointing: while there were expressions of interest by foreign investors, particularly in the minerals field, actual investments were very modest. In part in response to the poor performance, the government decided in 1980 to improve further the regime offered to mineral investors; a new set of regulations on mining property were proposed according to which the owner of a mining concession has a right over the mineral in the ground that is equivalent to civil ownership and therefore entitles the concessionaire in case of expropriation to compensation equivalent to the full value of the deposits. The initiative was surrounded with some controversy, as seemingly a sector within the military opposed it because it reversed the well-established principle of state ownership of mineral resources in Chilean law: as a result the actual enactment of the provisions was considerably delayed. In the end, however, the initiative was sanctioned

The State as Capitalist: the Role of Accumulator

We have already indicated that a major tenet of the economic model adopted by the military government was to dismantle the productive apparatus under state control. The process of privatisation advanced rapidly during the first stage of the economic policy, as Table 3.13 shows. The privatisation of state enterprises at an accelerated pace and in conditions of recession and high interest rates meant that only those with access to liquid resources or external credit – again, the large economic groups – could purchase the state companies being privatised; it further meant that the companies were sold at a considerably lower price than their real value. For a sample of 41 companies and banks representing about 60% of the value of all companies sold, it is estimated that the price of sale was of the order of 70% of the net value of assets of the companies. Privatisation thus entailed a substantial subsidy from the state to the emerging economic power groups.[36]

TABLE 3.13 *Chile: number of public enterprises, 1970–77*

Enterprises:	1970	1973	1977
With state equity participation:			
companies	46	229	45
banks	—	19	4
Under state control:	—	259	4
With state acting as receiver:	—	—	17
Total	46	507	70

SOURCE Foxley (1982), table 10, p. 54.

Privatisation, however, was not complete. From the beginning the government announced that certain activities regarded as strategic for national development and security would remain in the state sector; while the number of state companies went further down in the period 1978–82, by the end of the period it still included some 37 companies, whose current revenue amounted to nearly one-fourth of gross domestic product (Table 3.14). The exact definition of 'strategic' was seemingly disputed – with the 'Chicago boys' pressing for a minimal scope and other sectors, including military ones, trying to extend it – but it appeared that some 26 out of the 37 companies would be retained in the public sector; these covered public utilities, communications and transport, electricity, and major productive enterprises such as the oil, coal, steel and nitrate companies. They also included the largest state owned sector by far, the copper industry, whose case deserves a separate, albeit brief, discussion.[37]

TABLE 3.14 Chile: revenue of state enterprises as percentage of GDP, 1978–82

	Copper	Non-copper	All
1978	8.8	16.7	25.5
1979	10.4	16.8	27.2
1980	9.5	16.6	26.1
1981	6.1	14.9	21.0
1982	7.3	15.7	23.0

SOURCE Based on Ministry of Finance data.

As befits a government committed to re-establishing good relations with the United States and international capital, it was very shortly after the coup that the new military rulers of Chile started negotiations with the US companies nationalised by the Allende government to settle the compensation issue. The resulting compensation was in excess of what even the most favourable interpretation of the 1971 nationalisation the companies could have hoped for. Unexpectedly though, at that point there was no suggestion that the mines should be returned to foreign control. The reasons for this departure from the junta's general policy are complex: as already indicated, copper was perceived by the military as having strategic value for national security; the nationalisation had commanded widespread support among Chileans of all social sectors and political persuasions, and the new government was resorting to nationalist symbols to secure legitimacy; the copper industry was a potential source of power, patronage and wealth for the military themselves. Be that as it may, the fact is that it was only two years after the coup that reference was publicly made to the possibility of privatising the large scale copper mines. The issue came up in the context of proposals for the reorganisation of the state copper sector, and originated with groups close to the government economic decision-makers, by then clearly identified with the Chicago school of economics. At the same time, however, a change was taking place among the top echelons of the State Copper Corporation, which had been manned solely by civilian technical personnel throughout 1974. In 1975 Army Colonel Gaston Frez, who was reported to be personally close to Pinochet, was appointed General Manager. Frez quickly established himself as the main spokesman in defence of the state sector in the copper industry, and by November 1975 he was able to announce that the nationalised mines would definitely remain in the state sector, although adding that the latter was expected to operate as an efficient profit-maximising capitalist.

In one fundamental respect, though, the state copper sector was not allowed to operate as a private capitalist: its ability to expand and accumulate was subject to decisions by the government, which must approve any investment programmes of the state copper company. Despite the company having been very profitable, the annual investment programmes authorised by the government barely covered capital replacement; in effect, the state copper sector was condemned to stagnation – while foreign capital was invited to exploit new copper deposits – and at the same time became a major provider of general fiscal revenue. A similar situation can be observed with respect to the rest of the state enterprises, where, if anything, the restrictions on accumulation were even more drastic: while providing a substantial surplus to the government, they had to finance a major part of their authorised investment through external borrowing (Table 3.15). The extent to which transfers of surplus from the state enterprises became a major component of overall state revenue can be seen in Table 3.16. Despite the doctrinaire position of the 'Chicago boys' against any presence of the state in production, the state enterprise sector became highly functional to the objectives of reducing taxation without increasing the fiscal deficit. The dual requirement for the state enterprise sector to perform that role was that it should be profitable and that it should not accumulate. Both conditions appear to have obtained in Chile in the period 1978–82.

THE FORM OF THE REGIME: THE BASES OF DOMINATION

How do the preceding features of the economic role of the state relate to the features of the political regime and the stages through which the

TABLE 3.15 Chile: financial operations of public enterprises, 1978–82 (millions of current US dollars)

	Chilean Copper Corporation					Other public enterprises				
	1978	1979	1980	1981	1982	1978	1979	1980	1981	1982
Current revenue	1268	2076	2314	1770	1712	2561	3480	4582	4918	4166
Current expenditure	765	896	1196	1361	1139	2094	2734	3270	3713	2738
Operating surplus	504	1180	1118	410	573	467	747	1312	1205	1428
Payments to government	347	924	1015	465	613	333	774	994	1179	1237
Current account surplus or deficit	157	256	104	−56	−40	134	−27	318	25	191
Capital receipts	45	–	–	–	–	118	44	143	215	47
Capital expenditure	164	178	267	307	234	385	214	456	552	498
Overall surplus or deficit	39	78	−163	−363	−273	−131	−197	5	−312	−261

SOURCE Based on data in US dollars from the Chilean Copper Corporation and in Chilean *pesos* from the Ministry of Finance, the latter converted into dollars at the average annual rates. Totals may not add because of rounding.

TABLE 3.16 *Chile: financial operations of the consolidated public sector 1978–82 (millions of current US dollars)*

	1978	1979	1980	1981	1982
Current revenue	5948	6900	9355	10277	8382
General government	4977	4973	6925	8662	6381
Surplus of public enterprises	971	1927	2430	1615	2001
Current expenditure of general government	4662	5134	6750	8690	8498
Current account	1286	1766	2605	1587	−116
Capital revenue	329	505	616	1163	629
Capital expenditure	1379	1383	2001	2616	1706
Surplus or deficit	236	888	1220	134	−1193

SOURCE As per Table 3.15

latter has gone? It has been suggested above that a fruitful way of analysing the features of the political regime in relation to accumulation is to focus on the bases of domination of the regime and that they can be categorised in terms of coercion, ideology and welfare.

The Bases of Domination: Coercion

There is little dispute as to the extent to which the military government relied predominantly on naked force to impose its rule over the population as a whole and the workers in particular.[38] This was especially the case during the first stage of the economic model, which, as we have seen, was marked by a major attack on the standards of living of the workers. On 11 September 1973 the country was declared in a 'state of internal war', a concept that did not exist in the Chilean legal system until then but on the basis of which the military assumed emergency powers and introduced all the exceptional rules governing public order in wartime. These included a curfew and the operation of military courts exercising war-time jurisdiction and applying war-time procedure and penalties.

In September 1974 the state of internal war was formally ended and a decree issued establishing a 'state of siege in the degree of internal defence'; this was, in fact, no different from the 'state of internal war'. The decree also defined two other lesser forms of state of siege, and in September 1975 the state of siege was modified from the degree of internal defence to that of 'internal security', thus purportedly bringing to an end war-time procedures. The decree, however, also stated that war-time military courts retained jurisdiction with respect to certain offences, most notably that of 'subversion'. This, in turn, was defined in such wide terms as to be in the words of an official UN document, 'capable of providing pretexts for the arrest and trial of practically every person in Chile whom the authorities fear, dislike or wish to eliminate from normal life'.[39]

The provisions of the state of internal war and the state of siege allowed for the summary trial of large numbers of political opponents; in some cases, they resulted in execution. In addition, a form of generalised terror was introduced from the beginning, involving kidnappings, torture and killings. A particularly grim feature of the first period were the *desaparecidos*: individuals arrested by the security forces whose whereabouts became unknown after some time in custody. It is claimed that some 2000 persons disappeared in this way, most of them not heard of since. The largest numbers of disappearances took place in 1973 and 1974; the numbers then declined until no more cases are reported after mid-1977. The decline in numbers reflects first the extent to which the bulk of the more active opponents of the government were killed, jailed or exiled; but also the fact, already mentioned, that the initial uncoordinated repression carried out by the security services of the various branches of the armed forces was centralised in June 1974 in the National Intelligence Directorate (DINA). The modest relaxation of the economic policies with the move from the first to the second stages of the economic model was probably another factor in the relaxation of repression. As already suggested, though, it was only a full year after the end of the shock treatment that any non-negligible changes were introduced in the political arrangements, and that the second stage of the political regime started. Physical repression was less harsh in this stage, although detention and torture of political opponents continued to be the case, as was the forced exile or internal banishment of political activists. In March 1978 the state of siege was replaced with a less strict 'state of emergency'; non-judicial powers of arrest and the curfew, though, remained.[40] As the economy in the second stage was showing signs of improvement, some modicum of trade union and even political activity began to be tolerated, although overstepping the mark was dealt with harshly. Again it was only a year after the beginning of the third stage of economic policy that initiatives in the political front were undertaken, leading to the tolerance of some public debate on the options for institutionalisation. Coercion, however, remained very much present in the system; the plebiscite on the new Constitution in September 1980 was far from a genuine consultation of public opinion. With the onset of the crisis in the second half of 1982, the level of coercion in the regime increased again, but, as we shall see below, the government did not appear to be in a position to reintroduce the form of terror that it had employed in 1973-74.

The Bases of Domination: Ideology[41]

The ideological bases of domination of the system have also undergone stages, corresponding to the overall stages of the political regime and their interaction with the stages in economic policy. The main ideological principle under which legitimation of the regime in the first stage was sought was the doctrine of national security.[42] This entailed a view of the state as an organic whole, prior and superior to the individuals and to any groupings within it. 'Subversion' was then identified as the fundamental threat to the unity and therefore the security of the country, and the armed forces as the only social actor capable of facing the threat. It was, therefore, tantamount to a glorification of the military institution and a demand of total obedience to its commands; in effect, it posited a militarisation of society. To oppose the military was to become an enemy, not of the government, but of the nation.

The political ideology of national security coexisted uneasily in the official discourse in this period with the economic ideology of the market understood in a technocratic, 'scientific' sense. This was particularly the case after the introduction of the 'shock treatment' of April 1975. The dominant ideological principle, however, was the political; the national security view of society pervaded the official statements – particularly those of Pinochet – until the end of 1976, when, as indicated above, an attempt was made to formalise the unregulated and indefinite military power through the Constitutional Acts of September 1976. It was only after the failure of this attempt that the economic ideological pole started to become dominant.

The strong political ideological stance of the military in this period, however, was not accompanied by any attempts at using the ideology as a lever to mobilise organised mass political support; clearly, popular mobilisation of any kind – even in support of the government – was regarded as dangerous. The junta issued in March 1974 a Declaration of Principles of the Chilean Government, in which its philosophy of irrestricted defence of private property was expounded and an attempt made to link it with Catholic doctrine.[43] The document included a strong attack on what was termed 'naive democracy' which was viewed as fostering 'class struggle', and suggestions were made as to the need to replace it in due course by an 'organic democracy' based on corporations. But this fascist-like ideological stance was not followed, either in the document or in the actual practice of the junta later on, by any attempt at organising a mass movement based on a fascist ideology. This refusal to engage in legitimation by organised ideological mobilisation was a constant feature of the Chilean political regime under the military, straddling its various stages.

The uneasy co-existence of the doctrine of national security as the central political ideology and the ideology of economic freedom towards the end of the first stage was resolved in the second stage in favour of the latter. Pronouncements about national security by Pinochet were increasingly replaced by pronouncements about the efficiency of the market mechanisms and, especially, about the scientific management of the economy by the 'Chicago boys'; these could carry some more credibility – particularly *vis-à-vis* the bourgeoisie and the military – as the economy was recovering. The compatibility of the two sets of beliefs was attempted through the notion that an authoritarian state was required in order to establish the normal equilibrium under which economic freedom and its result, political freedom, could take place. Before the economy – and the polity – were cleared of perverse interferences, it was not possible to introduce full political freedom. The notion of a transitional character of the military government began thus to appear, but at this stage was not made explicit; instead, the economic ideology became the dominant pole.

The anti-democratic elements in the economic ideology were, on the other hand, apparent. If there are no fundamental contradictions in society and public decision-making is a matter of finding the 'right' technical solution to economic technical problems, large areas of public decision-making become not the province of the voter and public opinion but of the specialist, i.e., the trained professional economist. The whole area of money management was thus postulated as one that should, by constitutional provision, be excluded from the powers of the elected organs – whenever they might reappear – and left to a neutral, technical body such as the Central Bank. This was in fact incorporated in the 1980 constitution.

As it is obvious, this new ideological focus was even less appropriate for purposes of mass mobilisation than the one in the previous period. The case thus remained that the military did not attempt a process of legitimation by ideological mobilisation. A 'national consultation' called by Pinochet in January 1978 in response to criticism from the United Nations and international public opinion generally was less an attempt at democratic mobilisation than a crudely manipulated affair whose main purpose seems to have been to show the efficiency of Pinochet's personal power apparatus.

The third stage of the political regime was dominated by the social ideology of individualism and social fragmentation. This is, of course, linked to the economic ideology of the market; what was in fact being propounded was the transformation of all forms of social relations into market relations. But the ideology behind it was different; it did not emphasise so much the technocratic element as the utilitarian principle as a central component of social life as a whole. To that extent, it came again into conflict with some of the tenets of the other converging philosophies in the government ideology, notably that of Catholic integrism, which would emphasise the common good.

Together with this move to a utilitarian social approach, the official ideological discourse began to reintroduce some of the symbols of the democratic ideology. The notion of a 'protected' democracy of elections, parliaments, etc. began to reappear, although posited as desiderata to be achieved when the full transition, the cleansing of society, was completed. Such pretence, however, was not credible without some opening of the system if only in terms of the exchange of opinion among the political elite, and this in effect took place. This, however, increased the tensions in an already heated political system, and the latter at some point became incapable of dealing with those tensions and had to resort to repression once again.

The other novel element in the ideological front was the announcement by Pinochet, in the wake of the September 1980 constitutional plebiscite, of his intention to create a civic-military mass movement in support of the government. The fact that 2 years later such a movement had not yet been set up is an indication of the difficulties in trying to instrumentalise an essentially anti-participatory ideology through mobilisation.

The Bases of Domination: 'Welfare'

In terms of the 'welfare' function of the state as a basis for compliance, the figures already given on the evolution of public spending in the social services and more generally on the levels of wages and of unemployment give an idea of the extent to which 'welfare', particularly in the first period of the economic policy, was not regarded by the military government as a worthwhile avenue towards political legitimation. Such a view is reinforced by the figures in Table 3.17 showing the evolution of the level of the average pension, the number of hospital beds per person and the level of health services per person. All three indicators show a fall in the years 1974 and 1975; the fall is particularly large in the case of pensions.

TABLE 3.17 *Chile: indicators of welfare, 1974–81 (1970=100)*

	Average pension	Hospital beds per person	Health services per person
1970	100	100	100
1974	65	94.4	89.3
1975	n/a	91.7	84.5
1976	64.9	88.9	90.3
1977	n/a	86.1	91.3
1978	76.0	83.3	94.2
1979	n/a	n/a	n/a
1980	89.3	n/a	n/a
1981	97.4	n/a	n/a

SOURCE Ffrench-Davis (1982), table 5, p. 32; Foxley (1982) p. 42.

The only concession in the welfare front in the first stage of the regime was the introduction in 1975 of the Minimum Employment Programme, which employed part-time workers in such tasks as street cleaning, parks and gardens maintenance and the like. This was in accordance with the tenet of the economic doctrine of the government whereby the state should not intervene in the sharing of the social product except to help those sectors below the poverty line. The extent to which this programme was a device to reduce unemployment figures rather than a means of real relief for the poorest is shown by the fact that in 1981 the average remuneration in the Minimum Employment Programme was equivalent to 32·1% of the minimum wage.[44]

In the second stage of the regime, the figures in Table 3.8 above show a very modest move towards increasing transfer payments and therefore towards a use of the 'welfare' function of the state as a lever for legitimation. At the same time, however, the National Planning Office issued a document suggesting that the way out of unemployment was to reduce wages and salaries to the level that the market will bear, i.e. the clearing price of labour in the market (Kelly Plan).[45] Also, in September 1979 the government made the already discussed announcement about the 'modernisation' of the areas of social security, health and education, together with four other areas of the economy and the society; the modernisation would entail a reduction in the role of the state in their management.

In the third stage of the regime, the 'welfare' front was indeed dominated by the reform of the social security system and the related privatisation and commercialisation of health care. The state-run social security system was not dismantled, but in early 1981 a private system of insurance was introduced and strong incentives offered to the workers to transfer their social security funds to a company of their choosing in the new system.[46] This in fact happened on a large scale, the only exception being the workers with very long periods of contribution to the state system, for whom the transfer was not attractive. Contrary to the state system, which was based on earnings-related contributions and uniform benefits, the new system was based on individual saving accounts. The company invests the funds in the capital market and the returns to the individual are a function of the performance of the investment. The state guarantees a minimum level of returns but this is itself based on the overall performance of the financial system. The arrangement was set up with a view to co-opting the workers into the system inasmuch as their social security benefits depend on the performance of the financial market. It also entailed a major transfer of financial resources from the state to private groups. In the event, those groups were the same that had benefited from the policy on interest rates and the privatisation of the banks. By July 1981 the two largest economic groups were controlling 75% of the transfers of social security contributions, and all social security companies were subsidiaries of the largest groups controlling 71% of the capital and reserves of the private financial system.[47]

Another effect of the reform of the social security system was to increase pressures on the state budget. As the workers who remain in the state system tend to be the older ones, the system continues for a period paying out benefits at about the same level until the reform, but will have ceased to receive contributions from the younger workers. It has been estimated that the reduction in state revenue resulting from the change is of the order of 5% of GDP. These pressures, as indicated above, have been partially compensated by the surplus of the state enterprises.

The second element in the welfare policy of the government that must be mentioned in relation with the third stage of the regime is the reform of the national health system.[48] Until 1979 the government did not introduce fundamental changes in the working of the national health service, although it adopted a restrictive policy in terms of resources and particularly in terms of personnel. The first significant change was introduced in 1979, when the national structure that existed until then was replaced by 27 autonomous regional authorities, which were empowered to privatise parts of the operation of the service. With the reform of the social security system, another step towards privatisation of health was taken, as the workers who decided to transfer to the private social insurance system were also encouraged to transfer the payment of their compulsory national health contributions to private health care institutes. The government further announced that the charges in the national health service would be increased to market levels in order not to allow unfair competition *vis-à-vis* the new private health institutes. The initial impact of these measures was to attract to the private system the higher paid workers who are the only ones who can afford health insurance without state subsidy. Again, this means the national health service must face a significant reduction in their revenue, which can only partially be offset by the increase in the cost of the services and which must result in a deterioration of the level of health care offered.

The only indicator of welfare that, surprisingly, shows a marked improvement through the military regime is child mortality, whose rate went down from 65·8 per thousand in 1973 to 37·9 per thousand in 1979; in 1969 it had been 83 per thousand. This is due to a deliberate government health and nutrition programme for infants in risk categories.[49]

THE SOCIAL BASES OF THE STATE AND THE MANAGERS OF THE REGIME, 1973–82

The discussion so far should have shown the extent to which the policies of the Chilean state under the military exclude the interests of the workers, the peasants and the poor generally; these groups were under sustained attack and their standards of living seriously eroded. On the other hand, the military state is not an abstract expression of the interest of capital in general. It represents a more concrete articulation of the interests of some fractions of the capitalist class around a hegemonic pole; this articulation is further accomplished through the mediation of specific state institutions and of groups in charge of the state. The conflictive interaction among these various levels provides a crucial point of entry into the dynamics of the military state.

In Chile between 1973 and 1982 the process is firstly one of concentration of wealth and economic power in a small section of the bourgeois class; and secondly of consolidation of the financial fraction as the hegemonic one within the state. This was less clear in the first period of the first stage of the economic policy, when the state tried to balance the interests of all fractions of the bourgeoisie. The consolidation of the financial fraction begins in earnest with the shock treatment of 1975, and is accompanied by the slow development of conflict between the financial and the commercial fractions on the one hand – with the support of international banking and the IMF – and the industrial and agrarian fractions on the other. This conflict is at the root of the crisis of 1982, which in turn marks the apparent demise of the power bloc hegemonised by the financial fraction, and its temporary replacement with a highly autonomous military state. Let us look at these developments more closely.

The process of concentration of economic power in the Chilean economy since 1973 can be substantiated without too much difficulty. Figures on the publicly subscribed companies registered in the Stock Exchanges of Santiago and Valparaiso – the second largest city in Chile – show that in 1978 the assets of the companies controlled by the five largest Chilean groups plus the foreign-owned companies represented over 75% of the total assets of this sample of companies.[50] The two largest Chilean groups alone controlled some 50% of the total assets of the sample, and it is estimated that they controlled at least 37% of the assets of the 250 largest national and foreign companies in the country.[51] The value of the assets of these two groups doubled in real terms between 1978 and 1980. As already indicated, these same two groups attracted 75% of the social security savings and contributions transferred from the state sector to the newly created private social insurance companies; almost all of the latter, furthermore, were set up by the groups that controlled over 70% of the assets of the private financial system.

Who are, then, these new groups? The thesis has been suggested for other Latin American countries that the expression 'finance capital' must be understood in the sense given it by Hilferding, that is as the taking over of industrial capital by financial capital leading to monopoly.[52] In this sense, finance capital would be no less productive than industrial capital; only more monopolistic and controlled from the financial system. This is clearly not the case in the Chilean experience.[53] It is, of course, true, that the new financial groups took over large numbers of productive enterprises, and that in some cases, notably export industries, they ran them profitably. It is also the case that the history of Chilean industrialisation has always exhibited a high degree of interpenetration between industrial and financial capital. The main economic groups in the 1960s and 1970s were centred around banks, while comprising major industrial enterprises. The situation, however, experienced a qualitative change under the military government. The new financial hegemonic group was not composed of industrialists that moved into banking; it was composed of financial speculators for whom the acquisition of productive enterprises was simply a temporarily profitable way of investing liquid resources, to be liquidated again when the financial market changed. Industrial enterprises for these groups provided outlets for medium and even short term investment, as well as mechanisms for further speculation; thus, as will be discussed below, a large part of the unrecoverable debt of the banking system was contracted by enterprises controlled by the banks themselves. An indication of the extent to which these sectors profited from the policies of the government is provided by the following figures on the distribution of the mass of profits, rent and interests in the Chilean economy in the period 1960–81 (Table 3.18).

TABLE 3.18 *Chile: distribution of payments to capital by main sectors, 1960–81*

	Agriculture (%)	Industry (%)	Trade (%)	Banking (%)
1960–1970	10.5	30.0	22.4	1.0
1971–1972	9.5	24.3	31.1	2.4
1973	7.6	26.5	30.4	10.3
1974	6.2	29.9	30.2	11.1
1975	8.0	15.6	29.6	10.7
1976	12.1	24.9	20.4	9.1
1977	16.3	20.0	26.2	8.8
1978	10.0	23.0	27.2	9.7
1979	8.7	21.1	26.5	11.5
1980	9.6	20.3	25.0	15.0
1981	7.3	20.9	27.8	18.0

SOURCE Based on data in: 1960–74, ODEPLAN (1960–75) pp. 72ff; 1975–81, Banco Central de Chile (1983b) pp. 1625–8.

The increase in the share of the financial sector (from an average of 1·0 in 1960–70 to 18% in 1981) is dramatic; less so but still impressive is the drop in the share of industrial capital, with the share of commercial capital showing also some increase. Our previous discussion on the effect of differential internal and international interest rates on the relative position of local productive capital *vis-à-vis* the financial groups is also relevant here. Thus, the main lines of conflict within the power bloc were drawn; I shall come back to the meaning of this contradiction below.

At this point it is, however, important to relate this assessment of the composition and index of hegemony of the power bloc with the question of the control over the apparatus of the state and the relative autonomy of the latter. The two are separate questions, one having to do with the form of the state, the other with the form of the regime.[54] The groups in charge of the state in Chile between 1973 and 1982 were the military in the first place and (especially since 1975), the Chicago technocrats in the second place. They ran the apparatus of the state and made decisions on behalf of capital. In most cases, until the crisis, such decisions were effectively discussed with the representatives of the hegemonic fraction of capital, as well as other fractions. In fact, in many cases the technocrats themselves were either members of the hegemonic fraction or their employees. However, there was not always perfect coincidence between the groups in charge of the state and the hegemonic fraction; the state had a degree of relative autonomy, and this became particularly apparent when the crisis took place. Furthermore, the degree of agreement between the two components of the groups in charge of the state was not always perfect either. In some non-negligible issues, the military component imposed its view over that of the technocrats.

The question why the military should have relied on the 'Chicago boys' to run the economy until the crisis has exercised many analysts of the Chilean experience. In particular, the hypothesis has been suggested that at the time of the shock treatment decision the extreme form of monetarism propounded by those groups was the one that made possible to face the problems created by the gradualist approach – failure to control inflation, stagnant output, balance of payment difficulties – while retaining intact the power bloc, that is, not altering the essential lines of the free market economic policy followed until then.[55] While this 'conjunctural' interpretation no doubt points to a component of the explanation, it would appear that the elevation of the 'Chicago boys' to the place of economic policy-makers in the military government has deeper causes, closely linked with the process of emergence of the financial fraction of capital as the hegemonic one.

At the level of the fundamental logic of the new form of state adopted, the main element seems to have been the perceived political impact of the previous economic model. For the bourgeois class as a whole – and increasingly for the military as a specific social group – the essential cause of the social upheaval culminating in the Allende experiment lay in the model of development that had prevailed since 1940 and which had been provided with a sophisticated theoretical rationale by the Economic Commission for Latin America and the so-called 'structuralist' school of Latin American economics. It was a state-oriented, protectionist, industrialising model, where the growth of a protected industry producing for the internal market meant the growth of the proletariat and the need to expand internal demand. This created economic and political pressures, which the economic system – assumed to have been inefficient because of protection – could not meet and which the 'compromise state' increasingly could not contain. A radical departure from that model was thus required; a move away from protection of domestic industry, in fact, from industrialisation itself. The 'inefficient' national industrial capitalist was as much responsible for the *débâcle* as the populace. Financial capital was thus ready to take its place as the hegemonic fraction, and monetarism was the alternative economic philosphy.

This, of course, can explain why it was possible for the process to take the course it took, but it does not explain why it actually did so. In more concrete terms, the explanation needs to take into account the emergence of the 'Chicago boys' as a cohesive social and political group and their role in the framing of a radical right-wing economic alternative. The name 'Chicago boys' might mislead into thinking that most of them were trained in Chicago. In fact, only a few actually were. The rest were trained in the Department of Economics of the Catholic University of Chile – the private university of the Chilean upper class – which in the 1960s entered into an agreement with the Department of Economics at Chicago whereby lecturers from the latter would be seconded to the Chilean counterpart. The agreement was financed with US aid funds and had the explicit purpose of providing a kind of training for economists that could be regarded as an alternative to the structuralist approach taught in the University of Chile, the state university. The economist trained in 'Little Chicago', as the Economics Department of the Catholic University came to be known, were for the most part members of the bourgeoisie, and they maintained a high degree of social cohesion and economic interlinking. 'Little Chicago' soon began to be regarded as the economic think-tank of the right; when in early 1973 the opposition to Allende began to think seriously about the possibility of a coup, it was the 'Chicago boys' network that organised the putting together of an economic plan to be offered to the military and to the civilian opposition leaders.[56]

The formulation of the plan was well advanced at the time of the coup, although not all of its details had been worked out. Still, when the time came to give a strong direction to economic policy, the 'Chicago boys' appeared to be the only ones with a clear and coherent set of ideas and proposals. From then on, their influence was self-reinforcing: on the one hand the application of their policies required a growing influx of foreign loan capital; on the other, the enthusiastic reception of those policies among international banks and the international financial institutions made the 'Chicago boys' appear as the main brokers *vis-à-vis* the world financial system. Their power was thus increased, and with it the orthodoxy of the policies pursued. The self-reinforcing mechanism was only broken with the onset of the crisis, which pitched the financial bourgeoisie against the 'Chicago boys' and both against the rest of the bourgeoisie. At that point, the military state reclaimed its autonomy; the partial demotion of the 'Chicago boys' – demanded initially by the financial bourgeoisie – was followed by a direct attack on sectors of that same financial bourgeoisie.

ACCUMULATION IN CHILE, 1973–82: CONTRADICTIONS AND CRISIS

What had in the meantime happened to accumulation? Again, a straight comparison of the levels of investment in fixed capital with previous periods is difficult because of the change in the methodology of national accounting introduced in 1981. The new series of investment figures covers the period 1960–82 and entails a significant increase with respect to previous estimates, apparently due to differences in the measurement of construction investment. It would appear that, while the previous methodolgy did tend to underestimate investment, the new one probably overestimates it; it is not known whether the overestimation is biased with respect to particular periods.

Table 3.A1 (Appendix) presents the original series for 1960–76 and the revised series for 1960–82; the latter shows less of a fall in the level of investment as a percentage of GDP in 1974 as compared to 1960–64, and a certain recuperation after 1977, particularly in 1980 and 1981. Still, the performance of accumulation for the period as a whole is very poor, even when compared with the low levels of the Allende period. This is further confirmed by column 5 in Table 3.A1 (Appendix) showing the index of per capita gross domestic investment in fixed capital: the average for 1974–82 was less than 83% of the average 1960–64.

Two other features of accumulation in the period 1975–81 are worth noting. One is the high incidence of external savings (defined in terms of the surplus in current account) in its financing (Table 3.19); investment was therefore highly dependent on the inflow of loan capital, while direct foreign investment was very low throughout the period (Table 3.20). The second is the reduction in the proportion of public investment (Table 3.21). The military government maintained that the lower levels of investment were more than compensated by an increase in the efficiency of investment: from being mostly state investment in infrastructure and housing it became basically purchases of capital equipment by private entrepreneurs. It would seem, however, that a large proportion of the investment in the manufacturing sector was replacement capital, while a significant part of the purchase of transport equipment was done by industrial companies to take advantage of the fact that road transport does not pay profit tax; a number of companies ended up operating their own transport fleets at very low levels of utilisation. At the same time, the neglect of infrastructural investment was serious; the government's hopes to attract private capital to sectors such as railways did not materialise.

TABLE 3.19   *Chile: sources of savings, 1970–81*

	Gross domestic savings (%)	External savings (%)
1970	92.5	7.5
1974	97.9	2.1
1975	60.4	39.6
1976	113.6	−13.6
1977	74.1	25.0
1978	70.7	29.3
1979	69.9	30.1
1980	66.1	33.9
1981	32.1	67.9

SOURCE   Based on Chilean Central Bank data as reported in *Ecomanager*, vol I, table 4.4.11.2; and Banco Central de Chile (1983b) p. 1632.

TABLE 3.20 *Chile: authorised and actual foreign investment by sectors, 1974–83 (millions of current US dollars)*

Sector	Authorised investment		Actual investment		
	(1) mUS$	(2) %	(3) mUS$	(4) %	(5) 3:1
Mining	5 718	79.4	735	38.0	12.9
Industry	658	9.1	505	26.2	76.9
Services	632	8.8	553	28.6	87.5
Other	191	2.6	138	7.2	72.3
Totals	7 199	100	1932	100	26.8

SOURCE Based on data from the Committee on Foreign Investment as reported in Economic and Financial Survey (1983) p. 3.

TABLE 3.21 *Chile: public and private shares of gross domestic investment, 1970–81*

	public (%)	private (%)
1970	74.7	25.3
1974	100.0	0.0
1975	57.4	42.6
1976	56.7	43.3
1977	45.5	54.5
1978	36.6	63.4
1979	37.2	62.8
1980	32.2	67.8
1981	30.0	70.0

SOURCE ODEPLAN (1982) p. 13.

The poor performance of capital accumulation was matched by the poor performance of the economy generally. The much vaunted 'economic miracle' period, when the GDP grew at an average of 8·6% per year between 1977 and 1980, was in effect only a recovery of the aggregate levels of activity preceding the deep recession of 1975. Table 3.A4 (Appendix) shows that in 1981 GDP per capita was only 5% higher than 10 years earlier. Even this figure is an overestimate, however. Given the high levels of foreign indebtedness, particularly in 1980–81, nearly 20% of the per capita growth between 1974 and 1981 is really the payment of interests and profits abroad. The level of the per capita gross national product – as distinct from GDP – was therefore about the same in 1981 as in 1971. In addition, the main factors explaining the growth of GNP between 1974 and 1981 were the value added by the marketing of imported goods and by financial services, both a function of the distortions introduced by the model. If these two sectors are excluded, the per capita GNP in 1981 is about the same as in 1974, i.e. 96% of what it was in 1970.[57]

The situation is even more clearly visible in the behaviour of industrial production, where the per capita value added in 1981 was 85·4% of what it had been in 1971. With the onset of the crisis, of course, all indicators of economic activity were to plunge into historical lows.

We are now talking about the period beginning in mid-1982. The macroeconomic management tensions in the implementation of the model began to exceed the capabilities of the system. They exacerbated the social and political contradiction between the state and the working class that had underlined the whole of the military experience; more ominously for the regime, though, they brought to the surface the increasing contradictions within the power bloc and the dominant class.

An early danger signal was the bankruptcy in May 1981 of a large sugar refining company, owned by one of the major financial groups.[58] The immediate cause of the bankruptcy was the unsuccessful attempt by the company to speculate in the world sugar market; it was therefore discounted by government spokesmen as simply the result of financial malpractice and without significance for the economy as a whole. The incident, however, brought into light some of the deeper factors associated with the model and making for a highly unstable economic position: the fact that the company was used as a vehicle for financial manipulations; its enormous internal debt, much of it with banks belonging to the same group; and the lack of effective regulation of foreign transactions and commitments. It was precisely in those two areas – the internal financial system and the foreign sector – that the tensions exploded.

Between December 1979 and June 1981 the credit extended by the banking system to the private sector doubled in real terms.[59] Part of the credit went to productive companies struggling for survival; the bulk went to finance speculative deals, particularly in real estate. Large numbers of loans went to subsidiaries of the banks themselves, particularly those belonging to the two largest economic groups. At the same time, a crisis in the balance of payments was developing. The trade deficit in 1981 was US $2·6 billion, with imports of US $6·6 billion. This was fuelled by the effective revaluation of the Chilean peso due to the fixed rate of exchange and an internal inflation exceeding international inflation. The deficit in current account was US $4·8 billion, which was covered with inflows of loan capital, mostly going to the banking sector.[60] The foreign debt of the country was by then reaching US $14·7 billion, equivalent to about 57% of the gross domestic product, and its services represented over 80% of the value of exports of goods.[61]

The initial reaction of the 'Chicago boys' and in particular of their undisputed leader and intellectual mentor, Finance Minister Sergio de Castro, was to try and contain the financial deterioration by means of restrictions on financial operations which would nevertheless preserve the fixed exchange rate. This precipitated the first major rift between the 'Chicago boys' and the financial groups. In July 1981 the government announced restrictions to the granting of bank loans to related companies;[62] in November it took over the running of four small banks and four financial companies which were in serious difficulties because of bad loans, and imprisoned 3 of their major shareholders.[63] The two major financial groups, while not directly affected by the last measures, reacted with increasing hostility towards De Castro and began to campaign in favour of devaluation. This fuelled speculation about an impending move in this direction – despite official denials – and provoked a run on the dollar reserves of the Central Bank, since the Chilean peso was freely convertible.

The government responded by raising the interest rate to make the holding of pesos attractive. This did not prevent the run on dollar reserves but added to the already serious difficulties of the industrial sector and aggravated the recessive tendencies. The general index of manufacturing production (1968 = 100) fell from 127·3 in July 1981 to 90·8 in April 1982,[64] and unemployment soared from 10% in June–August 1981 to 19% in March–May 1982.[65] By March 1982 the unrecoverable debt of the banking system was also rising alarmingly.

In April 1982 Sergio de Castro resigned as Finance Minister and was replaced by another 'Chicago boy', Sergio de la Cuadra, who was more acceptable to the financial groups. The message of the new Minister was that the growing disequilibria were due to rigidities introduced by the level of wages in the automatic adjustment of internal and international prices with a fixed rate of exchange. The proposal was to remove that rigidity by decreeing a general reduction of wages. It would appear that this solution was vetoed by the military; the alternative was to abandon the fixed exchange rate and to devalue. Despite statements to the contrary by Pinochet himself, the peso was devalued by 18% in June. Also, to pacify the financial groups, the government offered to purchase through the Central Bank the outstanding debt of the private banking system.[66] Nevertheless, the instability continued and a second devaluation – this time by 30% – took place in August.

By then the government appeared increasingly divided, their economic policy in disarray and the contradictions within the power bloc all too evident. De la Cuadra was replaced in September 1982 by yet another Chicago-trained economist, Rolf Lüders, who did not, however, belong to the core group of the 'Chicago boys' and who had been an executive in a bank belonging to one of the two major financial groups. Responding to Pinochet's increasing annoyance with the behaviour of the financial groups, the new Minister brought two banks into receivership – including his old employer – and ordered the takeover of five other banks; the latter included the two largest ones, owned by the two major financial groups.[67] The groups, however, fought back, and Lüders himself was replaced after only five months in office by a more mainstream 'Chicago boy'. But the all-powerful position of the Chicago boys had been very seriously undermined by the almost unmanageable economic situation: GDP had fallen by 14·3% in 1982, unemployment – including the people in the Minimum Employment Programme – stood at nearly 30% in March 1983 and annual inflation in that same month had shot up to 25%.

At the same time, the crisis had profound political implications. In terms of the power bloc, it marked the break of the unity of the bourgeoisie under the hegemony of the financial fraction and around the military regime: a growing conflict developed between the industrial and the financial fractions. Since the regime appeared totally identified with the latter, a kind of 'revolt of the capitalists' began to take shape. It entailed a demand for an opening of the political system that would allow the various fractions of capital a formalised and recognised voice in the decision-making processes of the regime. The fundamental new element in the political front was therefore the fact that policital debate ceased to be a matter of nuances of opinion among staunch supporters of the regime; in mid-1983 sections of the bourgeoisie were openly challenging the very essence of the military government, Pinochet's rule and the 1980 Constitution, and began to coordinate their protests with the workers. The latter, furthermore, had reappeared in the political scene as a major actor, as had the parties of the left. The government appeared incapable of dealing with the new context by resorting to simple coercion of the kind applied in 1974 and 1975.

CONCLUDING CONSIDERATIONS

We can now come back to the main threads of the argument presented in the preceding pages, and to the main organising concepts used throughout the discussion. The military government that took over in September 1973 in Chile represented a fundamental break with the previous history of the country both in terms of the role of the state in accumulation and in terms of the bases of domination of the political country regime. It represented a new form of state as well as a new form of regime. It was a form of state that initially expressed the political interest that the bourgeoisie as a whole had in the interruption and prevention of the socialist attempt of the Allende government. It was, in O'Donnell's terms, a response to the threat from below.[68] But it went further than that. It attempted to change fundamentally the bases of functioning and reproduction of the Chilean society and economy. In this it reflected the hegemony of the financial fraction of the bourgeoisie, itself linked to the decision of the government to withdraw from the function of mediation with the world capitalist system. This was prompted, again, by political considerations; the 'interventionist' role of the state was equated, in the view of the bourgeoisie and the military, with the 'compromise state' and the latter with the 'threat from below'. The consolidation of a financial sector that could take over that mediation was an explicit aim of the military government.

The hegemony of financial capital was therefore a result of the combination of the political factor of the 'threat from below' and of external dependency, that magnifies the internal importance of the links with the capitalist system. It was a result of the operation of peripheral capitalism. Its project was not to proceed to a deepening of capitalist accumulation, but to seek a different form of insertion in the world capitalist system for which a reduction in the rate of accumulation and change in direction – away from industrial goods and into raw materials, minimal processing, commerce and services – was functional. It was, therefore, fundamentally different from the cases of state monopoly capitalism described for advanced capitalist countries, where the state devalues its own capital in order to increase the rate of profit of a dynamic industrial monopoly sector.[69] Nothing of the sort has happened in Chile. A financial bourgeoisie was able to hegemonise a power bloc composed of all fractions of the bourgeoisie inasmuch as it seemed to offer the only way to avoid a repetition of the Allende threat. Once in power, it started implementing a de-accumulation model which led it into conflict with the other fractions and allowed for a re-emergence of the popular sectors as credible political actors. When the conflict became acute, the ultimate managers of the state, the military, decided to downgrade the role of the 'Chicago boys' and to distance themselves from the financial groups, while attempting a rapprochement with the other fractions of the bourgeoisie. What was lacking was a viable politico-economic project that could reconstitute a power bloc and – increasingly important – that could incorporate, albeit partially, the popular sectors. This would, however, be tantamount to reinstituting the 'compromise state'. Whether the bourgeoisie and their military guardians can bring themselves to effect what, in their own terms, would be a reversal of history is clearly an open question.

NOTES

I am grateful to Alan Angell, Mónica Peralta Ramos, John Sheahan and Arturo Valenzuela for comments on an earlier version of the section on 'The State and Capital Accumulation in Chile Until the 1970s' on pp. 141–52 of this chapter, and to Christian Anglade and David Evans for comments on the full present version. None of them, of course, bears any responsibility for the final outcome.

1. Seers (1978). For a lucid discussion of the issue in Latin America as a whole, see Sheahan (1980). The view that there is no necessary connection between open economies and repressive regimes is argued in Díaz Alejandro (1983).
2. A great deal of the evidence is contained in the indispensable contribution of the Chilean social scientists grouped in the *Corporación de Investigaciones Económicas para Latinoamérica* (CIEPLAN) in Santiago. I shall use extensively their published work in the section on 'The Economic Role of the State in Chile Under the Military' on pp. 160–75. Syntheses of their main findings are presented in Foxley (1982) and Ffrench-Davis (1982). Other important overall assessments are Arancibia (1978) and (1981) and Pinto (1981). For accounts that are sympathetic to the junta's model see Balassa (1983) and Sjaastad (1983).
3. A general political history of Chile in English that has a good discussion of the period is Pike (1963). For a Marxist treatment see Jobet (1955). Stevenson (1942) remains one of the most readable and perceptive ac-

counts of the rise of the Chilean Popular Front. See also Drake (1978). Useful discussions of the economics of the period – from opposing analytical viewpoints – are included in Pinto (1962) and (1964) and Mamalakis (1976). Muñoz (1968) provides a history of the development of industry in Chile from 1914. The relevant section of Sater's detailed bibliographical study of post-1965 sources adequately covers most other items, although it contains some errors. Sater (1979).
4. CORFO features prominently in most economic histories of the period. See Pinto (1962) and (1964), Instituto de Economía (1956) and (1963). For assessments of the role of CORFO see Mamalakis (1967), (1969) and (1976) pp. 293–314.
5. Mamalakis (1976) p. 253.
6. See more generally Graciarena and Franco (1978), esp. pp. 34ff.
7. Mamalakis (1965) pp. 17–18. He argues, however, that agriculture was discriminated against in the 1940–73 period. ibid., pp. 138–9.
8. For a discussion of the large literature on the Alliance for Progress from the 'bureaucratic politics' viewpoint, see Lowenthal (1974). There is a dearth of serious comprehensive treatments of the Frei government, although most of the better analyses of the Allende experience contain some discussion of the 1964–70 period; see note 15 below. Ffrench-Davis (1973) covers Frei's economic policies. See also Ramos (1972) for a perspective from the Chilean left. In this section I will follow closely and will partially reproduce sections of a previous article on the topic (Fortin, 1979).
9. Based on figures in ODEPLAN (1973) pp. 32, 49 and 52.
10. Based on CORFO figures in Mamalakis (1978), table 62, p. 250.
11. Borón (1971) pp. 428–9.
12. See generally Angell (1972). The figures on unionisation are taken from Valenzuela (1978) pp. 28 and 30.
13. Borón (1971) p. 430.
14. United States Senate (1976).
15. The literature on the *Unidad Popular* experience is vast. For the economic programme of the government, see Martner (1971). Useful overall assessments include De Vylder (1976), Valenzuela and Valenzuela (1976), Roxborough, O'Brien and Roddick (1977), and Gil, Lagos and Landsberger (1979). They were all however written before the full extent of US government involvement in the destabilisation of the Allende government became public knowledge (see note 14). Sigmund (1977) takes account of US activities but argues that they were not a major determinant of the outcome. Assessments by Chilean social scientists who were involved in the Allende experiment are contained in Sideri (1979) and Bitar (1979). The economic history of the period is covered in Stallings (1978) and Mamalakis (1976), the former sympathetic and the latter hostile to the *Unidad Popular*. Valenzuela (1978) is a lucid discussion of the political dynamics of the period. Valenzuela and Valenzuela (1975) reviews among others a number of sources which provide a sample of Chilean partisan responses to the Allende attempt and to the coup.
16. On the events immediately preceding the coup, see Garcés (1975).
17. This periodisation was suggested by the one proposed in Foxley (1982) but differs in substantial respects from it.

18. See Frenkel and Johnson (1976); Kreinin and Officer (1978); Humphrey and Keleher (1982).
19. See Garretón (1980), from whom the periodisation is essentially taken.
20. A chilling detailed account of DINA's international activities is contained in Dinges and Landau (1981).
21. United Nations (1977), paras 240–60, pp. 98–106.
22. United Nations (1978), para. 641, p. 187.
23. Barrera and Henríquez (1982).
24. There are official Chilean figures on fiscal expenditures, but the distinction between state agencies and decentralised, autonomous and para-statal institutions – which are not included in the fiscal sector – is arbitrary. Also, transfers from fiscal to non-fiscal state organisations are counted as fiscal expenditure. For these and other methodological reasons, official fiscal figures are a misleading indicator of the level of state expenditure. There is, however, a study for 1969–79 (Marshall, 1981) which covers the whole of the public sector, excluding only public enterprises, local government and universities. I have used the figures in the study and I have extrapolated the figures on fiscal expenditure for 1981–82.
25. Marshall (1981) pp. 66–72; see also Vergara (1981).
26. McKinnon (1973) and (1981). On the 'structuralist' nature of McKinnon's approach, see FitzGerald (1983).
27. Lagos (1981) pp. 86–9.
28. Foxley (1982) pp. 44–5.
29. Zahler (1980); Herrera and Morales (1979).
30. Ffrench-Davis (1982) p. 17.
31. See Ffrench-Davis (1980) and Ffrench-Davis and Arellano (1981).
32. Calculated on the basis of data in Foxley (1982) p. 44.
33. Ffrench-Davis and Arellano (1981).
34. Foxley (1982) p. 58.
35. Vignolo (1980).
36. Dahse (1979).
37. See Fortin (forthcoming).
38. See generally United Nations (1976), (1977), (1978), (1979), (1980) and (1981).
39. United Nations (1976) p. 25.
40. United Nations (1978).
41. Moulian and Vergara (1980) offer an illuminating account of the relationship between ideology and economic policy in the military regime; my account, however, differs from theirs in important respects. See also Garretón (1981).
42. Arriagada and Garretón (1978).
43. For this and other junta statements, see references in Valenzuela and Valenzuela (1975).
44. Ffrench-Davis (1982) table 5, p. 32.
45. For a discussion, see Arancibia (1978) pp. 78–9.
46. See Arellano (1981) and Nash (1981).
47. Ffrench-Davis (1982) p. 34.
48. Morales (1981).
49. Raczynski and Oyarzo (1981).
50. Herrera and Morales (1979) p. 148.

51. Dahse (1979); pp. 138ff.
52. FitzGerald (1983) pp. 122–3.
53. Lagos (1981); see also the lucid analysis in Pinto (1981).
54. In his otherwise incisive analysis Garretón (1980) confuses these two questions when he maintains that the hegemonic group in the regime is composed of Pinochet and the economic technocrats.
55. Moulian and Vergara (1980) pp. 95–6.
56. Latin America Bureau (1983) pp. 38–41.
57. Ffrench-Davis (1982) pp. 29–30.
58. Mönckeberg and Paulsen (1980).
59. Banco Central de Chile (1982) p. 1502.
60. Banco Central de Chile (1983a) p. 1596.
61. See Banco Central de Chile (1982) p. 1404.
62. Banco Central de Chile (1981).
63. Vector (1981) pp. 33–6.
64. See Banco Central de Chile (1983) p. 973 and (1983b) p. 1643.
65. Economic and Financial Survey (1983b) p. 3.
66. See Economic and Financial Survey (1982).
67. Economic and Financial Survey (1983a).
68. O'Donnell (1978).
69. Boccara *et. al.* (1976); Herzog (1972).

REFERENCES

Angell, A. (1972), *Politics and the Labour Movement in Chile* (London: Oxford University Press).
Arancibia, A. (1978), 'Chile, 1973–1978: la vía chilena a la pauperización y la dependencia', *Economía de América Latina*, México, 1st. Semester, pp. 61–110.
—— (1981), 'Chile: mitos y realidades del proyecto autoritario', *Economía de América Latina*, México, 2nd Semester, pp. 169–95.
Arellano, J. P. (1981), 'Elementos para el análisis de la reforma previsional chilena', *Estudios CIEPLAN*, no. 6 (Santiago) Dec. pp. 5–44.
Arriagada, G. and Garretón, M. A. (1978), 'Doctrina de seguridad nacional y régimen militar', *Estudios Sociales Centroamericanos*, San José, Costa Rica; part I, vol. VII, no. 20, May–Aug., pp. 129–53; part II, vol VII, no. 21, Sept.–Dec., pp. 53–82.
Balassa, B. (1983), *Policy Experiments in Chile, 1973–83*, World Bank Discussion Paper, Nov.
Banco Central de Chile (1974), *Boletín Mensual*, no. 555 (Santiago) May.
—— (1980), ibid., no. 623, Jan.
—— (1980a), ibid., no. 628, June.
—— (1981), ibid., no. 641, July.
—— (1982), ibid., no. 653, July.
—— (1983), ibid., No. 662, Apr.
—— (1983a), ibid., no. 664, June.
—— (1983b), ibid., no. 665, July.
Barrera, M. and Henríquez, H. (1982), *Participación popular y autoritarismo*

político. El caso de la negociación colectiva de los sindicatos chilenos (Santiago: Centro de Estudios Sociales).
Bitar, S. (1973), 'La presencia de la empresa extranjera en la industria chilena', *Desarrollo Económico*, vol. 13, no. 50, Buenos Aires, July–Sept., pp. 243–284.
—— (1979), *Transición, socialismo y democracia: la experiencia chilena* (México: Siglo XXI).
Boccara, P. et. al. (1976), *Traité d'économie politique: le capitalisme monopoliste d'état* (Paris: Editions Sociales).
Borón, A. (1971), 'La evolución del régimen electoral y sus efectos en la representación de los intereses populares: el caso de Chile', *Revista Latinoamericana de Ciencia Política*, vol. II, no. 3 (Santiago) Dec.
Cortázar, R. (1980), 'Distribución del ingreso, empleo y remuneraciones reales en Chile 1970–1978', *Estudios CIEPLAN*, no. 3 (Santiago) June, pp. 5–24.
—— (1982), 'Desempleo,pobreza y distribución: Chile 1970–1981', *Apuntes CIEPLAN*, no. 34 (Santiago) June.
—— and Marshall, J. (1980), 'Indice de precios al consumidor en Chile: 1970–1978', *Estudios CIEPLAN*, no. 4 (Santiago) Nov., pp. 159–201.
Dahse, F. (1979), *Mapa de la extrema riqueza: los grupos económicos y el proceso de concentración de capitales* (Santiago: Editorial Aconcagua).
Díaz Alejandro, C. F. (1983), 'Open economies, closed polity?', in Tussie, D. (ed.), *Latin America in the World Economy: New Perspectives* (London: Gower) pp. 21–53.
Dinges, J. and Landau, S. (1981), *Assassination on Embassy Row* (London: Writers and Readers).
Drake, P. W. (1978), *Socialism and Populism in Chile, 1932–1953* Urbana, Ill.: University of Illinois Press).
ECLA (1949), *Economic Survey of Latin America* (New York: United Nations).
ECOMANAGER, published by Economic and Financial Survey, Santiago.
Economic and Financial Survey (1982), *Carta Semanal*, no. 1064 (Santiago) 19 July.
—— (1983), *Análisis. Diagnóstico Económico y Financiero*, no. 919 (Santiago) 3 Oct.
—— (1983a), *Carta Semanal*, no. 1090 (Santiago) 17 Jan.
—— (1983b), *Carta Semanal*, no. 1105 (Santiago) 16 May.
Ffrench-Davis, R. (1973), *Políticas económicas en Chile, 1952–1970* (Santiago: Ediciones Nueva Universidad).
—— (1980), 'Liberalización de importaciones: la experiencia chilena en 1973–79', *Estudios CIEPLAN*, no. 4 (Santiago) Nov. pp. 39–78.
—— (1982), 'El experimento monetarista en Chile: una síntesis crítica', *Estudios CIEPLAN*, no. 9 (Santiago) Dec. pp. 5–40.
—— and Arellano, J. P. (1981), 'Apertura financiera externa: la experiencia chilena en 1973–80', *Estudios CIEPLAN*, no. 5 (Santiago) July, pp. 5–52.
Fortin, C. (1979), 'The State and Capital Accumulation in Chile', in Carrière, J. (ed.), *Industrialization and the State in Latin America* (Amsterdam: CEDLA) pp. 15–48.
——(forthcoming), 'Copper Investment Policy in Chile, 1973–84, *Natural Resources Forum*.
Foxley, A. (1982), 'Experimentos neoliberales en América Latina', *Estudios CIEPLAN*, no. 7 (Santiago) Mar.

Frenkel, J. A. and Johnson, H. G. (eds) (1976), *The Monetary Approach to the Balance of Payments* (University of Toronto Press).
Garcés, J. (1975), *Chile: el camino político al socialismo* (Barcelona: Ediciones Ariel).
Garretón, M. A. (1980), *Procesos políticos en un régimen autoritario. Dinámicas de institucionalización y oposición en Chile 1973–1980*, FLACSO (Santiago) Documento de Trabajo no. 104, Dec.
—— (1981), 'El camino institucional y el sistema político', *Chile–América*, no. 74–5 (Rome) pp. 83–93.
Gil, F. G., Lagos, R. and Landsberger, H. A. (eds) (1979), *Chile at the Turning Point. Lessons from the Socialist Years, 1970–1973* (Philadelphia: Institute for the Study of Human Issues).
Graciarena, J. and Franco, R. (1978), 'Social Formations and Power Structures in Latin America', *Current Sociology*, vol. 26, no. 1, Spring.
Herrera, J. E. and Morales, J. (1979), 'La inversión financiera externa: el caso de Chile, 1974–1978', *Estudios CIEPLAN*, no. 1 (Santiago) July, pp. 103–50.
Herzog, P. (1972), *Politique économique et planification en régime cápitaliste* (Paris: Editions Sociales).
Humphrey, T. M. and Keleher, R. E. (1982), *The Monetary Approach to the Balance of Payments, Exchange Rates and World Inflation* (New York: Praeger).
Instituto de Economía (1956), *Desarrollo económico de Chile, 1940–1956* (Santiago de Chile: Editorial Universitaria).
—— (1963), *La economía de Chile en el período 1950–1963* (Santiago de Chile: Universidad de Chile).
Jobet, J. C. (1955), *Ensayo crítico del desarrollo económico-social de Chile* (Santiago de Chile: Editorial Universitaria).
Kreinin, M. E. and Officer, L. H. (1978), *The Monetary Approach to the Balance of Payments: A Survey* (Princeton Studies in International Finance no. 43).
Lagos, R. (1981), 'La burguesía emergente', *Chile–América*, no. 72–3, Rome, pp. 83–93.
Latin America Bureau (1983), *Chile: The Pinochet Decade* (London: Latin America Bureau).
Lowenthal, A. F. (1974), '"Liberal", "Radical" and "Bureaucratic" Perspectives on US-Latin American Policy: The Alliance for Progress in Retrospect', in Cotler, J. and Fagen, R. R. (eds), *Latin America and the United States: The Changing Political Realities* (Stanford University Press), pp. 212–35.
McKinnon, R. I. (1973), *Money and Capital in Economic Development* (Washington, D.C.: The Brookings Institution).
—— and Mathieson, D. J. (1981), *How to Manage a Repressed Economy* (Princeton University Essays in International Finance no. 145, December).
Mamalakis, M. J. (1965), 'Public Policy and Sectoral Development. A Case Study of Chile 1940–1958' in Mamalakis, M. and Reynolds, C. W., *Essays on the Chilean Economy* (Homewood, Ill.: Richard D. Irwin, Inc.) pp. 3–200.
—— (1967), 'Veinticinco anõs de la Corporación de Fomento de la Producción', in Instituto de Economía, *Ensayos sobre planificación* (Santiago de Chile: Universidad de Chile).
—— (1969), 'An Analysis of the Financial and Investment Activities of the

Chilean Development Corporation, 1939–1964', *Journal of Development Studies*, vol. 5, no. 2, Jan., pp. 118–37.
—— (1976), *The Growth and Structure of the Chilean Economy* (New Haven, Conn.: Yale University Press).
—— (1978), *Historical Statistics of Chile. National Accounts* (Westport, Conn.: Greenwood Press).
Marshall, J. (1981), 'El gasto público en Chile: 1969–1979', *Estudios CIEPLAN*, no. 5 (Santiago) July, pp. 53–84.
Martínez, A. (1979), 'The Industrial Sector: Areas of Social and Mixed Property in Chile', in Sideri (1979), pp. 221–74.
Martner, G. (ed.) (1971), *El pensamiento económico del gobierno de Allende*, (Santiago de Chile: Editorial Universitaria).
Mönckeberg, M. O. and Paulsen, F. (1980), 'CRAV', *Análisis*, IV, 36, Santiago de Chile, July, Supplement.
Morales, E. (1981), 'La salud', *Chile–América*, no. 74–5, Rome, pp. 73–7.
Moulián, T. and Vergara, P. (1980), 'Estado, ideología y políticas económicas en Chile, 1973–1978', *Estudios CIEPLAN*, no. 3 (Santiago), June, pp. 65–120.
Muñoz, O. (1968), *Crecimiento industrial de Chile, 1914–1965* (Santiago de Chile: Universidad de Chile, Instituto de Economía y Planificación).
Nash, J. (1981), 'La reforma previsional', *Chile–América*, no. 74–5, Rome, Oct.–Dec., pp. 44–59.
ODEPLAN (1973), *Balances económicos de Chile 1960–1970* (Santiago: Editorial Universitaria).
—— (1960–75), *Cuentas Nacionales de Chile 1960–1975* (Santiago).
—— (1972–77), *Cuentas Nacionales de Chile 1972–1977* (Santiago).
—— (1982), *Informe sobre proyectos y estudios de inversión del sector público* (Santiago).
O'Donnell, G. (1978), 'Reflections on the Patterns of Change in the Bureaucratic-Authoritarian State', *Latin American Research Review*, vol. XIII, no. 1, Winter, pp. 3–38.
Pike, F. B. (1963), *Chile and the United States, 1880–1962* (University of Notre Dame Press).
Pinto, A. (1962), *Chile, un caso de desarrollo frustrado* (Santiago: Editorial Universitaria).
—— (1964), *Chile, una economía difícil* (México: Fondo de Cultura Económica).
—— (1981), 'Chile: el modelo ortodojo y el desarrollo nacional', *El Trimestre Económico*, vol. 58(4), no. 192, México, Oct.–Dec., pp. 853–902.
Raczynski, D. and Oyarzo, C. (1981), '?Por qué cae la tasa de mortalidad infantil en Chile?', *Estudios CIEPLAN*, no. 6 (Santiago) Dec., pp. 45–84.
Ramos, S. (1972), *Chile: una economía de transición?* (Santiago de Chile: Centro de Estudios Socio-Económicos de la Universidad de Chile, *Cuadernos*, no. 15).
Roxborough, I., O'Brien, P. and Roddick, J. (1977). *Chile: the State and Revolution* (London: Macmillan).
Sater, W. F. (1979), 'A survey of Recent Chilean Historiography, 1965–1976', *Latin American Research Review*, vol. XIV, no. 2, pp. 55–88.
Seers, D. (1978), *Chile: the Rule of the Chicago Boys* (London: World University Service – UK), July.

Sheahan, J. (1980), 'Market-oriented Economic Policies and Political Repression in Latin America', *Economic Development and Cultural Change*, vol. 28, no. 2, Jan., pp. 267–91.
Sideri, S. (ed.) (1979), *Chile 1970–73: Economic Development and Its International Setting* (The Hague: Nijhoff).
Sigmund, P. E. (1977), *The Overthrow of Allende and the Politics of Chile, 1964–1976* (University of Pittsburgh Press).
Sjaastad, L. A. (1983), 'Failure of Economic Liberalism in the Core of Latin America', *The World Economy*, vol. 6, no. 1, Mar., pp. 5–26.
Stallings, B. (1978), *Class Conflict and Economic Development in Chile, 1958–1973* (Stanford University Press).
Stevenson, J. R. (1942), *The Chilean Popular Front* (Westport, Conn.: Greenwood Press Publishers).
United Nations (1976), *Protection of Human Rights in Chile: Note by the Secretary General*, Doc. A/31/253, 8 Oct.
—— (1977), ibid., Doc. A/32/227, 29 Sept.
—— (1978), ibid., Doc. A/33/331, 25 Oct.
—— (1979), ibid., Doc. A/34/583, 21 Nov.
—— (1980), ibid., Doc. A/35/522, 23 Oct.
—— (1981), ibid., Doc. A/36/594, 6 Nov.
United States Senate (1976), *Hearings before the Select Committee to Study Governmental Operations with Respect to Intelligence Activities*, vol. 7, 'Covert Action' (Washington D.C.: Government Printing Office).
Valenzuela, A. (1978), *The Breakdown of Democratic Regimes: Chile* (Baltimore: The Johns Hopkins University Press).
Valenzuela, A. and Valenzuela, J. S. (1975), 'Visions of Chile', *Latin American Research Review*, vol. x, no. 3, Fall, pp. 155–75.
—— (eds) (1976), *Chile: Politics and Society* (New Brunswick, N.J.: Transaction Books).
Vergara, P. (1981), 'Las transformaciones de las funciones económicas del Estado en Chile bajo el régimen militar', *Estudios CIEPLAN*, no. 5 (Santiago) July, pp. 117–54.
Vector (1981), *Informe de Coyuntura Económica* (Santiago) Oct.
Vignolo, C. (1980), 'Inversión extranjera en Chile, 1974–79', *Mensaje*, no. 286 (Santiago).
de Vylder, S. (1976), *Allende's Chile: the Political Economy of the Rise and Fall of the Unidad Popular* (Cambridge University Press).
Zahler, R. (1980), 'Monetary and Real Repercussions of Financial Opening: the Case of Chile, 1975–1978', *CEPAL Review*, no. 10, (Santiago) Apr., pp. 127–53.

APPENDIX

TABLE 3.A1 *Chile: gross investment in fixed capital as a percentage of GDP and index of per capita domestic investment in fixed capital, 1960–82 (1960–64 = 100)*

	(1) CORFO 1961 Prices	(2) ODEPLAN 1965 Prices	(3) Banco Central 1977 Prices		(4) Index of per capita gross domestic investment in fixed capital	
1940–44	8.0					
1945–49	9.9					
1950–54	9.6					
1955–59	9.9					
1960–64	12.2	16.1	21.4	21.4	100	
1965–70		14.5	19.3	19.3	101.7	
1971		13.9	18.3		115.9	
1972		11.8	14.8 ⎱	16.0	91.2 ⎱	89.4
1973		11.6	14.7 ⎰		84.2 ⎰	
1974		12.7	17.4		98.6	
1975		11.1	15.4		74.9	
1976		10.1	12.7		62.7	
1977			13.3		71.2	
1978			14.5	15.7	82.1	82.7
1979			15.6		94.4	
1980			17.8		113.1	
1981			19.1		127.5	
1982			14.1		78.9	

SOURCE Calculated from data in (1) Mamalakis (1978), table 5, pp. 43–6; (2) ODEPLAN (1960–75), table 12, pp. 33–4, and ODEPLAN (1972–77), table 13, p. 23; Central Bank data as reported in (3) *Ecomanager*, vol. I, tables 4.3.3. and 4.4.2, and Banco Central de Chile (1983b) p. 1623. Per capita index calculated on the basis of population series of the National Institute of Statistics as reported in *Ecomanager*, vol. I, table 2.1. Different series are not strictly comparable because of changes in methodology.

TABLE 3.A2 *Chile: sectoral shares of GDP, selected years, 1907–82 (percentages)*

	Agriculture	Industry	Services	(Banking)	(Trade)	Mining	Construction
1907–30*	14.0	16.0†	50.0	(n.a.)	(n.a.)	20.0	
1940	14.9	16.7	56.1	(n.a.)	(18.1)	8.6	2.3
1945	13.0	22.4	59.3	(n.a.)	(19.3)	5.8	2.7
1950	13.2	21.9	57.4	(n.a.)	(17.4)	5.7	2.4
1955	13.0	23.7	54.1	(n.a.)	(20.5)	4.1	2.4
1960	10.1	22.2	47.5	(3.0)	(17.1)	7.7	7.6
1965	8.6	24.8	46.3	(2.7)	(15.9)	7.5	7.8
1970	8.2	24.7	47.6	(4.6)	(16.5)	6.6	7.5
1971	7.4	25.7	48.1	(4.9)	(17.6)	6.4	6.9
1972	6.9	26.6	49.2	(4.2)	(18.5)	6.2	5.6
1973	6.6	26.0	50.6	(4.3)	(18.3)	6.4	5.3
1974	8.2	25.1	48.4	(5.2)	(14.6)	7.8	6.6
1975	9.9	21.5	52.2	(5.7)	(13.9)	7.9	5.6
1976	9.3	22.0	54.0	(6.1)	(13.7)	8.6	4.5
1977	9.3	21.7	52.4	(6.3)	(15.6)	8.0	4.1
1978	8.2	22.0	53.1	(7.0)	(17.3)	7.6	4.1
1979	8.0	21.9	53.5	(8.3)	(17.7)	7.3	4.6
1980	7.7	21.6	54.1	(9.4)	(18.5)	7.1	5.3
1981	7.6	20.9	53.9	(10.3)	(18.6)	7.3	6.1
1982	8.6	19.1	57.1	(11.0)	(17.9)	9.0	5.1

* As percentage of total income.
† Including construction.

SOURCE 1907–30, Mamalakis (1976), table 1.3, p. 15; 1940–55, calculated from CORFO data in 1961 prices in Mamalakis (1978), table 28, pp. 145–8; 1960–82, calculated from data in 1977 prices from the Central Bank of Chile, in *Ecomanager*, table 4.4.81 and Banco Central de Chile (1983b) p. 1621. The three series are not strictly comparable because of changes in estimating methodology.

TABLE 3.A3 *Chile: payments to labour as percentages of domestic income, selected years, 1940–81*

	(1) CORFO	(2) ODEPLAN	(3) Banco Central
1940	41.9		
1945	42.1		
1950	44.6		
1954	46.1		
...			
1960		51.6	51.6
1964		44.8	44.8
1969		48.6	48.6
1970		52.3	52.3
1971		61.7	61.7
1972		62.8	62.8
1973		47.2	47.2
1974		42.2	50.9
1975		41.9	54.6
1976		41.1	52.5
1977			53.3
1978			51.5
1979			46.5
1980			48.8
1981			51.7

SOURCE Calculated from data in (1) Mamalakis (1978), table 53, pp. 239–40; (2) ODEPLAN (1960–75), table 11, pp. 31–2 and ODEPLAN (1972–77), table 12, p. 22; (3) *Ecomanager*, table 4.37 and Banco Central de Chile (1983b) pp. 1625–8. All original data in current money.

TABLE 3.A4 *Chile: annual rate of change of GDP and per capita GDP (percentages) and indices of per capita GDP and per capita industrial value added, 1960–82 (1971 = 100) in real terms*

	% Variation GDP	% Variation per capita GDP	Index per capita GDP (1971 = 100)	Index per capita industrial value added (1971 = 100)
1960–64	4.6	2.1	79.9	72.2
1964–70	4.0	2.0	88.8	86.1
1971	9.0	7.1	100.0	100.0
1972	−1.2	−2.9	97.1	100.5
1973	−5.6	−7.1	90.2	91.2
1974	1.0	−0.7	89.6	87.4
1975	−12.9	−14.4	76.7	64.1
1976	3.5	1.8	78.1	66.8
1977	9.9	8.0	84.3	71.2
1978	8.2	6.4	89.7	76.5
1979	8.3	6.5	95.5	81.1
1980	7.8	6.0	101.2	84.7
1981	5.7	3.9	105.2	85.4
1982	−14.3	−14.2	90.2	67.1

SOURCE Based on data from the Central Bank of Chile reported in *Ecomanager*, vol. I, tables 4.3.1 and 4.4.8.1 and Banco Central de Chile (1983b) p. 1621. Per capita figures calculated on the basis of population data from the National Institute of Statistics reported in *Ecomanager*, vol. I, table 2.1 and Banco Central de Chile (1983b) p. 1680.

TABLE 3.A5 *Chile: variation of the consumer price index, 1950–82 (percentages, December to December)*

1950	16.5
1951	23.4
1952	12.0
1953	56.2
1954	71.1
1955	83.8
1956	37.7
1957	17.2
1958	32.5
1959	33.2
1960	5.5
1961	9.6
1962	27.7
1963	45.3
1964	38.5
1965	25.8
1966	17.0
1967	21.9
1968	27.9
1969	29.3
1970	36.1
1971	355.4
1972	n/a
1973	605.9
1974	369.2
1975	343.3
1976	197.9
1977	84.2
1978	37.2
1979	38.9
1980	31.2
1981	9.5
1982	20.7

SOURCE Banco Central (1983b) p. 1663 except 1970–73 taken from Cortázar and Marshall (1980) p. 161.

TABLE 3.A6 *Chile: foreign debt and reserves, 1960–81 (million current US dollars)*

	Foreign debt	Reserves
1960	746	119
1961	1 010	104
1965	1 781	182
1970	3 123	505
1972	3 602	271
1974	4 774	535
1975	5 263	427
1976	5 195	816
1977	5 434	871
1978	6 911	1 597
1979	8 463	2 792
1980	10 746	4 074
1981	14 653	3 775

SOURCE Banco Central de Chile (1980) p. 1050, (1981) pp. 1512 and 1526, (1982) pp. 1388 and 1403.

4 The Financial Constraint on Relative Autonomy: the State and Capital Accumulation in Mexico, 1940–82

E. V. K. FITZGERALD

THE FOUNDATIONS OF THE MEXICAN STATE

The activities of the state are widely regarded as a central feature in the remarkably rapid process of economic expansion experienced by Mexico in the 25 years after the outbreak of World War II, and thus must also be seen as such in the imbalance that has emerged over the last 15 years. In a mixed economy such as Mexico, where the state does not directly control production and the surplus accrues fundamentally to the private sector, the finance of these activities – particularly public investment – proves a significant constraint on the 'relative autonomy of the state', reflecting as it does the relationship between state and civil society in the sphere of circulation. Extensive state intervention in the process of capital accumulation during the period of industrialisation is common to the experience of Latin America as a whole,[1] but in Mexico the scale and scope of this intervention appear to have been greater than elsewhere. This has become the central theme of political debate in recent years. It also provides a significant case to be examined in the light of current theoretical discussions as to the relative autonomy and the fiscal crisis of the state in capitalist economies.

On the political plane,[2] although the reformism of Madero had been overtaken by the popular agrarian movements of Villa and Zapata during the revolutionary years, and the hegemony of the agrarian oligarchy distroyed, these movements had demonstrated their incapacity to form a government before being themselves suppressed by Carranza and Obregón. In this political vacuum, it took the bureaucratic-military elite a decade to build a national state, but the resultant interventionist (and perhaps 'intermediate' in the Kaleckian sense) regimes of Calles and Cárdenas managed between 1925 and 1940 to reduce substantially the degree of foreign ownership in the export sectors of mining and agriculture, nationalise oil, implement a large-scale land reform in favour of the subsistence peasantry, and establish local control over the banking system. The consolidation of the *Partido Revolucionario Institucional* in these decades provided the basis of both popular support for the new state and control over the labour force; but equally important was the new relationship established between the state and the emergent national bourgeoisie, and the consolidation of the position of the bureaucracy itself so as to effectively displace the military from power. The result was to create a state with considerable relative autonomy from both external (US) and internal (class) pressure.

Within this state, a relatively small and stable group of senior bureaucrats ('state managers') could make a politico-administrative career without great reference to party politics or direct links to class interests. Consequently ideology, and economic ideas in particular, was to play an important part in determining the form of state intervention in support of capitalist accumulation.

On the economic plane,[3] the 1925–40 period saw the decline of mining and oil as the 'leading sectors' and their replacement by commercial agriculture and manufacturing, although external trade remained highly dependent on the US. The Depression did not, as elsewhere in Latin America, foster the process of import-substituting industrialisation (because Mexico had no lack of access to US manufactures) but rather led to the restructuring of the fiscal and financial systems (basing public investment on domestic credit and creating state banks in order to finance industry, agriculture and foreign trade), a redistribution of income away from peasants and foreign export enterprises towards local profits, and the expansion of urban employment. This process was supported by massive public investment in irrigation and transport on the one hand, and the implementation of measures to stimulate industrialisation on the other. As a result, the rate of productive accumulation was already rising strongly in the 1930s.

Thus by 1940, a strong nationalist state had set the stage for a long period of sustained capital accumulation. Although historians disagree as to which social group managed to dominate the new state,[4] it was clearly orientated towards the fostering of capitalist growth: the subsequent industrial and agricultural growth was supported by low wages, appropriate infrastructure, development finance and favourable prices. Economic progress even allowed the gradual retraction of state intervention in production and investment and the strengthening of the private sector. However, when the contradictions of this growth-model began to become evident during the latter half of the 1960s – in the form of sectoral imbalance, excessive foreign ownership, worsening income distribution and internal migration – there occurred a renewed extension of state activity. In this essay, we shall argue that the underlying financial imbalance (despite enormous oil revenues at the end of our period), which might be termed a 'fiscal crisis of the state', prevented the required restructuring of the Mexican economy and a renewal of industrial accumulation; and that although this constraint on relative autonomy appears in the 'economic sphere', it is, in fact, the result of a political conflict over control of the surplus and the direction which accumulation should take.

To some extent, this appears to be a common feature of the large Latin American state in the post-import-substitution stage of industrialisation,[5] and thus the Mexican case may have some bearing on wider issues. None the less, the post-revolutionary nature of the Mexican state – which has retained its essential features over nearly half a century – and the relatively independent role played by senior state managers in particular, means that general conclusions are difficult to draw. We shall start by setting out the main economic trends for the two main periods under consideration; we will then look at the pattern of capital accumulation, and the fiscal crisis of the Mexican state in relation to this; from this analysis, we shall finally derive some tentative conclusions as to the nature of relative state autonomy.

THE MEXICAN ECONOMY, 1940–65: ESTABLISHING *DESARROLLO ESTABILIZADOR*

Between 1940 and 1965, Mexico enjoyed a remarkable rate of economic expansion: an expansion that was both sustained with relatively little interruption (although it did respond to depressions in the US economy such that of 1959–61) and experienced in a 'balanced' manner between different sectors – above all the growth of agriculture in line with industry. The former grew at about 5% per year and the latter at about 7%, leading to a GDP growth rate fluctuating narrowly around 6% – which as a sustained growth record must be almost unequalled in the post-war world. An inflationary period in the forties had the effect of reducing real wages quite sharply (see Appendix, Tables 4.A1 and 4.A6), through official trades union control over wage pressure (with the government imposing a minimum wage) on the one hand, and finance of state investment by monetary creation on the other. The devaluation of 1954, although it was brought about by a sudden decline in the external terms of trade, meant an excessive decline in real wages for the political system to contain, as the state managers realised. The resolution of this problem was a new strategy '*desarrollo estabilizador*'.

The transition was not a simple one, as it involved the state not only coming to terms with its own labour movement but also with the private banks, who had to be persuaded to finance the government through compulsory reserves (i.e. forced loans) in the Central Bank; a rapprochement with US investors was also finally reached.[6] For the subsequent decade the wage bill was contained by the progressive capital deepening resulting from the heavy investment programme, leading to sustained and high profit rates. Meanwhile, the balance of payments remained reasonably stable, imports declining steadily as a proportion of domestic output as the import-substitution process advanced. The modest deficit on current account was covered by steady inflows of foreign capital funds, although these only accounted for a fraction of total savings in the economy. In short, the Mexican economy appeared to have achieved sustained and balanced long-run growth; it became a textbook example to other developing economies and even entered the pantheon of the Rostovian 'takeoff'.

A considerable literature began to appear in the mid-1960s, analysing the causes of this success.[7] It was initially of Mexican origin although it became known internationally through the work of US economists associated with the *Banco de México*. The main thrust of this argument was that Mexican economic development was an almost unqualified success, the main long-run causes being the structural reforms before 1940 (above all the agrarian reform), the concentration of state investment on productive public works (such as irrigation), the provision of development finance so as to set up and sustain private enterprise in its 'infant' stage, and the channelling of foreign investment into selected industrial branches requiring advanced technology. Concern was expressed, however, lest this government intervention might deprive the private sector of resources and the required freedom of action for 'entrepreneurship'. Indeed the size of the public sector was seen as the 'dilemma of Mexican development',[8] in the belief that the historic task of state intervention was over and that Mexican capitalists could now manage for themselves.

The *technical* economic analysis of the Mexican economy by this 'orthodox' group concentrated on the financial and monetary aspects of state intervention.[9] Their version of events took into account structural factors but attributed macroeconomic stability (and thus 'business confidence' and rising private investment) to monetary policy; this to a considerable extent became established as the official Mexican version of events. In this model, government expenditure follows the 6-year cycle of presidential office (low at the outset and higher later on as new projects and programmes mature) but in the absence of major tax reform and with steady output growth and relatively low proportion of exports in total demand (private consumption expenditure is a stable and exogenous factor) stabilisation can only be achieved by adjusting private investment. Banks maintain a rate of interest (essentially linked to those on Wall Street) which is low relative to high enterprise profit rates, so they are always faced by excess demand for their funds; by manipulating credit rationing rules and reserve requirements for private banks the monetary authorities can absorb the proportion of private savings from the banking system required to finance the public sector deficit – itself the result of high state investment. Consequently, neither an inflationary nor a deflationary situation develops because variations in the fiscal deficit change the credit available for private investment. In addition, by limiting available funds on the Mexican capital market in times of external deficit, the monetary authorities oblige the private sector to borrow abroad, thus avoiding public external debt from rising. Hence, it was held that this mechanism allowed steady economic growth despite the deficits on both fiscal and trade accounts arising from that growth; but that attempts to raise government expenditure further would 'crowd out' productive private investment.

The contemporary critique of this approach came not as a criticism of the internal logic of this model but rather in the form of pointing out structural aspects of asset ownership and income distribution that formed no part of the official version. The first line of attack took the form of analyses of ownership in major enterprises,[10] which underlined the extreme degree of concentration in private industry, close links between banks and large enterprise groups, and a very high degree of foreign ownership in manufacturing. Domestic asset concentration generated less criticism than the fact that despite the nationalisation of oil, electricity, railways and agricultural estates, foreign control in other sectors was increasing. Official data indicated that half of manufacturing assets were controlled by multinational firms in 1972, and that the share of sales controlled rose from 38% in 1962 to 45% in 1970.[11] Close collaboration between foreign enterprise and state enterprise, and the dominance of foreign brokers in large areas of agricultural marketing – let alone the traditional diplomatic presence of the 'Good Neighbour' – were held to strengthen this dependency. Apart from the implications for national sovereignty, the critics also pointed to the outflow of profits and royalties, the gearing of the output pattern to the production of luxury 'branded' goods and the lack of integration between branches brought about by reliance on imported inputs. They also blamed foreign companies for the limitation on manufactured exports based on labour-intensive 'border' operations and internal enterprise transactions, which did not form the foundation for self-sustaining growth.

The skewed and deteriorating income distribution[12] provided the second line of attack. This was attributed to the growing imbalance of the economy as industry and urban services expanded more rapidly than agriculture (leading also to massive internal migration) on the one hand, and to the concentration of national income in profits, on the other. Apart from the social implications, it was also argued that this concentration of national income resulted in a 'narrow' domestic market for manufactures (particularly wage-goods) and thus limited the expansion of domestic industry; in other words, that underconsumption was acting as a constraint on accumulation. In this way, the two lines of the critique were combined to a single assault on the orthodox view of the Mexican growth process. The orthodox and critical approaches developed during the 1960s are still central to the debate.

The interpretation of the dominant class forces – or more precisely, the dominant fraction of capital since 1940 – remained a crucial point of dissent.[13] Some argued that the new industrial capitalist class was the main beneficiary of state support, and eventually achieved dominance within the power structure, while the industrialisation process was assisted not only by the containment of wage demands, tariff barriers and capital finance but also by the defence of domestic industry from foreign enterprise. In contrast, others argued that although some independent industrial capital did emerge (particularly the 'Monterrey group') the main beneficiaries of state support (and dominant faction within business) were the finance capital groups – not quite in the sense of Hilferding, but rather the dominance of groups of enterprises in a number of sectors linked by a bank – which undertook industrialisation in direct collaboration with foreign capital.

In sum, although there was disagreement on the achievements and causes of economic growth in Mexico during this period, it appeared clear that at least in its own terms, *desarrollo estabilizador* was a success, and that state support of national capitalists had been central to it. The size of the state, its functions or its financial weakness were not, as yet, a major topic of debate.

THE MEXICAN ECONOMY 1967–82: UNSTABLE GROWTH

No sooner had this debate taken place than the smooth growth path began to break up into contradictory and unstable tracks. For the next decade, the rate of national income growth was maintained at around 6% between 1966 and 1975 on average, but there were clear signs of manufacturing deceleration, despite the success with manufactured exports (which accounted for half of total exports by 1975) and most seriously, agricultural growth fell below the population growth rate from the mid-1960s onwards. Moreover, in relation to industry, the pattern of output was stagnating at the consumer goods and intermediate inputs stage, without progressing to the establishment of true capital goods branches. Both these phenomena contributed to a structural deterioration in the balance of trade, as industrial inputs and imported food forced up the ratio of imports to national income, a situation exacerbated by the effect on export volumes of the deceleration in the US economy and the transmission of inflation across the Rio Bravo in the early seventies. Attempts to maintain real income growth through government deficit expenditure and real wages by successive upward adjustments of the nominal wage only worsened the disequilibrium. Meanwhile, internal migration and emigration northwards accelerated, labour unrest appeared to be breaking the bounds of the PRI organisations, and there was growing resentment at the increasing transnational control of Mexican industry.

What had gone wrong in the 1960s? First, agrarian reform, and more importantly the massive investment in irrigation (and thus effectively land 'creation') had been responsible for the rapid growth in agricultural production; the relative neglect of this aspect of accumulation since the mid-1950s now made its effects felt. In addition, the concentration of farmers in northern areas (under the influence of US brokers) on fruit and vegetable exports further exacerbated urban food supply problems which had themselves become more urgent after decades of internal migration. Second, the end of the initial stage of import-substitution – that of consumer goods – meant a natural deceleration once the domestic market was covered by domestic supply, an effect strengthened by the slowing down of 'factory' expansion based on the elimination of 'artisan' activities as the Mexican economy was modernised. Third, the dominance of the more dynamic branches of industry by foreign enterprise resulted in a continued reliance on imported technology and equipment, effectively preventing the establishment of capital goods branches and limiting manufactured exports to labour-intensive products which required a cheap labour force to remain profitable. Fourth, the profitability of real estate development (in tourism and the Federal District itself) relative to more productive investments caused the diversion of an increasing proportion of private accumulation. Finally, the imbalance of the economy and the resulting internal migration led to serious strain on urban infrastructure and services. Interestingly enough, these symptoms were commonly felt elsewhere in Latin America rather earlier in the decade, after growth paths that had started later than in Mexico.

The response to these problems took the form of renewed state intervention, starting under the Díaz Ordaz administration (1964–70) but deepening to form an overall strategy under that of Echeverría (1970–76). This response consisted of five elements, all of which contributed to the fiscal crisis:

1. Much closer controls over the activities of transnational enterprises were imposed. Foreign ownership of electricity, utilities, communications and mineral rights was forbidden, and only minority ownership in heavy industry, transport, forestry, gas and automobile components allowed under the *Ley para Promover la Inversión Mexicana y Regular la Inversión Extranjera* in 1973. In addition, technology contracts were to be directly supervised and foreign ownership of new ventures only permitted in exceptional circumstances.
2. The state moved into oil exploration, petrochemicals and fertilisers on a large scale (availing itself of dormant legislation from the Cárdenas period) in order to restore the national resource base of the export structure as well as eliminate incipient oil imports at the higher world prices.

3. Infrastructure in agriculture was extended and renewed, particularly in marketing and storage facilities, which in combination with small-scale credits, fertilisers and new seeds would, it was anticipated, revive food supplies.
4. Through both state finance and direct parastatal ventures, a start was made on a capital goods branch – particularly railway stock, machine tools and electronic equipment.
5. By food subsidies and the massive expansion of urban services, health and education to the poorer classes, it was hoped to ameliorate the deterioration of personal income distribution and so to some extent recapture waning popular support for the PRI.

However, these measures did not succeed in restoring balanced growth, in the succeeding decade at least; the internal and external disequilibria became steadily more acute (manifesting themselves in inflation and trade deficits, both of which were linked to state finance, as we shall see) leading to a 'crisis of confidence' in 1975–76 accompanied by a massive outflow of capital, a forced devaluation in 1976 (the first for nearly a quarter of a century) and the imposition of an IMF-style stabilisation programme.[14] Another furious debate broke out among the state managers, further developing the themes of the previous decade. The radical economists[15] pressed for further state expansion and control, or at least for time for the previous measures to take effect, and pinpointed the part played by the banks in undermining the attempt at restructuring the economy; the contradictions of *desarrollo estabilizador* policies applied between 1950 and 1970 were blamed for the structural imbalance. The conservatives[16] argued in reverse, suggesting that it was the abandonment of free-market policies and the excessive expansion of the state sector that brought about the inflation and external debt of the mid-1970s, and prevented the private sector from restructuring production along appropriate lines of comparative advantage; *desarrollo estabilizador* was held up as a model which should be applied once more.

The López Portillo administration (1976–82) opened with a sharp deflationary shock in order to restore short-term equilibrium (which involved falling real wages and GDP per capita for the first time in 25 years), but the prospect of massive oil and gas exports from the new fields and higher world prices seemed to promise the relaxing of the financial constraint on state accumulation and thus on the restructuring of the Mexican economy. A ministry of planning was established[17] and an industrial plan approved,[18] and a comprehensive food supply system (the *Sistema Alimentario Mexicano*) set up. This implied that the oil resources would be channelled into state investment in order to resolve the two central problems of Mexican economic structure – heavy industry and food – and thereby provide for a structural change in the external trade situation once the energy boom was over. In the event, however, although GDP began to grow again at high rates, and the state investments in food and heavy industry did take place to some considerable effect, the funds arising from the new oil resources were channelled through the commercial banks from reserves into the private sector, and the state accumulated enormous new debts. Meanwhile, the non-oil balance of payments became alarmingly negative, and another massive flight of private capital in 1982 led to not only renewed devaluation but the virtual bankruptcy of the private financial sector, which was only averted by the nationalisation of all banks. Again, this failure to make proper use of the new resource was attributed both to excessive and to inadequate state intervention. The next president, De la Madrid (1982–88) was committed to budget cuts, encouragement to foreign investment, and an economic strategy based on a return to *desarrollo estabilizador*; the opposition, which had unified and established links with an increasingly militant labour movement, once again based its programme on a tradition of state intervention in the mixed economy stretching back to Calles and Cárdenas.[19]

THE PATTERN OF CAPITAL ACCUMULATION

Underlying the changes in any economic structure and distribution of income is the pattern of capital accumulation. As we see in Appendix (Table 4.A1), the rate of investment has risen steadily over the entire 1940–80 period, and an examination of this process of capital formation should both throw light upon the debate we have just outlined and provide a framework for the analysis of the fiscal crisis of the Mexican state which will follow. Curiously in all the vast literature on the Mexican economy, although capital accumulation is frequently mentioned, it is accorded little serious quantitative analysis.[20] Table 4.A2 (Appendix) indicates a number of significant trends in the composition of accumulation. The first is, that while up to the mid-1960s, it was private investment that grew more rapidly than public, afterwards the reverse was the case; in consequence the state share of total accumulation fell from 56% in 1940–44 to 32% in 1955–59, and rose to 44% in

1975–78 and 48% in 1979–81. Second, that while the proportion of private investment dedicated to productive sectors rose between 1940 and 1965 (reaching over two-thirds) thereafter it declined seriously as investor interest shifted from agriculture and industry towards real estate and tourism. Third, that public investment shows a different trend, shifting away from agriculture towards heavy industry through the period; the effect being to substitute for the private sector in industrial accumulation but to reinforce the neglect of investment in agriculture. We have, then, two superimposed but interconnected trends, a private shift out of productive accumulation (although capitalists retain control over the surplus in the economy) and a public shift from agriculture to industry. The result was that while the rate of productive accumulation had doubled from 5% of GDP in 1940–49 to 10% in 1975–78, the state share of that had risen from one-quarter towards two-thirds; the *Plan Industrial* represented, therefore, the culmination of a historical trend.

Given that both public and private aggregate investment rates have risen steadily, and that the state has expanded into generally unprofitable branches – even taking over bankrupt private enterprises in many cases – it cannot really be argued that the public sector has 'crowded out' private investment directly. Thus the earlier fears that we have noted do not seem to have been borne out in practice; on the contrary, public investment has been devoted in its greater part to sectors defined as *básicos de desarrollo*, while even *beneficio social* outlays are mainly concerned with improving the conditions of the urban workforce in medium and large enterprises – thus contributing indirectly to private profitability. However, the twin forces of low tax pressure and restraint on borrowing, as we shall see, kept public investment rates fairly low during the period of *desarrollo estabilizador* (1957–66), so that the necessary long-term support (i.e. in agriculture and exports) was run down in favour of short term profit-supporting activities such as cheap steel and electricity. In the subsequent 'disequilibrium' period (1967–82) investment in energy, heavy industry, food agriculture and infrastructure did not compete with the private sector either.[21]

Profit rates probably increased from their already high levels into the mid-fifties (see Appendix Table 4.A6) given that the profit share of GDP rose and capital–output ratios appear to have been fairly stable; capital–labour ratios subsequently rose, with new imported technology, which partly explains why underemployment became such a problem in the 1960s and 1970s.[22] From the mid-1950s onwards, however the wage-share began to rise, and although this was mainly due to the elimination of the small-scale (peasant and artisan) sector, the stable profit share probably represented a squeeze on profitability as the economy became more capital-intensive. In the 1970s the increase in the wage share was clearly at the expense of profits; the stabilisation programmes of the late-1970s and early 1980s seemed to have restored the balance at the cost of both wages and petty producer incomes (e.g. peasants and artisans). The attempts to legitimise the Mexican state by wage concessions were too late to repair the damage of decades of labour repression, and in any case did not help the unemployed. This would tend to throw doubt upon the common belief that the constraint on private productive investment (particularly industrial) is the 'narrowness' of the Mexican market. In the sense that early stages of import-substitution provided a more rapid market expansion than GDP growth itself, and that deceleration of GDP growth due to problems in other sectors discouraged industrial investment, this is undoubtedly true. However, the argument that there was some form of 'structural underconsumption' due to the skewed income distribution which impeded the development of a mass consumer-goods market – or that such a distribution was necessary in order to sustain 'luxury' production – is not supported by recent research.[23] Thus, it would seem plausible to suggest that it was the wage pressure on industrial profits and the increased profitability of other non-productive sectors that led to the slackening of private sector interest in productive accumulation, rather than a lack of effective demand.

In view of the importance of foreign enterprise in the Mexican economy,[24] it is unfortunate that we have no data on the volume of its investment. Given our knowledge of the extent of foreign control over individual production branches, weighted by the proportion of private investment allocated to each branch during the 1960s, we could derive a figure of between 3 and 4% of GDP, equivalent to about a third of private investment during that period; but there is reason to believe that this proportion may have fallen in the 1970s, as foreign investors became more interested in banking and services and industrial excess capacity was built up on a world scale. Because outflows of profits and royalties have exceeded the inflow of direct foreign investment over the period as a whole and in each decade therein, the financial benefit of foreign investment is not the main consideration; rather it is the transference of technology from the United States, above all into the manufacturing sector, that is crucial – and although this may have contributed to rapid industrial expansion, it has certainly contributed to widespread underemployment as well. The exact nature of the relationship between foreign, domestic and state firms if far from clear, because most studies seem to concentrate on one of the three; but it would appear that on the one hand the state enterprises limit their connections with foreign firms to technology contracts and have relatively little contact with domestic private business, while on the other the relationship between the 'groups' and foreign firms has been largely mediated by the private banks. In consequence, two largely separate systems of technology transfer were built up.

The financing of this rising rate of capital accumulation without destabilising effects on inflation or the balance of payments has been a major concern of Mexican policymakers throughout the period. As can be seen in Table 4.A1 (Appendix), the 'space' for this investment and for the less dramatic rise in proportion of the national product assigned to government consumption was provided by a quite astonishing decline in the proportion of national income assigned to private consumption despite the widening deficit on current account of the balance of payments. Private consumption as a proportion of GDP fell from 85% in 1939–46 to 65% in 1977–81. Mexican investment had relied upon the progressive skewing of the income distribution away from wages towards profits between 1940 and 1955 through inflation (see Appendix Table 4.A6) as well as the squeezing of the small-scale sector; between 1955 and 1965, real wages rose steadily, but less so than productivity (which increased with productive accumulation) so that the profit share was maintained; only after 1966, in the absence of an acceleration in productivity growth, did the profit share begin to fall slightly. Rising public accumulation must have pressed on consumption out of profits, therefore: this then explains the resistance of the private sector to government deficits financed through domestic banks and to taxation. The only alternative was a progressively greater reliance on foreign finance, particularly in the form of official borrowing abroad.

Within this overall framework, the contributions of the public, private and external sectors to the finance of capital formation are shown in Appendix (Table 4.A3). Throughout the period, public sector savings have been a fairly stable proportion of GDP, although this proportion has shown a tendency to fall gradually over the past twenty years. Broadly, current expenditure has been kept in line with income, but the resultant margin has become steadily less adequate to finance the growing public investment rate, covering three quarters at the outset but barely a quarter by the end to 1975. Foreign finance (i.e. the deficit on current account of the balance of payments) accounted for a rising proportion of total savings in Mexico up to the oil boom and stabilisation programmes of the late seventies; but they were not dominant. This did not arise solely because the restraint in consumption (either public or private), was insufficient, but also because of the high foreign exchange coefficient of investment; as the import coefficient of current production is considerably less than that for investment, reductions in consumption do not release corresponding amounts of foreign exchange in order to import capital goods. In other words, it is the external rather than the internal gap of the 'two gap model' that binds. It is ironic that after 1967, when the external disequilibrium became acute, it was to a great extent due to an investment drive that was intended through further industrial import-substitution and more natural resource exports to ease the problem in the long term but which actually exacerbated it in the short run. As is clear from Appendix (Table 4.A1) the rate of accumulation has steadily risen in Mexico over the past forty years: it is this rather than consumption which causes the disequilibria. The further irony is that when the gains in foreign exchange from oil and gas exports started to come through after 1975, they were not used to finance state acumulation: public deficits were financed abroad, the new funds were channelled to the private sectors through the banks; rather than stimulate private investment, these were used for transfer abroad in 1976–79, for luxury consumption in 1980–81, and again for capital flight in 1982.

Private savings have always been the main source of finance for investment in Mexico, not only for private enterprise capital formation, but also a substantial proportion of public investment in the form of draining of funds from the banks, which effectively centralise the profits and working capital of the private sector – especially those of the 'groups'. However, as household savings are mainly channelled directly into housing, and private firms finance their fixed investment from retained profits, the main impact of this transfer of funds from private to public sector is upon profits consumption, *not* the crowding out of private investment – a post-Keynesian rather than a neoclassical accumulation balance.[25] The remarkable rise in the private savings rate in post-war Mexico is also associated with the development of the capital market.[26] Already in the 1930s, the principal financial groups had been emerging in the shadow of the *Banco de México* and the *Nacional Financiera* but in the 1955–65 period they expanded extremely rapidly, channelling an increasing proportion of private savings through the financial system, as Table 4.A3 (Appendix) shows. The emergence of *financieras*, a species of 'merchant bank' associated with a particular clearing bank, and the sale of fixed-interest bonds that not only had a substantial real rate of interest (because the rate of inflation was low) but were also redeemable at par on request, encouraged a vast increase in savings by small businessmen and professionals that could be shifted into capital formation. However, there was no parallel development of a share market, as corporate ownership was still kept within a small group of banks, rich families and transnational corporations. Moreover, the bulk of increased saving was still derived from retained profits in the company sector. The monetary authorities were able to control the volume of bank lending resulting from these new bank assets by imposing extremely high reserve requirements, which not only restricted bank credit – particularly for consumer durables – but also provided a convenient means of financing the public sector deficit; further, differential reserve requirements were used as an incentive for banks to extend operating credit to productive sectors such as agriculture and industry. None the less the private banks did not always channel those resources towards productive capital accumulation in the private sector, but rather towards real estate and consumer durables (either directly through hire-purchase or indirectly as working capital so that firms could extend trade credit), due to the higher returns and lower risks involved.

The system worked well enough during the period of *desarrollo estabilizador* when the public sector borrowing requirement (PSBR) was modest. Even after 1967, when an expanded 'state offtake' from the banking system was based on obligatory bond purchases, the financial disequilibrium brought about by this form of financing public investment did not prevent the private sector from investing, as Table 4.A2 (Appendix) indicates – the problem was the composition of this investment. In other words, the 'monetarist' model of investment and savings balance, where the latter is an effective constraint on the former, does not apply to Mexico; public investment was not 'crowding out' private investment by draining investment funds off the capital markets. The key factor was the opposition of the private sector, articulated through the banks, to increased state control over the economic surplus and its use for consumption or capital flight.

Under those circumstances, where the availability of finance is not the constraint on private investment, and state access to domestic resources is blocked by the banking system, it is not difficult to understand why the enormous increase in oil income in 1976–80 did neither increase the rate of private accumulation nor resolve the fiscal problems of the state itself. In other words, the problem of accumu-

State and Capital Accumulation: Mexico, 1940–82

lation in Mexico has been more a 'neo-Ricardian' one of income distribution (between labour and capital on the one hand, and between state and capital on the other) than one of resource constraints in the structuralist fashion.

THE FISCAL CRISIS OF THE MEXICAN STATE

So far we have only approached the problem of state intervention in the accumulation balance tangentially. It should be evident, however, that this problem is central to the growing disequilibrium, which by the 1970s appeared to have become chronic. In order to carry out its task of restructuring Mexican capital, the Mexican state undertook a progressively greater investment burden, but as we have seen, it did not increase its rate of savings commensurately – in fact public sector savings as a proportion of GDP declined after the late-1940s, and even the oil boom at the end of the period did not really change this tendency for the self-financing of state accumulation to be inadequate.

The main elements of this problem are indicated in (Appendix) Table 4.A4: the first characteristic to meet the eye is the low and stable tax pressure throughout much of the period under consideration. Although local taxation – state and municipalities – and social security contributions are included in 'other public sector', they are small and largely spent by the entities concerned; the proportion of GDP acquired by the central government is very low indeed.[27] Two major attempts at tax reform, in 1964 and 1972, were frustrated by political pressure from business, professionals and the bureaucrats themselves, these three groups being very lightly taxed in Mexico. The Echeverría administration did make some headway in increasing efficiency of collection from these groups, which increased revenue only at considerable political cost.[28] Overtime, the process of import-substitution reduced the importance of customs income, while the introduction of value added tax in 1980 was basically a rationalisation rather than a change in the tax system as such. The structure of taxation remained remarkably stable between 1940 and 1980: about a third of revenue comes from direct taxation (although only half of this is borne by companies); sales taxes of various forms account for a further third; and the remainder is made up of a small amount of export duties and other non-tax revenues, including the distributed profits of state-owned enterprises. The increased tax pressure in 1977–81 was mainly due to the payments by PEMEX on its oil exports.

This failure to increase tax revenue sufficiently, and the political cost of achieving the little progress that was made, is particularly serious when the steadily rising rate of current expenditure is taken into account. Despite the populist tradition of Mexican politics, the level of expenditures on welfare is relatively low – benefits being effectively limited to that part of the workforce that is unionised and in the 'modern' sector (less than half the total) – and, perhaps because of this same tradition, expenditure on the military is remarkably small. None the less, there is commitment to universal primary (and increasingly, secondary) education on the one hand, and a tendency for bureaucratic salaries to rise with those of industry without any commensurate increase in productivity, on the other: the result has been gradually to whittle away the central government surplus ever since World War II. The expansion of current government expenditure in the seventies (doubling as a proportion of GDP) was due in large part to debt servicing and subsidies to decentralised agencies. In fact, the rest of the public sector has been able to generate a greater surplus in the form of state enterprise depreciation allowances and social security funds than the Federal government itself. None the less, the public sector surplus (i.e. its 'savings') has declined steadily as a proportion of GDP, despite increasing state intervention in the economy. This position was not reversed in the late seventies because the deficits of non-oil entities (not only enterprises such as steel, but also decentralised organisms such as the universities) increased. Although PEMEX itself was generating large surpluses on current account (i.e. 'saving') equivalent to a quarter of its own income and a fifth of all state savings, its investment programme required massive borrowing at home and overseas. The 1981–82 position was more serious because declining world oil prices reduced even the PEMEX surpluses and the mounting burden of debt service had also to be paid for.

Meanwhile, of course, public investment was rising very rapidly indeed. The central government commitment remained fairly steady, being mainly for roads and irrigation works, which declined in relative importance as we have already noted. The main expansion, therefore, was in *empresas públicas e instituciones autónomas*, a vast galaxy of state corporations (ranging from steel mills and oil refineries to hotels and shops), research institutions, development funds (*fideicomisos*) and welfare agencies. The bulk of the capital expenditure over the 1965–80 period was undertaken in the oil, steel, railways and fertiliser sectors; thus the half-dozen or so enterprises in those sectors were predominant, but the number of state enterprises also increased, particularly during the Echeverría administration.[29] The *central* government managed to maintain a reasonably balanced budget from 1950 onwards; the problem arose from the deficits of the parastatal sector, which effectively met its deficits by borrowing from the banking sector – especially the state banks – which in turn had recourse to the *Banco de México* or foreign borrowing, increasingly the latter.

This 'fiscal crisis'[30] was based upon the imbalance between the acceleration in state accumulation and the inadequacy of its own surplus to finance it; although welfare expenditure did expand in response to the problem of state legitimation, it did not form the heart of the macroeconomic imbalance as it did in the metropolitan countries. This deficit and the consequent borrowing requirement was the economic dimension of the problem, while the refusal of the private sector to accede to higher taxes (to pay for what are, after all, government activities designed to maintain and increase private profitability) was the political dimension. In other words, it was a conflict over the disposition of the surplus rather than over its size. Due to the rapid development of the financial sector in the 1950s and 1960s on the one hand, and the relatively modest scale of the public sector borrowing requirement on the other, the former could once quite easily absorb the latter; indeed, the expansion of the monetary base was necessary for the continued growth of the capital market in any case. However, after 1966, local borrowing rose sharply and, while during the 1947–66 period the public sector had 'drawn off' about a fifth of new bank assets,[31] this proportion rose to a third in 1967–71 and two-thirds in 1972–6. The effect of fiscal deficits was not, therefore, inflationary (this was mainly imported from the US and exacerbated by devaluation) but not surprisingly led to an aggressive response from the private banks in the form of capital flight not seen since the 1938 oil nationalisation. In 1976–77, the *Banco de México* officially recorded flight ('short term private capital movements' and 'errors and omissions') of 5 billion US dollars, compared to annual exports of about 7 billion US dollars. A consequence of this outflow and the 1976 devaluation was a weakening of the capital market, which reduced its usefulness as a means of forced saving and as a source of non-inflationary deficit finance for the Mexican government in subsequent years. A similar event in the early 1980s triggered off another massive exodus of funds: in 1981–82, the official record shows over 20 billion US dollar flight; but this brought the financial system into implicit bankruptcy, so that the state was forced to take over the entire banking system and apply exchange controls to prevent a collapse of the monetary system. It remains to be seen whether this extension of state ownership will resolve the problem (any more than oil income did); but it is doubtful, if the same groups retain effective control of finance, accumulated profits are still held abroad, and the large firms 'belonging' to the banks are not incorporated into the state enterprise sector.

Increasingly, then, the Mexican state was driven abroad to cover the public sector borrowing requirement, and this made up most of the net inflow of long-term capital to Mexico throughout our period. Most of this borrowing has been on behalf of state enterprises,[32] although this is more a convention than anything else as the loans are underwritten by the central government (that is, they do not depend upon the profitability of a particular project or firm) and release the government's 'own' foreign exchange acquired through the central bank for discretionary uses – including the finance of private sector imports. Moreover, this borrowing is linked to imports of capital goods and thus not substitutable by local borrowing or higher taxes unless consumption (particularly that of richer strata of the population) were to be cut disproportionately in order to effect the necessary savings of foreign exchange. As Table 4.A5 (Appendix) shows the result has been an exponentially mounting external debt, much of which was contracted in order to repay existing commitments. The greater part of the increase in debt has been arranged with suppliers and private banks, so that the proportion owing the multilateral and bilateral agencies (e.g. the IBRD, IMF and US aid fell from 26% in 1964 to 16% in 1976: private US banks were willing to lend so much not only because of the reputation that Mexico had gained during the 1957–66 period for 'sound' economic policies and the oil potential in subsequent years, but also because of their own high liquidity (itself the result of the recycling of petrodollars and the US government's own deficits, ironically enough) and the lack of domestic investment demand. The result was a total external debt equivalent to a quarter of GDP by 1976 and a debt service burden that was using up over a third of exiguous export income; these figures rose to a third and a half by 1981.

The 'cost' of foreign debt in interest charges was not low: despite the 42 billion US dollars increase in national external debt (four-fifths public) between end-1975 and end-1981, some 44 billion US dollars were paid out in debt service during the same period, for example. Moreover, the 'leverage' exercised by the international banking system over domestic policy was strengthened by the large debt and the necessity to refinance it at frequent intervals. Although it holds only a small proportion of Mexican debt, the International Monetary Fund has a particular importance in this negotiation process as a representative of international banking as a whole: in 1976, when the peso was massively devalued for the first time in over 20 years, this 'leverage' was particularly marked, as the IMF imposed stringent conditions on Mexican policy, particularly public expenditure cuts and tariff reductions, as a condition for a 'clean bill of health' being issued at all.[33] None the less, these policies – which represent an attempt to return to *desarrollo estabilizador* despite the fact that the problems were brought about by just that strategy – also reflect the strength of the 'financial fraction' of the state managers themselves, pressing for such measures against the 'nationalist state capitalism' of their more radical opponents within the bureaucracy with the support of the large business sector, both domestic and foreign. In other words, the external pressure to reduce the expansion of the Mexican state was effective to the extent that it supported particular domestic groups with a similar strategy.

In sum, the fiscal crisis in Mexico does not arise from a 'technical' problem of budget structure as such, but rather from the interaction of three of the underlying trends in the accumulation model. First the exhaustion of the post-revolutionary industrialisation model, requiring increased state investment to take the place of private investors who were moving their capital to more profitable but less productive sectors of the economy or even abroad. Second, the opposition of the private sector (led by the banks but aided by part of the state management group and aided by an open frontier) to greater state control over the surplus in order to finance that investment, whether in the form of taxes, bank loans, or use of oil income. Third, the inevitable consequence of attempting to reconcile these two trends by foreign borrowing (albeit with the willing support of US banks) was eventually to worsen both internal and external disequilibria which it was intended to resolve.

CONCLUDING REMARKS

We can now draw some tentative political conclusions from the economic material we have analysed, although the method of analysis has tried to avoid such a distinction. The first is that the object and result of state capital accumulation in Mexico since 1940 has been to support a process of industrialisation mainly carried out by a private sector made up of large Mexican entrepreneurs and transnational corporations. Initially this support involved a certain 'restructuring of capital' in the form of agricultural and transport investment, but during the 'miracle years' of 1950–65 the state share of investment declined and was mainly confined to industrial inputs such as energy, so that although the public sector ran a steady deficit, this was modest and easily absorbed by a capital market in any case under strong state control. The second is that when the apparently smooth path of economic growth began to lose both equilibrium and momentum as the underlying contradictions of capitalist industrialisation worked through, renewed state intervention became necessary after 1967. This took the form of a doubling of the rate of public accumulation (directed towards minerals, agriculture and heavy industry) in a new effort to 'restructure capital', accompanied by attempts to reduce the degree of foreign control over industry. This expansion of state investment was not accompanied by fiscal reform and a commensurate increase in public sector savings, so the resulting borrowing requirement placed undue inflationary strain upon the Mexican capital market and resulted in an excessive external debt. The third is that the foreign exchange resources provided by oil did not stimulate private productive investment (which was not constrained by shortage of profits or imports, and less attractive than speculation – itself stimulated by rising domestic demand), while the state was prevented from using these resources productively (i.e. in the *Plan Industrial*) by the banks and a fraction of the bureaucracy itself. The fourth is that *desarrollo estabilizador*, far from being typical of the period as a whole with desequilibrium as a deviation therefrom, really only obtained for a quarter (1956–66) of the four decades and when the structure of production, the income distribution and the fiscal balance would permit it.

The undoubted long-term stability of the Mexican state and the sustained industrialisation record of the Mexican economy (which brought it from a position of peripheral poverty in 1940 to that of tenth largest capitalist industrial power in 1980) should not disguise the fact that the class structure did change significantly in that period. Above all, the process of industrialisation led to both a strengthening of the private sector (banks, local groups and multinationals) and the emergence of a proletariat; both of these served to 'fill up' the political space and reduce the room for manoeuvre of the state. Further, the civil basis of state power which had been evolved as a substitute for military power and articulated by the PRI (the peasantry, public-sector trades unions and traditional bureaucracy) were eroded by new classes (landless labour, urban sub-proletarians, skilled unions and a professional class) which were not included (let alone coopted) in the political system. At the same time, the crucial group of state managers, who had been broadly united on the nature of state intervention between 1940 and 1968 became sharply divided thereafter. As a result, the degree of relative state autonomy was steadily reduced, from both without and within, so to speak; to the extent that it has been argued that Mexico had become 'almost ungovernable' by 1980.[34] It is too early to say at the time of writing[35] what the outcome of the De la Madrid administration will be, burdened as it is with an enormous external debt, falling oil prices and growing labour unrest; but the nationalised banking system, the maturing of a decade of state investment in heavy industry, and the exigencies of foreign policy may well produce an outcome rather different from initial expectations. However, the problem remains of securing state access to the surplus (itself the result of state intervention in both accumulation and income distribution) sufficient to finance the restructuring of capital necessary for the economy to move from one stage of development to another.

This difficulty brings us to what is perhaps the core of the problem of state intervention in capital accumulation. In order to undertake the restructuring of the economy, necessary in this case if industrialisation is to continue beyond the 'easy' stage of import-substitution to build up its own technological base in capital goods and self-sufficiency in food, the state requires a certain freedom of manoeuvre in order to acquire greater control over available resources. This 'relative economic autonomy of the state' involves economic and political costs to the private sector in the short term in order to achieve greater benefits for the same private sector in the longer run. However, this relative autonomy is a product of history and not the result of an economic strategy; it is not conjured up just because it is 'necessary' for accumulation to proceed. In the case of Mexico it was created by the particular circumstances of the reconstruction of state and economy between 1925 and 1940, which provided the basis of a remarkable process of sustained industrialisation for the next quarter-century. Despite the need for greater state autonomy in the 1970s in order to overcome the economic contradictions, there was no commensurate political change. This is the unexpected result of the durability of the system constructed by Calles and Cárdenas in the wake of revolution half a century ago.[36]

NOTES

I am grateful to Rosalía Cortés for research assistance, and to the Institute of Latin American Studies at Austin for their excellent library facilities. This essay represents a complete rethinking of, and hopefully an improvement on, my previous essay on this topic, FitzGerald (1978a). As should be evident from the bibliography, it is also part of a larger project on the economic aspects of the state and capital accumulation in Mexico since 1925.

1. FitzGerald (1980) surveys public and private investment trends in Latin America, while FitzGerald (1978b) examines the hypothesis that import-substituting industrialisation in Latin America has generated a structural 'fiscal' crisis of the state'.
2. Córdova (1972) is the key source on the political and social foundations of the Mexican state; Hamilton (1978) treats the relative autonomy issue specifically in a perceptive study of this early period.
3. An analysis of this period is presented in FitzGerald (1984); see also Velasco (1981).
4. Fragoso (1979) and Hansen (1971) argue that the industrialists became the dominant class fraction, under state tutelage; subsequent events, however, would seem to support Leal (1972), who suggests that it was the financiers, in close collaboration with certain fractions of the bureaucracy (particularly in *Hacienda* and *Banco de México*, but also in the state development banks), who became dominant; but all authors agree upon the special role of the senior bureaucracy – or 'state managers' as we term them.
5. See the other essays in this volume.
6. Thompson (1979) in his chapter V 'The transition from inflation to stability' sees this as the triumph of the 'monetarists' against the 'structuralists' and a recognition of real wage losses in previous years; Pellicer and Mancilla (1978) entitle their study of 1952–60 as 'the understanding with the United States and the birth of stabilising growth' and stress the encouragement of foreign investment and the suppression of what trades union autonomy remained.
7. Solís (1970) and Reynolds (1970) are good examples; both were written on the basis of data up to about 1967.
8. This is the title of Vernon (1965), a study which had a considerable influence on US academic opinion about Mexico.
9. Bennet (1965); Thompson (1979).
10. See Sepúlveda and Chumacero (1973) on the extent of foreign ownership; Fragoso (1979) on domestic ownership concentration, indentifies six main 'groups'.
11. Fajnzylber and Martínez (1976).
12. Hernández Laos and Córdova Chávez (1979) gives a full bibliography.
13. See note 4.
14. FitzGerald (1979).
15. Tello (1979); see also the essays in Cordera (1981).
16. Solís (1981), Cavazos-Lerma (1976).
17. The *Secretaría de Programación y Presupuesto* has been responsible for all budgetary expenditure, while *Hacienda* remained with fiscal income and borrowing. The first minister at SPP was Tello, to be succeeded by De la Madrid in 1977 after a political crisis over the size of the PSBR.
18. Sepafin (1979); this represented the culmination of a project put forward two decades earlier by the 'doyen' of the progressive group within the state managers; see Flores de la Peña (1975).

19. MAP (1981); see also Tello and Cordera (1981), upon which much of it is based, along with the work of Córdova.
20. An exception is Himes (1965), but he has little statistical data to work on; see the notes to Table 4.A1 (Appendix) for some recent sources.
21. Bennet and Sharp (1979); Villarreal (1977); Ayala (1977).
22. Solís (1970).
23. CIDE (1980); Lustig (1979); Villarreal (1976).
24. See notes 10 and 11.
25. FitzGerald (1981); see also the next section.
26. Thompson (1979); Bennet (1965).
27. See FitzGerald (1978c) for more details on the Mexican public sector. Including additional revenue sources, total current federal government income was 13% of GDP in 1965 and 19% in 1976, compared to (say) 27% in Brazil in 1970.
28. Solís (1981); Tello (1979).
29. Villarreal (1977); but note that much of this increase may come from the computation of firms under indirect state ownership not previously registered separately for budgetary purposes.
30. FitzGerald (1978b).
31. That is, 'local borrowing' (Appendix, Table 4.A4) as a proportion of 'financial intermediation' (Appendix, Table 4.A3).
32. Green (1976).
33. FitzGerald (1979).
34. Whitehead (1980).
35. Easter (1983).
36. Which helps to explain why the opposition now refers back to the 1925–40 period: see MAP (1981), particularly part 2 'El sistema'.

REFERENCES

Ayala, J. (1977), 'Límites y contradicciones del intervencionismo estatal, 1970–76', *Investigación Económica*, México, no. 3, July–Sept.
Banco de México (1982), *Informe Anual* (México: Banco de México, S.A.).
Bennet, D. and Sharp, K. (1979), 'El estado como banquero y empresario: el carácter de última instancia de la intervención económica del estado mexicano, 1917–70', *Foro Internacional*, vol. xx, no. 1 (Mexico) pp. 29–72.
Cavazos Lerma M. (1976), 'Cincuenta años de política monetaria', in Fernández Hurtado (1976) pp. 55–122.
CIDE (1980), *Economía Mexicana*, no. 2, México, Centro de Investigación y Docencia Económicas.
Cordera, R. (ed.) (1981), *Desarrollo y crisis de la economía mexicana: ensayos de interpretación histórica* (México: Fondo de Cultura Económica).
Córdova, A. (1972), *La formación del poder político en México* (México: Era).
ECLA (various issues), *Economic Survey of Latin America* (Santiago de Chile: United Nations).
Fajnzylber, F. and Martínez T. (1976), *Las empresas transnacionales: expansión a nivel mundial y proyección en la industria mexicana* (México: Siglo XXI).
Fernández Hurtado E. (ed.) (1976), *Cincuenta años de banca central* (México: Fondo de Cultura Económica).

FitzGerald, E. V. K. (1976), 'Some Aspects of the Political Economy of the Latin American State', *Development and Change*, vol. 7, no. 2, Apr., pp. 119–33.
—— (1978a), 'The State and Capital Accumulation in Mexico', *Journal of Latin American Studies*, vol. 10, no. 2, pp. 263–82.
—— (1978b), 'The Fiscal Crisis of the Latin American State', in Toye J. F. J. (ed.) *Taxation and Economic Development* (London: Cass) pp. 125–58.
—— (1978c), 'Patterns of Public Sector Income and Expenditure in Mexico', *ILAS Technical Papers Series* (Austin: University of Texas).
—— (1979), 'Stabilisation Policy in Mexico: The Fiscal Deficit and Macroeconomic Equilibrium 1960–77', in Thorp, R. and Whitehead, L. (ed.), *Inflation and Stabilisation in Latin America* (London: MacMillan) pp. 23–64.
—— (1979a), 'Acerca de la Periodización del Desarrollo Capitalista en México' (Mexico City: SPP, unpublished).
—— (1981), 'El déficit presupuestal y el financiamiento de la inversión', in Cordera (ed.), (1981) pp. 214–39.
—— (1983), 'The Functional Distribution of Income in Mexico 1940–80: a Preliminary Analysis', ISS Working Papers, The Hague.
—— (1984), 'Restructuring through the Depression: the State and Capital Accumulation in Mexico, 1925–40', in Thorp, R. (ed.) *Latin America in the Depression* (London: MacMillan).
FitzGerald, E. V. K., Floto, E. and Lehman D. (eds) (1977), *The State and Economic Development in Latin America* (Cambridge: University Printer for Latin American Studies Centre).
Flores de la Peña, H. (1975), *Los obstáculos al desarrollo económico* (Mexico City: Fondo de Cultura Económica).
Fragoso, J. M. (1979), *El poder de la gran burguesía* (Mexico City: Era).
Green, R. (1976), *El endeudamiento público externo de México, 1960–1973* (Mexico City: Colegio de México).
Hamilton, N. (1978), 'Mexico: the Limits of State Autonomy', (Doctoral Dissertation, Wisconsin University).
Hansen, R. D. (1971), *The Politics of Mexican Development* (Baltimore: Johns Hopkins Press).
Hernández Laos, E. and Córdova Chávez, J. (1979), 'Estructura de la distribución del ingreso en México' *Comercio Exterior*, México, vol. 29, no. 5, May, pp. 505–20.
Himes, J. R. (1965), 'La formación del capital en México' *El Trimestre Económico*, México, vol. XXXII, no. 125, pp. 153–79.
IBRD (1975), *World Bank Debt Tables* (Washington, D.C.: World Bank).
Leal, J. F. (1972), *La burguesía y el estado mexicano* (México: El Caballito).
Lustig, N. (1979), 'Distribución del ingreso, estructura de consumo y características del crecimiento industrial', *Comercio Exterior*, México, vol. 29, no. 5, May, pp. 535–43.
M.A.P. (1981), *Tesis y programa* (Mexico City: Movimiento de Acción Popular).
Nafinsa (various issues), *La Economía Mexicana en Cifras* (México: Nacional Financiera S.A.).
Pellicer, O. and Mancilla E. L. (1978), *Historia de la revolución mexicana, vol 23: El entendimiento con los Estados Unidos y la gestación del desarrollo estabilizador* (México: Colegio de México).

Reynolds, C. W. (1970), *The Mexican Economy: Twentieth Century Structure and Growth* (New Haven: Yale University Press).
Sepafin (1979), *Plan nacional de dessarrollo industrial, 1979–82* (México: Secretaría de Patrimonio y Fomento Industrial).
Sepúlveda, B. and Chumacero A. (1973), *La inversión extranjera en México* (México: Fondo de Cultura Económica).
Solís, L. (1970), *La realidad económica mexicana: retrovisión y perspectivas* (México: Siglo XXI).
—— (1981), *Economic Policy Reform in Mexico*, (New York: Pergamon).
Tello, C. (1979), *La política económica en México, 1970–76* (México: Siglo XXI).
Tello, C. and Cordera R. (1981), *México: la disputa por la nación* (México: Siglo XXI).
Thompson, J. K. (1979), *Inflation, Financial Markets and Economic Development: the Experience of Mexico* (Greenwich, Conn.: JAI Press).
Velasco, C. (1981), 'El desarrollo industrial de México en la década 1930–40: las bases del proceso de industrialización' in Cordera (1981) pp. 45–64.
Vernon, R. (1965), *The Dilemma of Mexico's Development* (Cambridge, Mass: Harvard University Press).
Villarreal, R. (1976), *El desequilibrio externo en la industrialización de México, 1929–75* (México: Fondo de Cultura Económica).
—— (1977), 'La empresa pública' in Bueno, G. M., *Opciones de política económica en México* (México: Tecnos).
Whitehead, L. (1980), 'Mexico from Boom to Bust: A Political Evaluation of the 1976–79 Stabilization Programme', *World Development*, vol. 8, no. 11, Nov., pp. 843–63.

APPENDIX

TABLE 4.A1 *Mexico: sectoral growth and expenditure composition*

	1939–46	1947–56	1957–66	1967–76	1977–81
Annual average growth (% per annum)					
Gross Domestic Product	5.5	6.9	6.7	5.9	7.4
GDP per capita	2.8	2.9	3.3	2.3	4.4
Agriculture	3.2	7.8	4.8	0.1	5.0
Manufacturing	7.1	7.2	8.5	7.1	7.7
Price level*	12.7	7.6	4.3	9.8	24.6
Composition of GDP (% of GDP)					
Investment	7.6	14.6	16.9	20.1	22.0
Stockbuilding	1.5	1.3	2.7	1.9	3.1
Govt. Consumption	6.0	4.5	6.9	9.0	10.9
Private Consumption	85.4	80.3	75.3	71.9	64.7
Imports *less* exports	−0.5	−0.7	−1.8	−2.9	−0.7

* GDP deflator, 1960 = 100.

SOURCE Nafinsa (various issues); ECLA (various issues).

TABLE 4.A2 Mexico: gross fixed capital formation by institutional sector (percentage of GDP)

	1940–44	1945–49	1950–54	1955–59	1960–64	1965–69	1970–74	1975–78	1979–81
Productive Investment*									
Public	1.0	1.6	2.5	2.2	2.9	3.2	3.5	5.8	7.5
Private	2.7	4.8	6.2	7.1	5.6	6.3	4.5	4.2	...
Total	3.7	6.4	8.7	9.3	8.5	9.5	8.0	10.0	...
Other Investment									
Public	3.1	3.1	3.7	3.1	3.6	3.1	3.4	3.8	4.1
Private	0.5	1.5	3.2	4.3	4.3	6.1	8.3	7.8	...
Total	3.6	4.6	6.9	7.4	7.9	9.2	11.7	11.6	...
Total Investment									
Public	4.1	4.7	6.2	5.3	6.5	6.3	6.9	9.5	11.6
Private	3.2	6.3	9.4	11.4	9.9	12.4	12.8	12.0	12.6
Total	7.3	11.0	15.6	16.7	16.4	18.7	19.7	21.5	24.2
Public Share of Investment									
Productive	27%	25%	29%	24%	34%	34%	43%	58%	...
Total	56%	41%	40%	32%	40%	34%	35%	44%	48%

* Primary and secondary sectors.

SOURCE Secretaría de Programación y Presupuesto statistics; FitzGerald (1979).

TABLE 4.A3 Mexico: sources of savings

Percent of GDP	1939–46	1947–56	1957–66	1967–71	1972–76	1977–81
Public sector	3.0	4.3	3.8	3.5	3.1	3.0
Private sector	4.3	9.6	11.3	13.5	14.6	21.4
External sector	0.3	0.7	1.8	2.2	3.3	0.7
	7.6	14.6	16.9	19.2	21.0	25.1
Financial intermediation*		2.6	3.7	5.4	5.6	8.9

* Annual increase in peso resources of the domestic banking system, excluding interbank transactions.

SOURCE As for Tables 4.A1 and 4.A4.

TABLE 4.A4 Mexico: public sector accumulation account (percentage GDP)

	1939–46	1947–56	1957–66	1967–71	1972–76	1977–81
Federal government						
Current income	6.4	7.5	7.2	7.8	10.8	14.2
Current expend	4.6	4.3	5.7	6.3	8.6	12.6
Surplus	1.8	3.2	1.5	1.5	2.2	1.6
Other public sector Surplus	1.2	1.1	2.3	2.0	0.9	1.4
Total public sector Surplus	3.0	4.3	3.8	3.5	3.1	3.0
Investment						
Federal government	2.3	3.1	2.7	2.7	3.2	3.3
Other public sector	1.7	2.3	3.4	4.7	5.8	6.2
Total public sector	4.0	5.4	6.1	7.4	9.0	9.5
Public sector deficit (financed by)	1.0	1.1	2.3	3.9	5.7	6.5
Domestic borrowing	0.8	0.5	0.8	2.1	3.8	...
Foreign borrowing	0.2	0.6	1.5	1.8	1.9	...

SOURCE FitzGerald (1981).

TABLE 4.A5 Mexico: external debt (US $ millions)

	1960	1967	1970	1973	1976	1979	1981	1982
Disbursed debt								
Public sector								
Long-term	816	2 514	3 227	5 416	15 923	28 315	40 041	48 982
Short-term	..	..	..	..	3 677	1 442	8 671	9 006
Private sector	..	..	..	..	19 600	29 757	48 712	57 988
					6 213	9 235	19 000	..
Total external debt	..	..	..	..	25 813	38 992	67 712	..
Debt service								
Public	..	508	692	945	2 188	10 174	11 307	
Private	..	..	..	..	1 396	2 618	4 314	
					3 584	12 792	15 621	
Debt service/exports*	16%	24%	25%	27%	51%	83%	54%	

* 1960–73, long term public debt only; 1976 for total debt.

SOURCE 1960–73, IBRD (1975); 1976–81, ECLA (1982), Banco de México (1982).

TABLE 4.A6 Mexico: functional distribution of income, 1940–80 (percentages)

	1940	1945	1950	1955	1960	1965	1970	1975	1980
Wagebill (W)	32.0	25.4	26.3	29.3	34.3	35.9	40.0	45.4	43.0
Small-enterprise (Z)	31.5	26.7	24.8	23.1	21.2	18.7	15.7	14.8	12.0
Surplus (R)	36.5	47.9	48.9	47.6	44.5	45.4	44.3	39.8	45.0
Total income (X)	100.0	100.0	100.0	100.0	100.0	100.0	100.0	100.0	100.0
Distribution in the corporate sector (D)*	46.7	34.7	35.0	38.1	43.5	44.2	47.4	53.3	48.9

* $D = W \div (W + R)$

SOURCE FitzGerald (1983).

Index

ABC strikes, in Brazil, 104
abertura, in Brazil, 71–3
agrarian reform
  in Brazil before 64, 60–1
  in Chile, 144, 147
  in Mexico, neglected until the mid-60s, 216–17
  resistance against, in Latin America in the 60s, 38
  see also under land reform
alcohol programme in Brazil, 115
Aguirre Cerda, P., 141
Alessandri, A., 31
Alessandri, J., 142, 143, 145
Aliança Renovadora Nacional (ARENA), 72
Allende, S., 39, 139, 140, 143, 146, 147, 149, 151, 157, 189, 195, 196
Alliance for Progress, 39, 144
Altvater, E., 19–20, 21
Amin, S., 9
anti-statism
  campaign, in Brazil, 87, 95–6, 117, 122, 133n.85
  in Chile, 140
  in Mexico, 229
Antonio Ermirio de Moraes, 122
Argentina, 5, 28, 29, 31, 32, 33
Asociación Latinoamericana de Libre Comercio (ALALC), 39
Asian industrialising countries, 7, 8, 52, 134n.95
asynchronies between economic and political models in Chile, 140, 153
authoritarianism in Latin America, 40
  see also under authoritarian state, bureaucratic–authoritarian state, military government
authoritarian state
  in Chile, 180
  false paradox of, in Latin America, 139

balance of payments
  in Brazil (capital account and debt servicing in the 70s, 82–6; crisis in the 50s, 56; current account, 82–3, 85, 103, 108; deficit, 73, 75, 81–6, 104, 106–10, 118–19, 127; services account, 82–5, 108; trade account, 70, 74, 82, 83, 107, 118–19)
  in Chile (under Allende, 150; under the military, 155, 170–1, crisis of, 192–3)
  crisis of, in Latin America after 1930, 32–3
  in Mexico, 213 (deficit, 213, 216, 218, 219, 222–3)
  see also under foreign debt, public deficit, state–fiscal crisis
  see also economic policy–stages of, economic crisis, public firms
Balmaceda, J. M., 27, 31
Banco Central (Brazil), 85, 89, 111, 117, 127
Banco de México, 213, 223, 227
Banco do Brasil, 75, 111, 114, 117, 118, 119
Banco Nacional de Desenvolvimento Econômico (BNDE), 106, 116
Bank for International Settlements, 128
bankruptcies
  in Brazil, 121, 122
  in Chile under the military, 192
banks
  in Chile (and industrial enterprises, 186–7; lending policies of, under the military, 192, restrictions on, 193; nationalisation of, under Allende, 147, 148; privatisation of, under the military, 167–8, 183; takeover of, by military government, 193, 194)
  foreign, in Brazil, 82, 84, 85, 129
  in Mexico, 213, 219, 224, 227
Baran, P., 9
Benedito Moreira, 104
Benefícios Fiscais para Exportação (BEFIEX), 75, 113
Bonelli, R., 76
Boschi, R., 96
'bosses strike' in Chile, 149

Brazil, 14, 17, 32, 39, 41–3, 52–138
  southern, 29
Brizzola, L., 61
budget
  in Brazil (deficit, under Kubitschek, 59, and the deficit of public firms under Figueiredo, 111–16; recessionary 104, 105–6; unorthodox accounts, 111)
  in Chile, *see under* public expenditure
  in Mexico (cuts in the 80s, 210; deficit, 227)
  see also under foreign debt, public deficit, public firms
bureaucratic–authoritarian state, 15, 19
  see also under authoritarian state
  see also military government

calote oficial in Brazil, 115–16, 121
Calles, P.E., 211, 219, 231
capital
  foreign, *see under* foreign investment
  private, *see under* private capital
capital accumulation
  in Brazil (contradictions of, under Geisel, 70–100, acceleration under Figueiredo, 100–29, concluding remarks on, 130; control over, domestic, 53, foreign, 90; key problems and issues, 53; questioning of model of, 95–100)
  and capital formation, 1–2
  in Chile (under Allende, 147, 149, 150; under Frei, 144–6; under the military, 188–92)
  concept, 1–2
  contradictions and crises in, 10, 13–14, 67
  key issues in, 11–14
  in Latin American analyses, 1
  in the capitalist periphery, debate on, 2–14 (in early development economics, 3–9; in Marxist economics, 9–11; monistic assumptions in, 3–4, 9)
  and the state in Latin America (in the primary-export period, 28–32; in the populist period, 32–40; in the post-ISA period, presentation of the cases of Brazil, Chile and Mexico, 40–5)
  in Mexico, 211, 217, 219–25, 229–31, 236 (financing of, 222, 236, 238; and income distribution, 225;

  trends in the composition of, 219–20, 237)
  see also under capital formation, foreign firms, private capital, private firms, public firms, state, state capitalism, state enterprises, subsidies
  see also industrial production, inflation, investment
capital formation
  in Brazil, 69, 89, 91–2, 116–17
  in Chile, *see under* capital accumulation
  in Mexico, 219
capital goods
  in Brazil (under Geisel, in the II PND, 74; excess capacity in, in the early 80s, 121)
  in Mexico, 217, 218 (state investment in, after 1966, 226–7, 230, 231)
  see also under industrial production
capital market
  domestic, *see under* credit, financial system, *financieras*
  international (Eurocurrency, 82, 85, 134n.95; liquidity of, 82, 95)
  see also under credit–international, foreign debt
capital outflows
  in Mexico, 215, 218, 219, 223, 227
  see also under capital transfers abroad
capital resources, scarcity of
  in Hirschman, 6
  in Lewis, 4
  in 19th century Latin America, 28–32
capital transfers
  abroad, in 19th-century Latin America, 29
  see also under capital outflows
  from agriculture to industry in Latin America after 1930, 33–4 (in Brazil, 56)
Carajás mining project, 114
Cárdenas, L., 211, 217, 219, 231
Cardoso, F. H., 14, 16–17, 18, 19; *see also under* 'dependent associate' development
Carranza, V., 211
Carteira de Comércio Exterior (CACEX), 75, 94, 104, 118
Castelo Branco, H., 64, 67, 68
Castro, S., de, 193
Cavalcanti, L., 94
Central Bank

Index

Chile, 172, 180, 193, 194
Mexico, 213
Central Intelligence Agency (CIA) in Chile, 146–7, 149
Central Unica de Trabajadores, in Chile, 161
'Centre-periphery', 9, 10; *see also* dependency theory
'Chacarillas speech', 158, 159
Chenery, H., *et al.*, 8
Chicago school of economics, 167, 188
Chicago technocrats, in Chile, 187, 188–9, 193–4
Chile, 27, 31, 32, 34, 38, 39, 43–4, 139–209
class
  differentials, reinforced under populism, 36–7
  dominant, 23, 24, 25 (in 19th-century Latin America, 28–32)
  structures, in Mexico, 230
Claudio Bardella, 122
coercion
  as basis of domination, 18, 23–4, 140
  in Chile, 144, 151, 152 (under the military, 177–9)
  in 19th-century Latin America, 30–2
  see also under repression
coffee prices, in Brazil, 56
Comisión Económica para América Latina (CEPAL), 188
  and agrarian reform, 38
  emphasis on industrialisation, 6
  questioning of 'general equilibrium' assumption by, 3
'compromise state' in Chile, 141–3, 188, 195, 196
Congress
  in Brazil, 63, 111, 130
  in Chile, 39, 147, 148, 149, 151, 152, 160
  in Latin America, 31–2
cooptation
  in Brazil, 56
  of industrial labour by populist regimes, 37
  use of, in 19th-century Latin America, 32
copper, in Chile, 141, 143, 144, 170, 174–6
  nationalisation of, 147, 148
  prices, 150, 151, 170–1
Corporación de Fomento de la Producción (CORFO), 141

Costa e Silva, A., 67, 68
cost of living
  in Brazil (index (INPC) and inflation, 101, 120, 124, 125, 126, 134n.114, and the middle classes, 134n.112; and wage increases under Geisel, 74)
  in Chile, 208
credit
  domestic
    in Brazil (expanding under the 'miracle', 68; restricted, under Geisel, 74; subsidised, to private firms, 79; expensive, 116, 119, 121)
    in Chile, *see under* banks, debt, financial system
    in Mexico (restricted, 214, 220; development of *financieras*, 223–4)
    see also under financieras, interest rates, money market
    see also domestic entrepreneurs, demand, inflation, state, subsidies
  international
    in Brazil (used to cover balance of payments deficits, 84; and foreign firms, 93, 94, 95)
    see also under balance of payments deficit, credit worthiness, debt, domestic firms, foreign firms, interest rates, LIBOR
  see also economic crisis, inflation
creditworthiness
  of Brazil, 82, 84, 103, 105, 108–10, 121
  of Mexico, 228
'crisis of confidence', in Mexico, 218
Cuadra, S. de la, 193, 194
Cuban revolution, 39, 63
current transfers, in Brazil, 89
  see also under public deficit

data reliability questioned, in Brazil, 75, 81, 85, 101, 102, 110–11, 115, 120, 124, 125, 126
debt
  foreign, *see under* foreign debt
  internal, *see under* internal debt
debt peonage, 31
deflation, in Mexico, 218
Delfim Neto, A., 81, 100, 101, 102, 103, 104, 105, 120, 126
demand
  in Brazil (domestic, and sustained growth, 130; excess, and inflation, 63–4, 73, questioned, 76; falling for

demand-*cont.*
  industrial goods, 58, 59, 60, 101, 120)
  in Chile (contraction, in the 1950s, 142, under the military, 153–4
  insufficient aggregate, general problems of, in the periphery, 8, 12
  in Latin America (nature and role of, in the 19th century, 28–30; insufficiency of, for industrial goods in the 1950s, 38)
  in Mexico (domestic, and income distribution, 215; underconsumptionist argument questioned, 221)
  see also under market
  see also income distribution, industrial production, inflation, recession
Departamento Intersindical de Estatística e Estudos Sócio-Econômicos (DIEESE), 69, 97, 124, 125
dependency
  and capital accumulation, 13
  in Chile, 195
  'dependent-associate development', 14, 41
  and 'development of underdevelopment', 9
  reassessment of, 14
  'theory' of, and 19th-century Latin America, 9–10, 27–8
depression, in Mexico, 211
  see also under economic crisis of 1930
desarrollo estabilizador, in Mexico, 212–16
  analysed as an unqualified success, 213
  contradictions of, after 1966, 216–19
  discussion of the role of the state in, 213–16
  limited in time, 230
  return to, in the 1980s, 219, 229
development economics early debate on accumulation in the capitalist periphery, 3–9
'development of underdevelopment' criticised, 10
  in 19th-century Latin America, 28
Díaz Estrada, N., 161
Díaz Ordaz, G., 217
Diniz, E., 96
Dirección de Inteligencia Nacional (DINA), 157–8, 159
domestic capital, in 19th-century Latin America, 28–32
domestic entrepreneurs
  in Brazil (under Kubitschek, 57, 60–1; under Geisel, 80, 94–5; under Figueiredo, 119, 120–1; in anti-statism campaign, 87, 95–6, 122, 133n.86; demands to the government in the early 80s, 120, 121; hit by recession, 120–3; taken over by foreign firms, 57, 88, 90, 93, 119, 121, 122, 130)
  see also under credit, industrial production, interest rates
  in Chile, *see under* industrial bourgeoisie (*see also under* industrial capital, private capital)
  in Mexico, *see under* private capital
dominant classes
  in Brazil, before 64, 60–3
  in Chile, *see under* hegemony
  in 19th-century Latin America, 29–32
  under populism, 36, 39

Echeverría, L., 217, 225, 227
economic crisis
  in Brazil (and the ABC strike, 104; and the balance of payments deficit, 81–6; first signs, under Geisel, 52, 72, 73; and inflation, 75–81, 90, 100; lesson from, 130; and the *pacote do Natal,* 102–3; in 1983, 127–31)
  in Chile under the military, 153, 156, 189, 192–4
  in Mexico (leading to a 'crisis of confidence', 216–19)
  of 1930, in Latin America, 32–3
  see also under balance of payments deficit, demand, inflation, public deficit, recession, state–fiscal crisis, subsidies
'economic miracle'
  in Brazil, 52, 54, 63–70, 88, 90, 96
  in Chile, 156, 191
economic model
  in Brazil, post-64, 63–70 (choice of export industrialisation, 53; export-led growth limitations, 110; import cuts as the new 'model' in the 80s, 118–19; concluding remarks on, 129–31)
  in Chile (reformist, 143–7; socialist, 147–52; free-market, 152–3)
  in Mexico (establishing *desarrollo estabilizador,* 212–16; unstable growth, 216–19; axed on oil and

Index

gas exports in the late 70s, 218; exhaustion of, in the 70s, 229)
see also under economic policy, stages of

economic policy, stages of
in Brazil post-64 (expansion, 54–5, 67–70; expansion *plus* stabilisation, 70–95; attempt to stabilise, 100–6; failure of stabilisation, 106–18; recession, 118–26; collapse, 126–9)
in Chile under the military (liberalisation with contraction of demand, 153–4, 161, 166–7, 169, 173; opening of the economy with partial recovery, 154–5, 161; integration in the world economy with emerging contradictions, 155–6, 161)
in Mexico (*desarrollo estabilizador*, 212–16; renewed state intervention, 217–18; deflation *plus* primary exports, 218–19; return to *desarrollo estabilizador*, 219)
see also under economic model

economic power, concentration of, in Chile, 185

elections
in Brazil, 71, 72, 96, 105, 117, 125, 130
in Chile, 141, 143, 146, 151, 159, 160

Emmanuel, A., 9–10

Engels, F., 15

entrepreneurs, *see under* domestic entrepreneurs, foreign firms, industrial bourgeoisie, industrialists, private capital

Eurocurrency market, *see under* capital markets

European Economic Community (EEC), 75, 107, 109

Evers, T., 20

exchange rates
in Brazil ('maxi' devaluations, in 1979, 102–3, in 1983, 119, 122, 131n.108; overvalued, under Geisel, 75, under Figueiredo, 124; problems of a suggested devaluation, 129)
in Chile (devaluation, 155, 156, 193, 194; fixed, 156, 193; operations and money supply, 155; revaluation, 155, 156, 193)
in Mexico, devaluations of (1954, 213; 1976, 218; 1982, 219)
in Latin America, under populism, 35

export promotion
and adequate demand, 8
and capital accumulation in the periphery, 12
in Chile, 156, 170
and labour control, 65
in Latin America, 7, 28, 32, 40 (compared with Asia, 8)

exports
in Brazil (under the 'miracle', 68–9; myth of export-based expansion, 109–10; policy, under Geisel, 74–5, backed by anti-statism campaign, 96, Rischbieter plan, 102, as a solution to all problems in the 80s, 106–7; restrictions on, imposed by the USA and the EEC, 101–2, 107–8, 109, 113; subsidies, and public deficit, 75, 113, end of, 102–3, reintroduced, 107–8; in 1983, 127)
in Chile (copper, 143, 170; non-copper, 170)
in Mexico (fall in, and the US economy in the early 70s, 216; manufactured, 216, and foreign companies, 215; of oil and gas as a solution to all problems in the late 70s, 218)
see also under subsidies

fascist ideology, in Chile, 180
financial bourgeoisie, in Chile, 185–7, 194
financial crisis, and export promotion in Latin America, 7
see also under state–fiscal crisis
financial market, *see under* credit, money market
financial packages
in Brazil, 122
in Mexico, 228
financial repression, McKinnon on, 167
financial system, in Chile
crisis of, under the military, 192–4
restructured by the military regime, 167–9
financieras
in Chile, 167–8
in Mexico, 223–4
firms, *see under* foreign firms, private firms, public firms
see also under domestic entrepreneurs
fiscal crisis, *see under* state
fiscal incentives, in Brazil, 68
Fishlow, A., 64
food
in Brazil (imports, under Geisel, 78–9;

food—*cont.*
    prices, rising, under Geisel, 77–8, 99, under Figueiredo, 101, 124–5, as a result of cuts in subsidies, 120, 126; production, neglected for the home market, 77–8, subsidised for exports, 78)
    in Mexico (import and export of, 216–17; *Sistema Alimentario Mexicano,* 218–19; self-sufficiency in, 231)
    see also under balance of payments, inflation, subsidies
    see also economic crisis, income distribution, inequality, savings
foreign debt
    in Brazil, 58–9, 69, 82–6, 91, 116, 129 (profile, and growth of, in the 70s, 84–5, deterioration of, in the 80s, 108–10; service, in the 70s, 84–6, 90, 91, deteriorating, 103, 108, for 1984, 127)
    in Chile, 143, 156, 172, 193, 209 (economic groups and, 168, 172; service, 193)
    as a constraint on relative autonomy, 26
    in Mexico, 222, 226, 227, 229, 230, 231, 239 (profile, 228; service, 226, 228)
    see also under balance of payments, capital markets, credit, creditworthiness, public deficit, public firms, state–fiscal crisis
foreign exchange, insufficiency of, in Mexico, 223
    see also under foreign reserves
foreign firms
    in Brazil (debts of, 94; profits, 90, 93, operational, 93–4, non-operational, 80, 94–5; takeovers of domestic firms, 57, 88, 90, 93, 119, 121, 122; trade deficit of, 94)
    in Chile, *see under* foreign investment, multinational corporations
    in Mexico (control of production by, 212; control by the state over, 217; lack of data on investment by, 221)
    see also under private firms–large, industrial production
    see also credit–international, foreign investment, recession, speculation, subsidies

foreign investment
    in Brazil, 57–8, 93, 95
    in Chile, 145, 172–3
    and ISI in Latin America, 36, 38
    in Mexico, 211, 219, 229
    in the periphery, 11
    after populism, 38, 40
    see also under foreign firms
foreign reserves
    in Brazil, 104, 109
    in Chile, 193, 209
    see also under foreign exchange
Frank, A. G., 9
free market, in Chile, 152–3
    in labour market, 162
    and political repression, 139
Frei, E., 140, 143, 144, 145
Friedman, M., 167
Fundação Getulio Vargas (FGV), 69, 97, 126
Fundação Instituto Brasileiro de Geografia e Estatística (FIBGE), 71, 123
Fundo de Garantia do Tempo de Serviço (FGTS), 99
Furtado, C., 8

Gazeta Mercantil, 94, 133n.83
General Agreement on Tariffs and Trade (GATT), 75
Geisel, E., 70, 71, 72, 73, 90, 91, 126
    administration, 70–100
González Videla, G., 142
Goulart, J., 60, 61, 62, 63
Gramsci, A., 15, 23
growth
    'balanced' vs. 'unbalanced', 6–9, 39
    in Latin America (model of, before 1930, 28–30, after 1930, 33)
    for individual countries, see under economic model, economic policy–stages of

hegemony, 23
    in Chile
    of financial bourgeoisie, 185–8, 194, 195, 196
    of industrial bourgeoisie, 142, 143
Hilferding, R., 185, 216
Hirschman, A. O., 35
    'unbalanced' model of growth, 6–7
    criticism of, 6–7

Ibáñez, C., 142

Index

ideology, as a basis of domination, 18, 23–4, 140
   in Chile, 144, 151, 152, 179–81
imbalance, in Mexico, in the 60s, 212, 217
imports
   policy, in Brazil (controls reinforced under Geisel, 74; cuts, introduced in 1980, 105, scaled up in 1981, 108, and 1982, 118, and balance of payments deficit in the 80s, 118–19, and industrial production, 118, 121)
   in Chile, 150, 155, 170, 171; *see also under* tariffs
   see also under balance of payments, economic crisis, economic model, recession
import substitution industrialisation (ISI)
   in Brazil, 61, 95 (incentives to, under Geisel, 74; setback in 1981, 106)
   in Chile (exhaustion of, 143)
   in Latin America, after 1930, 33–6 (contradictions of, 38–9; exhaustion of, 40)
   in Mexico (stagnating in the mid-60s, 216, 217)
income distribution
   in Brazil (in 1960, 68; under the 'miracle', 68–9; under Geisel, 95, 96, 97–9, criticised, 95; in 1980, 123–5, 127; and aggregate domestic demand, 130)
   in Chile, share of labour in GDP, 206 (under Alessandri and Frei, 145; under Allende, 147; under the military, 164)
   in early development economics, 4, 5, 7
   under ISI, 33
   in 19th-century Latin America, 28–30
   and role of the state in capital accumulation, 64–5
   in Mexico (in the 30s and 40s, 211; under *desarrollo estabilizador*, 214–15, and domestic demand, 215; in the late 60s, 218; profits and wages shares of GDP until the 80s, 220–1, 222)
   see also under wage policy, wages
   see also cost of living, demand, food, inflation, popular unrest, savings, welfare
individualistic ideology, in Chile, 181

industrial bourgeoisie, emerging in Chile, 142; *see also under* hegemony, industrial capital, private capital
industrial capital, in Chile, 144, 148, 154, 166, 185
   indebtedness *vis-à-vis* financial capital, 156, 168
industrialisation
   in Brazil, *see under* industrial production
   in Chile, 141; *see also under* industrial production, manufacturing industry
   in Latin America, 5–6 (recommended by CEPAL, 6; limited, in 19th century, 29–30, 32; by import substitution, after 1930, 33–6, 38)
   in Mexico, 211; *see also under* industrial production
industrialists, in Latin America
   alliance with landowners, after 1930, 33–4
   conflict with landowners in the 50s and 60s, 38
   for individual countries, see under domestic entrepreneurs, industrial bourgeoisie, private capital
industrial production
   in Brazil (capital intensiveness in, and unemployment, 57–8; concentration of, 57, 64, 80, 92–3; excess capacity of, 59, 60, 64, 76, 105, 121, 127; growth of, 54–5, 67, 70–1; and import cuts, 118–19; overheating of, 70, 76–7)
   in Chile (decline under the military, 156; increase in capacity utilisation in 1971, 147; per capita value added in, 192, 207)
   'empty spaces' of, 65–6
   in Latin America (nature of, in 19th century, 29–30; unused capacity of, before 1930, 30, utilised, after 1930, 33)
   in Mexico (concentration of, 214; excess capacity of, 221; foreign ownership in, 214, 215, 217; stagnation of, 216, 217)
inequality
   in Brazil, 68–9, 97–9, 120, 123–5
   see also under income distribution, wage policy, wages, welfare
   see also food prices, inflation, popular unrest, subsidies

inflation
  in Brazil (before 64, 59, 60, analysed
      by the military government, 54–5,
      63–4; under the 'miracle', 70, 73;
      under Geisel, 75–81, 96, 'demand
      pull', 76, 'cost push', 77, food
      prices and, 77–8, and savings, 78;
      under Figueiredo, 103, 116, 126,
      127, and food prices, 101, 104,
      120, 126, and INPC, 101, 120,
      126, 134n.114, priority of government policy after 79, 104–5, up in
      the 80s, 105; impact on Brazilian
      society, 120; and high cost credit,
      116, 119; and money supply, 81,
      116; and public deficit, 119; and
      subsidies to private sector, 114,
      133n.66)
  in Chile, 143, 153–4, 155, 194 (in
      monetarist approach, 153–4; and
      inflationary expectations, 155; and
      fixed exchange rate, 156)
  in Mexico (in the 40s, 213; up in the
      70s, 218; as a method of forced
      savings in the 40s and 50s, 222)
  as a method of forced savings, 36
  and wages in the 50s and 60s, 38
  see also under cost of living, credit,
      food prices, money supply, money
      market, oil prices, savings
  see also economic crisis, demand,
      industrial production, public deficit, recession
institutional crisis, in Brazil
  in the early 60s, 61–3 (and anomaly of
      the constitution, 61, 62)
institutionalisation, in Chile
  political, 160
  social, 160–2
  see also under 'seven modernisations'
*Instituto Argentino para la Promoción del
  Intercambio* (IAPI), 34
*Instituto de Planejamento Econômico e
  Social* (IPEA), 89
interdependence, 26
interest rates
  in Brazil (domestic, free under Geisel,
      79, 95, and subsidies to private
      firms, 79–80, high, 116, 119,
      134n.105; international, 84–5, 110,
      121)
  in Chile, 167–8, 193
  in Mexico, 214
  see also under credit, LIBOR, money
      market, subsidies

  see also domestic entrepreneurs, inflation
internal debt
  in Brazil, 116
  in Chile, 156, 168, 186, 192, 193, 194
  in Mexico, 227, 238
international division of labour, in 19th-century Latin America, 28
International Monetary Fund (IMF), 8,
  105, 109, 111, 125, 126, 127–8, 129,
  130, 228–9
  'package' in Brazil, 127–8
'intervention', legal procedure in Chile,
  147–8
investment, domestic
  in Brazil (insufficiency of, in the 50s,
      56; high, under the 'miracle', 69;
      declining, in the late 70s, 89, 91–2;
      low, under Figueiredo, 116–17)
  in Chile, 201 (in agriculture, compared
      with industry in 1960s, 145;
      efficiency of, under the military,
      190; falling, under Allende, 150;
      financed with external savings,
      under the military, 190; financed
      with public sector savings in
      1940–60, 141, in 1960s, 145, under
      the military, 190, 191; low, under
      Alessandri, 143; low, under Frei,
      146; lowest, under the military,
      190; neglect of infrastructural,
      under the military, 190; problems
      of measurement, 189–90)
  in Latin America (in 19th century,
      28–32; and domestic savings under
      ISI, 35–6; insufficiency of, in the
      50s, 38)
  in Mexico (in the 40s, 211; low, in production, in the 60s, 217; private
      vis-à-vis public, 219, 220; and savings, 225–6, 230
Irigoyen, H., 31

Kelly Plan, 183
Korean war, 56
Kubitschek, J., 41, 54–61, 64, 80

labour
  in Brazil, 57–8, 123–7
  in Chile, *see under* workers
  in Latin America (industrial, coopted
      by populist regimes, 37; rural,
      exploited, in the 19th century, 30,
      31, 32, under populism, 36–7;
      unlimited supply of, 5, in the 19th

century, 28–32, after 1930, 33–4, and wages, 36–7; *see also under* labour surplus; Lewis)
  in Mexico, 211, 216, 221, 231
  see also under labour movement, labour surplus, popular unrest, repression, strikes, wages
  see also income distribution, recession, welfare
labour control
  in Brazil, before 64, 56
  and export-orientation, 65
  in 19th-century Latin America, 30–2
  under populism, 36–7
labour movement
  in Brazil, 99–102
  in Chile, *see under* workers
  see also under labour
labour policy, as an indicator of the role of the state in accumulation, 65
labour surplus, in Latin America, 5
  absence of, in Argentina, 33–4
  role in the 19th century, 28–32
  role after 1930, 33–4, 36–7, 55–6
landowners
  in Brazil, 56, 63
  in Chile, 141, 142, 143, 144
  in Latin America (in the 19th century, 27; alliance with industrialists after 1930, 33; conflict with industrialists over agrarian reform in the 50s and 60s, 38)
  see also under dominant class
land reform, in Mexico, 211
  see also under agrarian reform
land rent, 31
land tenure
  in Brazil, before 64, 60–1
  in 19th-century Latin America, 28–32
Langoni, C., 68
law 4131, in Brazil, 94
law of similarity, abolished in Brazil, 103
leasing, 115
legitimacy challenge, in Brazil, 72–3
Leighton, B., 157
Lenin, V. I., 3, 4, 9, 15, 18
Léniz, F., 154
Letelier, O., 158
Lewis, W. A., 6, 8, 36
  theory, 4–5 (criticised, 5; relevance of, to Latin America, 5)
liberal economics
  and capital accumulation in the periphery, 2–3

linkage effects
  in Hirschman's theory, 6
local bourgeoisie
  subsidiary role in Latin America in the 70s and 80s, 40
London Inter Bank Offered Rate (LIBOR), 84, 85, 121
Lüders, R., 194

McKinnon, R. I., 167
Madero, F., 210
Madrid, M. de la, 219, 231
Malan, P., 76
Mandel, E., 19
manufacturing
  in Brazil, 87
  in Chile, 141, 190
  in Mexico, 211, 216
  see also under industrial production
market
  in the primary export economies of Latin America, 28–30
  insufficiency, in the 50s and 60s, 38
  internal vs. export, and accumulation, 12
  see also under demand
market concentration and profits, in Brazil, 92–5
  see also under industrial production–concentration, foreign firms
Marx, K., 3, 4, 9, 10, 24
marxist economics
  classical assumption of, 3
  debate on capital accumulation in the periphery, 9–11
Médici, E. G., 67
Mexico, 32, 34, 39, 44–5, 210–40
middle classes
  in Brazil (pre-64, 63; and recession, 125, 129, 130, 134n.112)
  in Chile (and Popular Front, 141, 142; in charge of the state, 142; and Allende government, 151–2)
  in Latin America, 32
migration, in Mexico, 216
military
  in Chile, 139, 140, 151, 152, 153, 154, 157, 158, 159, 160
  coup (in Brazil, 39, 55, 63; in Chile, 140, 150, 151, 152, 155, 157)
  government, in Brazil, 54, 55, 71–3, 95, 96, 105, 116, 117, 118, 124, 127–8
'minimum food ration', in Brazil, 124–5
mining
  in Brazil, 86, 87

mining–*cont.*
  in Chile, 172–3
  in Mexico, 211
mobilisation, social and political
  in Brazil, 60–3, 72, 102
  in Chile (under Frei, 146; under
    Allende, 150; no attempt at, by
    military government, 179–80, 181
  see also under popular unrest, strikes
monetarism, in Chile, 154, 156, 180
see also under Chicago school of economics
monetary approach to the balance of
  payments, in Chile, 156
monetary policy, in Brazil, under Geisel,
  79–81
money market
  in Brazil, 79–80, 94–5, 116, 119, 121,
    122
  in Chile, see under financial system,
    financieras
  in Mexico, 223–4, 227
  see also under credit, interest rates
  see also domestic entrepreneurs, economic crisis, inflation
money supply
  in Brazil, 59, 70, 79–81, 91, 103, 105
  in Chile, 155
  in Mexico, 213
  see also under inflation
Monterrey group, 215
Morgan Guaranty Trust Company, 108
Movimento Democrático Brasileiro
  (MDB), 71, 93
multinational corporations
  control by, over accumulation in the
    periphery, 2, 11, 12, 13, 41
  see also under foreign firms

Nacional Financiera, 223
National Intelligence Directorate
  (DINA), 157, 158, 159, 178
national security doctrine, 179
  in Chile, 180
nationalisations
  in Chile, 147, 148, 149
  see also under copper
  in Mexico, 211, 219, 227
nitrate economy, in Chile, 142
Nurkse, R., 8

*Obrigações Reajustáveis do Tesouro
  Nacional* (ORTNs), 116, 119
O'Connor, J., 20–1

O'Donnell, G., 195
oil industry, in Mexico, 211, 219, 223,
  224, 230, 231
oil prices, and inflation in Brazil, 52, 70,
  73, 76, 77, 81, 114
oligarchy, in Chile, 141, 142
  see also under landowners
oligopolies, in Brazil, 57, 64, 80, 92
  see also under industrial production–concentration, market concentration
Organisation for Economic Cooperation
  and Development (OECD), 129
Organisation of Petroleum Exporting
  Countries (OPEC), 82

Pacote do Natal, 102–3
Partido Movimento Democrático Brasileiro (PMDB), 126, 130
Partido Revolucionario Institucional
  (PRI), 211, 216, 218
Partido dos Trabalhadores (PT), 130
patronage, in Latin America, 32
Paulo Villares, 122
payments for technical assistance, 94
peasantry, in Chile
  and military government's policy, 184
  mobilisation of, 144, 146
  political exclusion of, 142
Perón, J. D., 33
Petrobrás, 86, 114, 115
  foreign debt of, 115
petrochemicals
  state enterprises in, in Brazil, 86
Petróleos Mexicanos (PEMEX), 225, 226
Pinochet, A., 154, 157, 158, 159, 160,
  173, 179, 180, 181, 194
Plan Industrial, in Mexico, 220
Plan Laboral, in Chile, 161–3
Plano Nacional de Desenvolvimento
  (PND), 70, 79, 86, 95, 114
plebiscite, in Chile, 151, 179, 181
political institutions, in 19th-century
  Latin America, 31–2
political liberalisation, in Brazil, *see
  under abertura*
political crisis
  in Brazil, 130
  in Chile, 157, 160, 194
political opposition
  in Brazil post-64 (within the government, 95–6, 133n.84, outside, 93,
    111, 129, 130; divided, 130
  in Chile, *see under* political parties
  in Mexico, 219

political parties
  in Brazil (before 1964, 62–3; after 1964, 71, 72, 93, 126, 130)
  in Chile (banned by the military, 152, 157; Christian Democratic, 140, 143, 144, 148, 151, 152, 157, 159; Communist, 141, 143, 146, outlawed, 142; National, 157; Radical, 141, 146; Socialist, 141, 143, 146)
Popular Front, in Chile, 141
popular support, for the PRI, 211, 218
popular unrest
  in Brazil, 72, 97, 99–102, 127
  in Chile, 160, 194
  in Latin America, in the 50s and 60s, 38–9
  see also under food prices, income distribution, recession, strikes, unemployment
populism
  in Brazil (contradictions of, 56–63 role of labour surplus in populist pact, 55–6; reactivation under Goulart, 61–3; of Delfim, 101
  in Chile (in Ibáñez's government, 142; in Christian Democratic model, 145
  in Latin America (nature of, 33–4; contradictions of, 38–9)
  in Mexico, 226
  see also under populist state
populist state
  in Brazil (lack of autonomy of, 61; end of the system of compromise of, 63)
  in Latin America, 32–40 (crisis of, 37–40)
Portales, D., 27
Poulantzas, N., 17–19
power bloc
  in Brazil, 42
  and Cardoso's pact of domination, 18
  and form of state, 18, 23
Prats, C., 157
primary export model, 5
  in Latin America, 28–32
private capital, 64–7
  in Brazil, 72
  in Chile, 145, 149, 150, 151
  in Mexico, 212, 224, 225, 226, 230
  see also under domestic entrepreneurs, investment–domestic, industrial bourgeoisie, industrial capital, firms, state
  see also capital accumulation, subsidies
private firms
  large (market power of, 64; in Brazil, increasingly foreign, 93, market power of, 80, 88, 92–3, 105, subsidised credit for, 79, subsidised industrial inputs for, 88–90, 113–14; see also under foreign firms, subsidies; see also industrial production)
  small and medium, in Brazil, 122 (see also under domestic entrepreneurs; see also recession)
profits
  and accumulation in Lewis, 4
  in Chile (mass and rate of, under Allende, 147; distribution of, 1960–81, 186–7)
  in 19th-century Latin America, 28–32
  under populism, 33–8
  see also under foreign firms, income distribution, investment, subsidies
  see also wage policy, wages
Programa de Metas, 58–9, 64
'protected democracy' in Chile, 158
protectionism
  against Brazilian exports, 101–2, 107–8, 109, 113
  and industrialisation in Latin America, after 1930, 34–5
public deficit
  in Brazil (under Geisel, 88–92; under Figueiredo, 110–18, 119–20; impact of public firms deficit on, 112–16; and inflation in the 80s, 119–20)
  in Chile, under Allende, 149 (and nationalised companies, 149–50)
  in Mexico, 238 (caused by public firms, 226–7; financed abroad, 223; and private savings, 214)
  see also under balance of payments deficit, budget deficit, foreign debt, internal debt, public expenditure, public firms deficit, state-–fiscal crisis
  see also credit, inflation, money supply, savings, subsidies
public expenditure
  in Brazil, 104, 106, 123–4
  in Chile, 154, 165–6
  see also under public deficit

public firms
  in Brazil (budget of, 111, 112; characteristics of, 89–90; control of, by government, 112, 117; cuts in investment, in the 80s, 105, 106; deficit of, 87–8, 89–90, 111, 112, 113–17; foreign borrowing by, 89, 112, 113; impact on public deficit, 111–18)
  in Chile, *see under* state enterprises
  in Mexico (debate on role of, 218; and foreign debt, 228; and public deficit, 226–7; role in production, 217, 226–7)
  see also under balance of payments deficit, budget deficit, foreign debt, state, treasury transfers
  see also credit, inflation, industrial production, investment

Quadros, J., 61, 62

recession
  in Brazil, 103, 104, 105, 121 (and cuts in food subsidies, 120; impact on labour, 123–7, on local business, 120–3; without stabilisation, 118–20)
  in Chile, 154, 156, 191, 193
  in Mexico, *see under* economic crisis
  see also under domestic entrepreneurs, economic crisis, economic policy–stages of, labour
  see also balance of payments deficit, inflation, public deficit
reformism, in Latin America, 40
  postponed, 131
  see also under populism
reformist model of accumulation, in Chile, 143–7
regime
  bases of domination of, 23–4, 140
  in Brazil, *see under* military government
  in Chile, 144, 176–84 (stages under the military, 157–60)
  form of, 18–19, 140
Reis Velloso, J. P. dos, 89
repression
  in Brazil, 73, 99
  in Chile, 144, 157, 158, 159, 161, 178 (financial, 167)
  see also under coercion
  see also wage policy; wages

Rischbieter, K., 102, 104
Rey, P. P., 30
Rostow, W. W., 4, 213
royalties, 94

savings
  and accumulation, in the periphery, 11
  in Brazil (domestic, before 1964, 56, under the 'miracle', 69, under Geisel, 92, under Figueiredo, 116–17, 120, and inflation, under Geisel, 78, public, under Kubitschek, 59, in the late 70s, 92, 117; foreign, *see under* capital market–international, foreign debt)
  in Chile (public, and investment in 1940–60, 141; external, and investment in 1975–81, 190)
  and investment in the ISI period, 35–6
  in Mexico (under *desarrollo estabilizador*, 213, 214; public, 225, 226, 230; sources of, 222–4, 238)
  see also under capital accumulation, capital formation, investment
  see also inflation
Secretaria para o Contrôle das Estatais (SEST), 112, 117
'seven modernisations', in Chile, 160
'shock treatment', in Chile, 154
Siderbrás, 114, 115, 116
  foreign debt of, 115
Simonsen, M. H., 73, 82, 84, 95, 100, 101, 120
'Socialist Republic', in Chile, 147
'social question', in Brazil, 102
speculation
  in Brazil, 80, 94
  in Chile, 186, 192
  see also under foreign firms, money market
stabilisation
  in Brazil, *see under* economic policy–stages of
  in Chile, 153, 155
  in Mexico, 218
  see also under economic crisis, recession
state
  in Brazil (fiscal crisis of, under Geisel, 75, 79, 86–92, under Figueiredo, 110–18, 128; intervention in the economy, debate on, 95–6, impact on capital accumulation, under

Index

Geisel, 75–81, 81–6, 86–91, 91–2, 92–5, under Figueiredo, 106–10, 110–18, 118–19, 119–20, 130)
bureaucratic–authoritarian, 15, 19
and capital accumulation in Latin America, 28–40
in Chile (autonomy of, under the military, 185, 187; class nature of, 154; economic role of, 139–40; and industrialisation, 141; under Frei, 144; under Allende, 147, 151; under the Military, 152, 159–76, 195)
dependent–capitalist, 16, 17
fiscal crisis of, in O'Connor, 20
form of, in Poulantzas, 18
functions of, 19–21
intervention in the economy, 64–7
Marxist theory of, 15–21
in Mexico (fiscal crisis of, 212, 223, 225–9, 238; foundations of, 210–12; intervention in the economy, debate on, 213–16; impact on capital accumulation, debate on, 213–16, 220, 223, 224, 229, stepped up economic role in the 70s, 217–18; relative autonomy of, 210, 211, 230–1)
and regime, 16
relative autonomy of, 24–6, 67 (in 19th-century Latin America, 27, 31)
roles in capitalist accumulation, 21–4, 64–7
social bases of, 16, 25
type of, in Poulantzas, 18
see also under capital accumulation, capital formation, coercion, credit, exchange rate, exports, import policy, income distribution, interest rate, investment, money market, money supply, public expenditure, public firms, repression, savings, subsidies, tariffs, wage policy, wages, welfare
see also balance of payments, budget, economic crisis, foreign debt, inflation, internal debt, public deficit, recession
state bourgeoisie, 16, 41
in Brazil, 42
state capitalism, in Brazil, 53, 86–7
questioned, 87–90
state enterprises

in Brazil, *see under* public firms
in Chile (under Allende, 148, 149, 150; under the military, 173–6; *see also* copper)
in Latin America, 41
in Mexico, *see under* public firms
state managers, 16, 24, 25
in Mexico, 211, 212, 229, 231
state monopoly capitalism, 18
in Brazil, *see under* state capitalism
in Chile, absence of, 195–6
'state of internal war' in Chile, 152, 177–9
steel production, in Brazil, 86
excess capacity in, 114–15
see also under Siderbrás
Strassman, W. P., 8
strike, right to, in Chile, 161–2
strikes, in Brazil, 72, 99–100, 101, 104
subsidies
in Brazil, 78, 79–80, 87–90, 93, 95, 102–3, 107–8, 120, 122–3, 125, and inflation, 133n.66, and public deficit, 113)
in Mexico, 218, 229
Superintendência da Moeda e do Crédito (SUMOC), 57, 93
surplus, 1, 9
distribution of, under populism, 36, 38, 39
sources of, in the periphery, 11
surplus value, extraction of, 11, 21, 64–5
see also under income distribution, profits, wages
surveys, in Brazil, 97–9
Sweezy, P., 9

tariffs, in Chile, 155, 156, 169
tax reform
and the Alliance for Progress, 39
in Mexico, 225, 230
tax revenue
in Brazil, 91, 116
in Mexico, 225, 226, 227
tax system
in Chile, 167
in 19th-century Latin America, 32
after 1930, 35–6
technology
choice of, and accumulation, 12–13
costs of, 7 (in Brazil, 88)
torture, in Chile, 152, 161, 178–9
transfer pricing, in Brazil, 93–4

treasury transfers to public firms, in Brazil, 89, 91, 113, 114
Trebat, T., 89
'triple alliance', in Brazil, 134n.108
  demise of, 120–3

'underdevelopment, development of', 9, 10, 28
  orthodox marxist critique of, 10
underemployment
  in Brazil, 58, 127
  in Mexico, 220, 221
unemployment
  in Brazil, 57–8, 125, 127, 132n.42
  and changes in the techniques of production, in Latin America in the 50s and 60s, 38
  in Chile, 163–4, 193, 194 (and Minimum Employment Programme, 164, 182, 194; and Kelly Plan, 182–3)
Unidad Popular, 146, 149
United States of America (USA), 101, 102, 109, 113, 141, 144, 148, 161
Uruguay, 5, 28, 29

Vargas, G., 55, 86
Villa, P., 210
Von Doellinger, C., 94, 112

wage policy
  in Brazil, 68, 69, 73–4, 97–100, 100–1, 123–5, 128, 129 (and middle income groups, 124, 125, 127, 129, 130)
  in Chile, *see under* labour policy
  and export orientation, 65
  in Mexico, *see under* wages

wages
  in Brazil (before 1964, 56, 59, 60; after 1964, 69–70, 73–4, 97–9, 101, 104, 120, 123–5, 127, minimum wage, 69–70, 72, 97–8, 124–5, 127, structure of, in 1980, 124)
  in Chile, 161, 162–3 (share of national income, 147, 164; *see also under* workers)
  in early development economics, 4, 5, 7
  under ISI, 33
  and inflation in the 50s and 60s, 38
  in Mexico (before *desarrollo estabilizador,* 212, 213, during, 222, after, 216, 219, 221)
  in 19th-century Latin America, 28–30
  see also under income distribution
  see also cost of living, demand, food, inflation, popular unrest, savings
Wallerstein, I., 9
Warren, B., 10
welfare
  as basis of domination, 18, 23, 140
  in Brazil, 123–4, 127
  in Chile, 152, 164, 183, 184
  in Mexico, 218, 226, 227
  under populism, 36–7
Wells, J., 55
workers
  in Brazil, *see under* labour, labour movement
  in Chile (in the 40s, 142; repression of, 144; and military government's policies, 184; trade unions, 146, 161, 162)
  in Mexico, *see under* labour

Zapata, E., 210

Ruth Dome
456-9593
Daughter Helen
3:00 pm